strange
situation

strange situation

a mother's journey
into the
science of attachment

bethany saltman

BALLANTINE BOOKS
NEW YORK

2021 Ballantine Books Trade Paperback Edition

Published in the United States by Ballantine Books, an imprint of Random House, a division of Penguin Random House LLC, New York.

BALLANTINE and the **HOUSE** colophon are registered trademarks of Penguin Random House LLC.

Originally published in hardcover in the United States by Ballantine Books, an imprint of Random House, a division of Penguin Random House LLC, in 2020.

The estate of Mary Ainsworth has granted permission for the use of all archival materials.

Portions of this work were originally published as "Can Attachment Theory Explain All Our Relationships?" (*New York* magazine, July 5, 2016) and "A Mean Animal Practices the Hard Way" in "Flowers Fall: Field Notes from a Buddhist Mother's Experimental Life" (*Chronogram* magazine, October 2009).

ISBN 978-0-399-18146-7
Ebook ISBN 978-0-399-18145-0

Printed in the United States of America on acid-free paper

randomhousebooks.com

2 4 6 8 9 7 5 3 1

For Thayer, my secure base.
And for Azalea, my delight.

I'm going to be interviewing you about your childhood experiences, and how those experiences may have affected your adult personality. So, I'd like to ask you about your early relationship with your family, and what you think about the way it might have affected you. We'll focus mainly on your childhood, but later we'll get on to your adolescence and then to what's going on right now . . .

—*Introduction to the "Adult Attachment Interview Protocol"*

My own peculiar addiction to science takes the form of wanting to understand the individual case. And if an individual turns out not to match what one's hypothesis would predict, I want to know why.

—*Mary Ainsworth in a letter, 1983*

Things are not as they seem. Nor are they otherwise.

—*Shakyamuni Buddha*

foreword

Daniel J. Siegel, MD

In this marvelous, important book, you'll find a blend of clear, concise, and insightful summaries of the science of attachment woven beautifully with the essential inner journey of our intrepid guide, Bethany Saltman, who comes to make sense of her life during the course of writing the book. It is at once an intellectual and deeply personal account of our knowledge of attachment and its influence on human development. Our author's captivating approach and courage invite us to do exactly what attachment studies have powerfully demonstrated is a key aspect of attaining "secure attachment" at any age: reflecting on our past is how we develop more flexibility in our attention in the present and free ourselves to become who we want to be in the future. This "mental time travel" that links past, present, and future is how we make sense of the experiences of the past, the ways we've adapted to those events, and how we have been affected by our early relationships throughout our development.

The power of attachment theory and research, first formulated and organized by John Bowlby, MD, and Mary Ainsworth, PhD, is in their rigorous exploration of human development, their focus on empirical findings across cultures and across generations, and their continual updating of ideas as new scientific discoveries and techniques become available. When Bethany Saltman first contacted me to discuss this science over a decade ago, we discussed how she might learn more about attachment and make these academic findings accessible to a broader audience than the scholars and students who usually read these in-depth empirical reports. We discussed the insights of attachment research that revealed how we can have suboptimal attachment histories yet come to make sense of those challenging experiences—no matter how painful—as we integrate new insights into a way of being more present with our moment-to-moment experience internally and with our own children. This finding of learning or "earning" security is often surprising to those who hear it for the first time. Why, people often inquire, if the past is past and done and cannot be changed, would remembering those experiences, painful or not, be in any way helpful to the individual? The answer is quite simple yet profound. Yes, you cannot change the past. And, amazingly, yes, making sense of the past changes your relationship to those events and how they affect you, now and in the future. You *can* change how you are affected by the past. This making-sense process begins with knowing the nature of attachment, the ways memories become encoded and stored, and how these events influence our autobiographical narratives—the stories of our lives, the ways we come to get a "sense of who we are" in the world, especially the interpersonal world.

All of this might sound somewhat abstract and dry. And this is both why and how the magic of this book can work its way into your own understanding of the broad field of attachment, and, if you are open to it, into your own way of making sense of your personal life history. Our minds have the capacity to process both factual knowledge and personal knowledge. Because these types of knowledge are mediated in different networks in the brain, you may find, as I did, that quite different sensations arise as our author moves between very smart discussions of the science—just enough for you to get a clear and detailed idea without being flooded by unnecessary facts that can later be obtained, as desired, by a review of the extensive endnotes—and the compelling autobiographical journey she invites us to join her on as she weaves this research framework with her own personal reflections. Implicit in this tapestry of the scientific and the personal is a deeper, more compelling, and likely more effective way of acquiring insights into attachment at each of these levels of understanding.

In this book, you'll learn about many aspect of our lives, including how the sensitivity of parents in response to the dependency of infants in the early years shapes how children learn to regulate their emotions and come to know their own minds—as well as the minds of others—and also shapes how children develop self-regulation, insight, and empathy. You'll become familiar with how research strategies utilizing the "gold standard" of the infant Strange Situation (an infant being in an unfamiliar place with unfamiliar people) are correlated with the parents' own making-sense process as revealed in the Adult Attachment Interview. You'll come to know how these parent-shaped developmental experiences influence how children come to interact with their peers, their teachers, and even their romantic partners later in life. As you learn about these fascinating and important insights from science, you'll also be given the privilege of following Bethany Saltman's personal reflections as a guide to the autobiographical reflection process the research shows is central to how we as parents can learn to be present with our children—to show up for them as we emotionally connect, keep them safe, and provide the interactive repair following ruptures that is the basis for their developing security in their attachment with us.

Our insightful guide goes even further in what she offers to us, the fortunate recipients of her decade-long journey to construct this book. Beyond her background in Buddhist meditation and her contact with teachers such as Jon Kabat-Zinn, Bethany Saltman reaches out to leaders in the field of attachment and becomes trained in both the Strange Situation and the Adult Attachment Interview, connecting with luminaries in the field such as Miriam and Howard Steele, Bob Marvin, and Alan Sroufe, and obtaining permission to dive into and cite the personal files of Mary Ainsworth. The direct input of these leaders in the field in the form of dialogue and email communication with our author is part of the book's way of weaving the personal and the scientific into one powerful and dramatic tale.

In my professional development as a child psychiatrist, educator, and parent, learning about attachment was the most important discovery in my own education. At one evening's dinner gathering during my research training, I had the transformative experience of sitting for a three-hour meal between the two Marys of attachment—Mary Ainsworth and Mary Main. It was a bustling, noisy restaurant, and the two Marys leaned in so that the three of us could hear one another as we discussed everything from trauma and the brain to the development of the self and consciousness. That evening revealed for me the power of development in shaping our understanding of our lives. Attachment theory and research are based on deep science built from carefully collected empirical observations, embrace cultural variations and longitudinal perspectives, and offer us insights into how people develop and change across the lifespan. Essential to attachment is the fundamental reality that relationships are central to human existence and the development of the mind. As the interdisciplinary framework of interpersonal neurobiology in which I work was being formed, attachment theory was one of the cornerstones of knowledge that helped us see connections across fields as disparate as anthropology, sociology, linguistics, psychology, biology, physics, and even mathematics.

It is an honor to invite you to dive into the exploration that is *Strange Situation*. If you are open to taking part in this journey of discovery, Bethany Saltman will be your guide and your companion, your confidante and your inspiration. Welcome to the science of making sense of our lives from the inside out. Enjoy the fascinating journey ahead!

contents

prologue

It was a Friday when the home pregnancy test told me the time had come. My husband, Thayer, drove home early from his job as a hospice social worker to receive the news and saw me sitting on the big rock that was our front stoop, holding the pink stick in my hand like a magic wand poised to change our lives forever.

I had not spent my life longing for a baby. Instead, my considerable passions—as a writer, as a person, and as a Zen student—had always been directed at being born as myself. And then, at thirty-six years old, I came to believe that becoming a mother would teach me something necessary about being alive.

I was right.

When my daughter, Azalea, was born in 2006, I was relieved to see that even though I had approached motherhood with a bit of distant curiosity, I absolutely, unreservedly loved her with a squishy-hearted, swooning love: *Those perfect human ears; those dark blue, deep-set eyes; her sweet, milky breath; those miniature fingernails!*

But it wasn't long before I also started to sense that something was missing. When she cried, I resented the interruption. When she wouldn't settle down, the heat of my frustration unnerved me. One time, when she was six months old, she was supposed to be taking a nap but instead was trying to pull herself up in her crib, nonstop crying. I was frazzled, running on fumes. I sat on the floor in her room and seethed, yelling at her to *just go . . . to . . . sleep!*

I thought back to all the difficulty I'd had with relationships—starting with family, with friends, with boyfriends, with myself—and wasn't surprised to find that this was hard, too. I had always feared I was a damaged person, the victim of an unloving and maybe even dangerous childhood, crippled by something I couldn't name. I believed I was broken, unable to truly give or receive love. It was no surprise, I told myself, that I was a terrible mother, especially since my own mother was so cold and rejecting. She and my dad threw me to the wolves—my two older brothers—who never loved me. Then, when I was thirteen—Azalea's age as I write this—my parents divorced and my dad moved across the country, which didn't bother me at all. Because I had always felt alone.

That was my story.

And then I discovered the science of attachment. As I began to immerse myself in the decades of rigorous research that lie far beneath the popular "attachment parenting" movement—and in fact, in many ways, contradict it—I started to wonder if the thing I was missing was in my understanding of who I was rather than in my DNA.

AT THE HEART of attachment theory is an evolution-based explanation for the sometimes unbearably up-close identification we feel with our children. All newborn mammals attach to their caregivers in order to be fed and kept safe from predators—to stay alive. For human infants, born incapable of everything but the most basic bodily functions, our early dependency on a loving caregiver is so total that parent and child must operate, in a sense, as a unit for many years. And yet, as my Italian American, Jersey-born-and-bred Zen teacher used to say, "You and I are the same thing, but I am not you, and you are not me."

How painful that reality became when Azalea was born. Our indisputable one-thingness—when she was in utero we shared everything, including food and oxygen—crashed into the rough physicality of being, in fact, two things: me over here, feeling angry that she, over there, was a bundle of need demanding something of me that I didn't think I had or wanted to give.

What kind of mother am I? What kind of person? These were the questions that plagued me.

When I stumbled onto the science of attachment, something called to me, the shadow of a question not yet formed. In my reading, I began to see mentions of a laboratory procedure called the Strange Situation that was used in clinical research to observe and assess attachment patterns between caregivers—mothers, mostly, in the beginning—and their one-year-old babies. A mother and her baby enter a room with two chairs and some blocks on the floor. The mother sits down and the baby plays. Or not. A stranger comes in and the mother leaves. The baby is left with the stranger, and then alone. What happens next has been found to reveal something so profound about the relationship between the two that it will impact that baby forever. And, as I would later learn, the mother, too.

I was instantly drawn to the promise of this very strange situation to tell me what kind of mother I had been. I hoped that what I learned would let me off the hook for the damage I was afraid I was inflicting upon my daughter. But even more, I wanted to learn everything I could about the Strange Situation, because I thought it could point me to something important about love. And I was immediately drawn to the "lady professor" named Mary Ainsworth who'd created it.

Ainsworth was born in 1913 and died in 1999, when she was

eighty-five years old, a celebrated expert in her field and by all accounts a brilliant researcher and theoretician. Her *New York Times* obituary described her as a "developmental psychologist whose work revolutionized the understanding of the bond between mothers and infants." Inspired both by her own questions about the nature of a child's relationship to its mother and by a passion for the scientific method, she spent her career observing, then developing an understanding of, the parent-child dynamic—first for a few months in Uganda in 1954, then in Baltimore from 1964 to 1967—with a depth and a rigor considered "unparalleled." Her work in Africa was what she called "an experiment of opportunity," inspired by a Ganda ritual regarding weaning that intrigued her, but turned out to be a rumor. The truly fortuitous opportunity lay in the fact that she was in Africa only because her younger husband had insisted on going for a project of his own and she, being a dutiful 1950s wife, went with him. Never one to squander a moment, she decided to do a study of her own—a research project about the early love that forms between parent and child.

Visiting and chatting with twenty-six Ganda mothers and their babies every couple of weeks, watching the babies crawl, scramble, and toddle back and forth across the floor to their mothers' laps, Ainsworth began to wonder what made some of the relationships feel so easy and pleasant, while others felt disconnected and fraught, and she started to form a hypothesis. Though her Uganda study was a little scrappy and off-the-cuff, it was the first of its kind, and it set the stage for what is now the long, complicated history of attachment research.

And for the insights that have changed my life.

IN THE OPENING of the third edition of the *Handbook of Attachment* (2016), Jude Cassidy and Phillip R. Shaver write of

Mary Ainsworth and her colleague John Bowlby that "it seems unlikely that [either of them] dreamed for a moment that their theoretical efforts would spawn one of the broadest, most profound, and most creative lines of research in 20th- and 21st-century psychology."

While there is no way Ainsworth could have imagined that an online search—which of course did not exist in her lifetime—for "attachment" would turn up millions of entries, she did know she was onto something big. On January 2, 1968, she wrote in a letter to her graduate student and research partner Sylvia Bell, "This is really a tremendously difficult, subtle, and yet highly significant area of research we have gotten into . . . We can't really miss!"

And she was right. As the boom in attachment research now reports, pretty much everything we do—how we love, work, marry, create, lead, pray, scroll, drink, eat, study, sleep, have sex—can be seen in light of our earliest attachment relationships. And the field itself has evolved to become ever more subtle and fine-tuned, influencing other areas of study such as psychopathology, physical health, neurobiology, and genetics. While mothers were the original parental figures studied, it is now widely accepted that babies form the same attachments with fathers and nonbiological caregivers as well. Today, researchers believe that our pattern of attachment, entrenched enough by one year of age to be observed and classified, is more important to a person's development than temperament, IQ, social class, and parenting style. According to Marinus van IJzendoorn, attachment's most prominent statistician, the Strange Situation has been used for research in approximately twenty thousand studies around the world, with many kinds of children and parents—neurotypical and non-neurotypical, perfectly ordinary and uniquely challenged, rich and poor. It's simply the gold standard in psych labs everywhere for assessing security between children and their caregivers. Some researchers have even used the Strange Situation to look at the relationships between humans and their companion cats, dogs, and chimps.

To give just one example of the wide-ranging application that attachment theory has achieved, a study recently published by a team in South Korea considers Airbnb hosts' attachment relationships to the Airbnb brand:

> To build a robust attachment to the platform company, the firm manager should realize and acknowledge hosts (i.e., individual product owners) as business partners who deserve to be known, connected, shared with, updated, and collaborated with regarding any matters of the company. This sense of belonging leads hosts to be attached to the firm or peer hosts, finally resulting in citizenship behaviors.

I'm not sure if Mary would chuckle at such an extrapolation of her research or quibble with it. I'd love to ask her. I know she'd have something clever and surprising to teach me.

AS I BEGAN to travel into Mary Ainsworth's world, my interest in attachment started to grow and shift. I started to admire not just her work, but who she was. Far from being some aloof genius who theorized from an academic perch, Ainsworth was a brave intellectual who loved to roast chicken and drink bourbon and talk all night long and dance and watch tennis on TV. She was a real mush, a sucker for beauty who loved clothes, pretty things, people, and ideas. I was captivated by the sound of her frank but formal voice as I pored over her letters and the raw data from her studies of mothers and babies. And I was in awe of the way she began to discern these universal patterns of attachment out of the wilderness of her observations of families and her own very real relationships. And it was through the flutter of my own heart in reading about her life and her work that I started to really understand attachment, and how close to the bone it is, and must be.

If fact, I became so smitten with Ainsworth, this woman I would never meet, that I started to feel as if she were teaching me from the great beyond. I began to internalize her, approaching my life with her eyes, trying to understand the attachments of my own heart as she might. We became intimate, in my mind, even though she had been dead for ten years when I started my research. And as scary as it was, I wanted to be seen by her—the kind, sympathetic, but disarming expert—and to see myself and my relationships as she might.

It was my desire to merge with Ainsworth's wisdom that inspired me to go on this journey into the science of attachment. I white-lied my way into an attachment lab in New York City in order to see a real live Strange Situation. I flew to Akron, Ohio, to read Mary Ainsworth's letters in her own tidy handwriting and typing. I signed up for a training usually reserved for psychologists to learn how to code the Strange Situation. I also traveled to Charlottesville, Virginia, where Ainsworth's protégé and executor, now white-haired, showed me the boxes of her original Strange Situation notes and her parents' silver tea set. When I heard about the Adult Attachment Interview (AAI), which identifies an adult's attachment classification—like a Strange Situation for grown-ups—I maneuvered my way into going through it myself with one of the world's experts, even though it's not usually administered to random individuals, nor do people usually receive their "score," like I did. Still not satisfied with someone else's assessment of who I was, I attended— with Thayer and a group of PhD students and clinicians—a two-week intensive to learn how to code the AAI myself.

At every step along the way, I held Azalea in my heart and

in my mind—noticing the person she was becoming, watching our life together, imagining her future—all in the context of what I was learning.

"Are you a psychologist?" people ask me all the time.

"No," I say.

"A social worker? Therapist?"

"Nope," I tell them. "Just a writer. And a mother. And a daughter, trying to understand how attachment works."

Just a woman knocking on the door of Mary Ainsworth's lineage.

AT THE HEART of Mary Ainsworth's impressive legacy is something deceptively simple, and charmingly unscientific:

> It is interaction that seems to be most important, not mere care, and particularly conspicuous in mother-child pairs who have achieved good interaction is the quality of mutual delight which characterizes their exchanges.

It is this quiet but revolutionary notion of *delight* that has changed everything for me. Delight, as an aspect of attachment, took me years to understand and absorb, and even longer to experience. Today I approach my entire life through the question of delight. Do I delight in Azalea? Do we delight in each other? Do I delight in my life the way Mary delighted in her own, and in those wonderful babies and their imperfect mothers? Do I delight in myself? Even a little?

I do. Not all the time, but every day some flash of delight comes over and through me. Azalea laughs. I laugh. *Delight.* Butter sizzles in the pan. *Delightful.* My new shoes fit perfectly. Someone watches someone else as they tell a story from their day. I yell, I recover. A book I'm excited to read comes in the mail. Azalea kicks her first goal in a soccer practice I happen to be watching. I sleep. I awaken. We all do. The sun falls behind the trees. My heart moves along with it. To be truly delighted is to let it all in, even the end of a day. I hear Thayer drive up to our house in the cold winter dusk and I know we have an evening together to look forward to.

What I've learned by loving Mary Ainsworth is that I don't have to work so hard to love. I've learned that love, when working well, is automatic, intrinsic to who we are, almost imperceptible, stitched into our very being like digestion or respiration. If only loving were as simple as breathing.

But it's not simple. In fact, love is so nuanced, it's taken me almost fifty years and an expert spirit guide to find it; at the same time, it's so a part of my very being that it's taken me almost fifty years to see it. In fact, what I used to consider my anguish *is* my love, because of the way it reaches toward love. It's like that optical illusion I used to stare at in the backs of magazines when I was a little girl hiding out from my family in the privacy of my room. One moment it's two faces staring at each other in profile, a mirror image. The next, the outline between them becomes a lamp. Then two faces again.

Anguish turns to love. Separation becomes connection. Without the pain of aloneness, I never would have discovered the depth of my relatedness.

OVER THIS PAST decade of studying the science of attachment, I've come to understand that, though it is one of the most important schools of thought to come out of the twentieth century, at its core is a mystical insight: Attachment is not something we *do*, but a state of mind. The securely attached "autonomous" adult is simply of the mind to *value attachment*. That's it. And as the Vietnamese Zen master Thuong Chieu said, "When we understand how our mind works, the practice becomes easy." So while what follows is about me, my hope is that it will be read like a proof, clarifying an important theory of mind that will make the practice of love easier, as it has for me.

Which is not to say that the journey's been easy, or direct; far from it. My path these past many years has often felt more like a dreamscape than a straight line. As I've held the jewel of attachment up like a prism through which I could see the world—my world—in its shimmering, always changing light, I've questioned and requestioned my understandings and assumptions. And I've often wondered why I was going to all the trouble. Why so much effort to understand something so foggy and elusive and complex?

It's only now that I can see that it's because I love Azalea so much that I've spent the past ten years of my life trying to get to the bottom of that love, only to see that it's bottomless.

And though I had always felt broken, by studying attachment I've learned that we are all born with something utterly, totally, miraculously unbreakable, which is why my story of loneliness, of something being wrong, of the shame of feeling separate, has fallen apart.

This is the untelling.

part i

untelling

I had thought that she would be a very intellectual mother, but although her understanding of B [Baby] has been helped by her reading . . . she has learned quite a lot about the way her baby signals his states . . . She likes to touch B and does frequently. She kisses his head and shows all sorts of little gentle, affectionate signs. There is no indication whatsoever that she considers this baby a burden, but on the contrary I think she is surprised at how much she is enjoying him.

—Mary Ainsworth, Case 18

chapter one

In 2005, I lay in bed beneath the Christmas lights in the loft of our little house in the Catskills, *The Baby Book* propped against my giant round belly. This encyclopedic volume by Dr. William Sears and his wife, Martha, a nurse, is the seminal guide to what they call "attachment parenting," the controversial approach to raising kids that encourages mothers to breastfeed, co-sleep, wear their babies in a sling, and engage in what they call the "Seven Baby B's of Attachment Parenting," all designed in response to an infant's innate need to be close. That made good sense to me, though I knew that many people felt some resistance to this method, especially the fact that it seemed to ask an awful lot of parents and particularly women.

I, however, welcomed the Searses' invitation to wholehearted—though some said over-the-top—parenting and their insistence that "when a hungry or an upset baby cries, he cries to be fed or comforted, not to control." And they made it sound so simple: "All parents, especially mothers, have a built-in intuitive system with which they listen and respond to the cues of their baby." What would it be like to listen to my baby's cries? I wondered. Would I sink into this magic realm of knowing what to do? I had heard so many stories about colicky babies and tantruming toddlers and parents losing their shit. And I had seen *that mom* in the grocery store, the one who ignored her crying child. I thought, *Just pick the kid up! How hard can it be?*

While Dr. Sears says that attachment is an "intuitive system," the technical term is a "set goal" behavioral system, and, as I have come to understand, we all have it, not "especially mothers." Caregiving, attachment, sexuality, affiliation, fear—these are called set-goal behavioral systems. We are all equipped with these whole body/mind organizations that kick in when needed to work tirelessly until they reach their goal. When we lose track of our child in Target, there will never come a moment when we say, *Oh well, now that my kid's disappeared I get to sleep in on the weekends,* and give up the search. Likewise, there will never come a time when our lost child settles in among the school supplies or wanders off with a stranger, never looking back. Attachment works like fear, which, once ignited, never stops until the threat is gone, or like a state of sexual arousal, which won't rest just because we want it to.

When Azalea was seven years old, she and Thayer were riding the chairlift up a mountain at our local ski area. Lost in a daydream, Azalea missed the spot where she and Thayer had planned to get off, leaving her on the lift without her dad, who had skied off the chair, only to discover with a start that Azalea was not right behind him. Realizing that she was alone and her beloved father was gone, rather than wait until she got back to the bottom of the mountain, the next safe place to get off, Azalea jumped! Falling ten feet through the air, luckily she landed safely on her skis. That's the kind of commitment attachment inspires. That's the kind of danger love incites.

Once we get riled up, like Azalea alone on the chairlift, the only thing that slows the caregiving and attachment systems' primordial effort is reaching its set goal—of togetherness, of safety, of intimate connection, of what researchers so tenderly call "felt security." And when that goal isn't reached, we keep searching for it. Forever.

Felt security. It's not up to anyone but us to say when we get there.

LYING PREGNANT IN the winter sun with our cats, the snowy mountain outside our bedroom window, I didn't know any of that. It just felt good to imagine devoting myself to the needs of my unborn baby. It felt healing. After all, I knew the pain of feeling unloved. And something really resonated with me when I read from *The Baby Book,* "Studies have shown that infants who develop a secure attachment with their mothers during the first year are better able to tolerate separation from them when they are older." A "secure attachment" sounded like something worth having, and I wondered if I had one. Thinking back to my own childhood, and with a quick scan of all the trouble I'd been in and caused, I figured probably not.

One of my earliest memories is of being in the kitchen with my mother and asking her a question. She was busy. I was not. It's a posture that defines my childhood—her back to me, her motion; my stillness. Her *just going about my business* stance; my *something's missing* longing to be rescued from the pain of feeling alone in the house, unseen by my parents and shut out by my older brothers. My mom always said that being a mother was her true calling, which I found odd, since she really didn't seem all that into it. Regardless of the insults or violence that rose up between my brothers and me—their taunts sometimes led to physical aggression—she watched from the sidelines, choosing to stay moving and focused on taking care of *things* instead of me. Even as a little girl climbing onto her lap, I often felt disappointed. Her distracted, stiff cuddle just didn't satisfy me, and I would get down, still searching for something. As adults, my two brothers and I don't see one another much, and we see eye to eye on even less, but one thing we can all agree on is that my mom was obsessed with housework, particularly vacuuming, and especially in the morning, when her house of teenagers was asleep. And we can even—sometimes—chuckle about how she once told my brothers to go "clean up" the woods surrounding our house.

When I was pregnant, I was determined to be a warmer, more present, and more loving mom than mine had been. I had a feeling it might be tricky, since I also knew how much we tend to be just like our own parents. And in fact Azalea wouldn't dream of eating in my new car, and she scrambles for the paper towels whenever she spills something. But there's so much more to our relationship than cleaning up, I tell myself. And she doesn't need protection, I tell myself. Not like I did.

"HEY, BETH, YOU'RE UGLY," Sam, my oldest brother, reminded me one typical Saturday morning from his seat on the couch, wrapped in Grandma Beryl's afghan, our cat Tasha curled in his lap. I was eight years old, though even today, at forty-eight, I can hear his voice when I look in the mirror. I had just walked in from my room down the hall, looking for a place to sit, to settle, to be. No such luck. Matt, my middle brother, sat on the floor as they watched Abbott and Costello, the comedy duo. He hissed a laugh, like a balloon letting out air. We were all in our pajamas, our parents still asleep. Two empty cereal bowls sat on the coffee table, bathed in snow-light.

I went to the kitchen and poured myself a bowl of cereal and sat at the snack bar alone, my throat tingling, tears starting to well up, yet again stirred by the familiar frustration, the pain of not finding my place. When my mom finally came into the kitchen in her robe and poured water into the coffeepot, tears started sliding down my cheeks.

"Mom," I said, trying to be quiet.

"Mmm . . . hmm?" she asked, studying the faucet.

"They're *so* mean to me," I said. "I hate them."

"Just ignore them, honey," she said, spooning coffee grounds into the filter.

Just then my dad walked in, wearing his bathrobe, his knees crackling. He sat down next to me and opened the paper, then lit a cigarette.

"It'll make you tough," he said, then exhaled a stream of smoke across the breakfast bar.

GROWING UP IN a house with two older brothers who had their own demons to fight, and who weren't the least bit interested in me, did make me tough. And guarded. And very angry. Though they were just kids themselves, they were bigger and stronger than I was, and they regularly, and sometimes viciously, told me how much they hated me. They harassed me at school, seeming to take pleasure in embarrassing me in front of my few friends. Their marked lack of interest was humiliating. What kind of person is rejected by her own brothers? Sometimes I worried there was something seriously wrong with me. The rest of the time I dreamt of beating them up, even though I didn't stand a chance. So I turned to myself and fantasies of revenge, of a future when they would rue the day.

And it wasn't just my brothers who made me feel painfully awkward within my own family—self-conscious, like a ghost floating around the periphery.

My dad also made me uncomfortable, and I felt ashamed of my discomfort. Once, he took me for a ride in the vintage Jaguar he couldn't afford and went speeding down the country roads where we lived, ignoring my cries of "Dad, please slow down!" His nonresponse made me feel as if it was my fault I felt unsafe, and that I was ruining his good time.

Another time, we were visiting Ann Arbor and he yelled something at the skinhead neo-Nazis distributing anti-Semitic materials on a corner. Then he flipped them the bird. His rage made me nervous, but it was nice to feel protected by him for once—a strange brew.

Another time, I was taking a bath in the bathroom at the end of the hall with the yellow-and-silver foil wallpaper. I was old enough to be left alone in the tub, but young enough to still need checking in on. He poked his bald head into the steamy bathroom and I instantly responded with "No. Get Mom."

As a therapist I used to see once said to me, "Little girls aren't born not loving their daddies." I thought something must have happened to make me not love mine. For many years I believed that the clue to that something, and the difficulties that followed, could be found in that bathtub memory.

I mean, what has to happen to a little girl to be so rejecting of her father? What kind of relationship leads up to such a clear and resounding *No*?

WHEN I WAS PREGNANT, I dreamt about Azalea a lot. I wrote in my journal every day, wondering what she was going to be like, cataloging my growing belly, how difficult it was to walk, learning more about myself and my body as I wrote and reflected. I wrote about how much I loved Thayer, and how being pregnant made me feel vulnerable. I wrote about where our little girl, whom we had already named Azalea, might sleep, and how we might try "sleep training," though I wondered whether she would become "attached" if we did.

I needn't have worried that Azalea wouldn't become attached. Even my 1970s mom and dad were attachment parents. There's no other kind. We're all attachment children, too.

But how could I have known?

When I was pregnant, I just wanted to be a good mother. Better than my own—more attentive, a better listener, a true—a *fierce*—protector. I couldn't bear the thought of my unborn baby feeling as alone as I had, so I determined to give her a different kind of life, a different, better kind of love.

I had no idea how the past and present, comfort and disappointment, security and sadness would entwine into such an elegant knot.

chapter two

When Azalea was seven, she and I sat on the deck with my mom, who was visiting us from Michigan. The occasion for the trip was Azalea's Grandparents and Special Friends Day. My mom had been driving me crazy. She made innocent "suggestions" about how I could do everything better, from setting the table to cooking the burgers to being nicer to Thayer, who rolled his eyes when she wasn't looking but probably loved it. I still felt like she didn't see me at all. And I still felt like she was cold, unattuned. She never meant to be bossy or intrusive or rude, of course, but she couldn't help it. One day she snidely told me she thought my skirt was ugly, which really threw me. For the rest of the day, I silently fumed as we cooked and then ate, and then at night, as Thayer put Azalea to bed, my mom and I sat out on the deck, sipping our drinks—me a glass of wine, her a VO and water—and just watched the bats swoop across our yard, listening to the birds sing into silent darkness. As we sat there, I told her that I thought she was out of line in insulting me like that, especially in front of my family, and she took it in, then apologized.

A couple of days later, we sat chatting over guacamole and

chips. Azalea had been telling us about how her teacher counted "blurts" on the board, and then withheld recess from the kids who talked out of turn the most.

"It's not fair!" she said.

My mom and I agreed, saying that those were the kids who probably needed recess the most.

All of a sudden, my mom said, "Oh my gosh, Azalea, have I ever told you about Miss Patterson?"

Azalea shook her head and looked at me. I had never heard the story, either.

"Well," my mom began, reaching for her sparkly cigarette pouch, "when I was in fifth grade, Miss Patterson—who ran an old-fashioned classroom—hit kids with a strap for talking."

"Really?" Azalea asked, looking at me, her soft blue eyes open wide. She grabbed a chip. "Kids got hit?"

"One day," my mom said, nodding, "I must have whispered something to a friend, and Miss Patterson told me to go put an X next to my name."

My mom's voice got stern, and she dropped her chin. " 'That's almost your third, isn't it, Libby?' said Miss Patterson, and then Bobby Connor piped up, 'That *was* her third, Miss Patterson.' "

Azalea laughed, maybe thinking of the know-it-all brown-nosers in her class.

"How the hell did he know?" my mom snorted, putting her cigarette to her lips, then inhaling, her long fingers hovering near her mouth.

"And of course," she added, exhaling, "he was always in trouble."

Watching my mom's silver smoke disperse in waves, then bits, wondering where it goes, I listened as she told Azalea about how the worst part was that her parents' policy was that if she or her sisters got the strap in school, they would get it again at home, and she knew that her sisters would hardly be able to wait to snitch on her. They were older than she was and in a different class, but it was a small school in the tiny Ontario town where she grew up, and news traveled fast.

"Oh my gosh!" Azalea said.

"The next day," my mom continued, "Miss Patterson said, 'We have some unfinished business to attend to, Libby.'

"My poor little heart was pounding as she took me to the hall outside the class," my mom said, taking another drag.

But when she got to the hall, Miss Patterson gave her a package to take down the hall to the third grade teacher, Mrs. McIntosh, which she did, dutifully, if a little confused.

And then as my mom, wearing a perfectly pleated wool skirt from Scotland and brown lace-up shoes—just a few years older than Azalea was now, sitting next to her in shorts and flip-flops—walked through the hall, she heard the strap hitting the wall.

My mom made the noise. *Whack. Whack. Whack.*

"When I got back to her classroom, Miss Patterson was waiting for me." Putting her hands out in front of her, my mom said, "She gave me a light tap on each hand, and not another word was spoken about the matter. I wonder," she mused, "if the night before, she pondered what to do and hatched the plan with her friend Mrs. McIntosh."

Azalea grabbed another chip, munching away triumphantly for her grandma. But I was beginning to smell a rat. All of my mom's stories seemed to revolve around her youthful delicacy, and I wasn't buying it. She was somehow so vulnerable that even mean old Miss Patterson couldn't bear to give her a whack on the wrists?

My mom always talked about me the same way. She would show Azalea pictures of me as a little girl, standing alone at a table with all my cousins, looking totally sad and utterly alone, and say things like "Awww . . . your mom was so sweet. Wasn't she?"

And I would think: (a) You don't know me; I was hardly sweet—more like angry as hell, even then—and (b) if you thought I was so damn cute, why didn't you pay more attention to me? Or protect me?

I was also hurt by the fact that my mother didn't seem to remember anything about my infancy or early life, or anything, for that matter, that I asked her about. "That was a long time ago, honey," she'd say when Azalea was born and I asked her about the minutiae of sleep training or nursing or anything at all about taking care of the babies she swore gave her life meaning. But then she'd bust out with great advice, which I hardly took in, like the afternoon when Baby Azalea was crying after a feeding, and my mom, who was visiting, suggested I try burping her.

"Nah," I said, figuring that since none of the doctors or midwives had mentioned it, burping was no longer a thing. But after her relentless encouragement to try it, I finally gave in. Practically rolling my eyes like an irritated teenager, I put Azalea up on my shoulder, gave her a few pats, and the cutest little sound came out of her mouth. Then she went to sleep.

By the time my mom was pregnant with me, she had already given birth to two sons—Matt two years earlier and Sam two years before that—which I figured had something to do with why she remembered so little. For instance, when I asked my mom what it was like to give birth to me, she would always tell me the same pat story about how she was so excited I was a girl. And about how the rabbi came in to meet me and said, "She is very intelligent." I have always loved this part of the story—because of my great longing to be seen as smart, of course, but mostly because of my even greater longing to simply be *seen*. I like to think of this papery old man looking into my face and asking himself a question. A question about me.

In a picture taken after my birth, my mother lies in the hospital bed, holding me in her arms, a kidney-shaped bedpan and a pack of Tareyton cigarettes on the bedside table. She looks relaxed, happy, not sweaty or particularly emotional. I was her third, after all, and she was numb, having received the full "saddle block" treatment. This is the woman who told me, when I was pregnant with Azalea, that labor pains felt like when you had to "go to the bathroom," as in pressure "down there." In this picture, I can see that she was not kidding—she looks like someone who was just relieved of a minor burden.

My mom's sister, Aunt Brenda, who was a nurse at the time, told my mom about the benefits of breastfeeding—which was not de rigueur at the time, or even encouraged—so Matt and I were nursed. And then, when Azalea was a baby, my mom, who had been smoking since grade school—really!—admitted to me that she had even smoked while nursing me. I told her I could imagine that a few puffs here or there wouldn't be so terrible. And she said, "No. I mean, I smoked *while* nursing. As in at the same time."

It's hard to imagine nursing a newborn baby while holding a cigarette. Did she think to blow the smoke away from my little face? Did the ash ever fall onto my soft, wrinkled forehead?

Was she even looking?

chapter three

Azalea was born on January 27, 2006, at 6:15 P.M. It was nothing at all like sitting on the toilet.

After a day of painful pushing, with the help of Thayer and one of my best friends at my side, the midwife realized that Azalea wasn't coming out on her own, so I was wheeled into the operating room, and soon nearly seven pounds of human life—my daughter—was lifted from the ocean of my body.

As I lay on the surgical table, a green cotton screen pulled taut between my face and my exposed guts, Thayer, in scrubs, held our tiny baby bird in his arms, looking at me, and though I couldn't see it, I knew his mouth was open, halfway between a smile and a sob. I looked at our baby. Her eyes were closed. I finished vomiting into a tray in time to smile for a picture.

Life in the hospital was grand. I loved being awakened every few hours to nurse my baby into this world. It was like a moon-filled Arctic day, totally unmarked by time. And Azalea was perfect: her ears, eensy-weensy fingernails, and crinkly thighs, that musky little mammalian neck.

Holding Azalea's tiny sleeping body in my arms, I called another dear friend, who was stuck in Vermont instead of being there with me, as we'd planned.

"Tell me," she said.

"Girl, I had no idea," I cried. "I love this baby so much."

"Whoa," she said.

"I know," I said, sucking in some air. "Whoa."

IT WAS A few short/long months later when I changed Azalea's diaper on the pad on top of our old dresser, and she looked around the room, then at me, hands waving, feet jerking in little socks the size of a snail. I smiled into her sweet little face, then sat down and nursed her, her eyes fluttering lightly until she fell asleep, her warm, whistly nose-breath long and heavy on my breast, her eyes closed tight. Then I laid her gently down in her crib, surrounded by the soft white bumper. I had already closed the curtains against the spring sun.

Pulling the door quietly behind me, I snuck out to the cedar deck in the backyard, journal in my hand, as hot tears rose up in my throat. I sat down and cried, looking out toward the greening May mountain rising above us, hoping it would protect Azalea against the terrible words that circled in my head, the words I was afraid to write. I loved this child with all my heart, and yet I was miserable. How could both be true?

So that Azalea would never have to know how difficult being her mother was for me, I made a deal with myself: I would allow myself the comfort of writing it all out, but only if I made it disappear. And indeed, I recently found that old journal, with a section of pages ripped out, leaving a row of little paper teeth along the spine, dotted with edges of handwritten o's and t's and s's. Specks of words.

I remember that day well—the relief of truth spilling onto the page. And the pain of what the words said.

It had never before occurred to me to erase something I had written, because my words had always been my periscope, and to cross something out would have submerged me into darkness.

Until I became a mother.

Then I was writing as a prayer to save my life, and my daughter's. That's how much I loved her—I was willing to risk facing a dark truth because I knew even then, at the beginning of this journey, that in order to save her, I had to save myself.

I didn't yet know why or how it was so, but I knew that in some deep way, she and I will always be in the same boat, rowing against the same tide, toward the same shore.

beautiful child

In Swahili, the lingua franca of East Africa, any journey is called a safari. Whenever I left Kampala to spend an afternoon with a village family I made a safari. These many small safaris were, however, only the beginning of a much longer safari . . . a journey in understanding . . . What has emerged is a new way of viewing the origins and early growth of first love—the attachment of a baby to his mother.

—Mary Ainsworth, *Infancy in Uganda*

chapter four

One of the first phrases Mary Ainsworth learned when she arrived in Uganda was *"Omwana mulungi nnyo nnyo."* In Luganda this means "Oh! What a *beautiful* child!" Mary was seeking subjects for what would soon become one of the most important studies of mothers and babies ever completed, and though not a mother herself, she knew how to get a woman's attention.

It was 1954 when she and her husband, Len, finally docked in Kampala. Because all of Mary's writing about this time is so vivid, and because she took black-and-white pictures of the people she met in the villages surrounding Kampala, I have been able to imagine what these important few months might have been like for her. For instance, throughout her field notes, she manages to tuck mentions of the heat into many descriptions, some of which are ostensibly about other things. In addition to "The climate is tropical but surprisingly moderate," she writes, "Increasing numbers of the wattle-and-daub houses have roofs of corrugated iron or aluminum . . . even though they make for a hotter house." Or "Babies were often clothed, although midday temperatures did not require clothing for warmth . . . [Others] were usually naked . . . [but] put into clothes for special occasions, or for warmth when the sun got low in the sky in the late afternoon."

I can only imagine how the African sun beat down on her like a torch as she and Len stepped down the gangplank upon their arrival. It would have been quite a contrast to the rainy days of Halifax, where the two of them had begun their journey on New Year's Day. Though this trip would set her entire life and career in motion, she was "not enthusiastic" about it.

But she had an idea. While in Africa, she would try to answer some questions that had been nagging at her—some questions about the nature of love. And she was eager to try out the naturalistic research methods she had recently learned about from her colleague Jimmy Robertson, whom she had met on the job in London, where she was a research associate. John Bowlby and his team were studying maternal separations as he developed a new theory of parental bonds he called "attachment," and, though she was part of the team, she was skeptical.

Mary had heard that Ganda mothers send their children away when weaning, usually when another child is born. She thought this would be a very tidy way of studying a sudden, possibly traumatic separation that she could then compare with the more ordinary everyday separations that occur in every child's life, which she hoped to observe in her home visits. She had believed that by comparing these two types of separations, she would be able to better understand Bowlby's ideas about "attachment."

Once she arrived, she was able to "scrape together" the funds she needed for the home study of infant-mother behavior she had begun to envision. With the help of someone at the East African Institute of Social Research, she received just enough to support herself and an interpreter, Mrs. Katie Kibuka, a Ganda mother who had studied in the States and who would become Mary's beloved assistant and translator.

However, she soon learned that the sudden weaning in these Ganda villages never really happened. What she had conceived as the control or baseline to this variable—ordinary separations—became the study itself: everyday life for babies in Uganda.

MARY FORGED AHEAD. Her first order of business was to find subjects willing to be visited and interviewed by this "European"—the way all white people were described in the villages where her research took place—woman scientist in their home for two hours every two weeks. Though Mary describes these interactions as more like social occasions than clinical interviews, the women still had to be willing to answer all kinds of questions about their households, their children's births, their parenting decisions, their children's development, health, and—most important—separations.

She was led around the villages by a tribal chief who had agreed to help her find mothers willing to be part of her study—perhaps the same male elder who appears in one of Mary's photographs wearing a Western blazer, holding a baby, and looking very serious. She—impressively—had learned enough Luganda to write and recite a speech about how interested she was in the pros and cons of parenting practices in two very different cultures, framing her study in simple, neutral terms: "As you know, your own customs differ in many respects from European customs. I am especially interested in different customs about caring for infants."

Mary was riveted by the people and the families she met. She saw babies who looked like they were just nine months old walking in bare feet, a string of bells around their ankle jingling. She would later learn that Ganda parents put these bells on their babies' ankles because the babies like the music of it, and it inspires them to walk. She writes of the families and their lives in attentive, loving detail:

> Their house, although made of wattle and daub with a thatched roof, gave an impression of both grace and substance. Flowers grew in the front yard, and there was a graceful shade tree. Inside it was comfortable. There were simple but comfortable chairs. A woven reed ceiling lent coolness [!] to the rooms. Family pictures covered the walls, and there was one colorful painting that one of the children had done at school. There were several little tables with cross-stitched covers. There was always a vase of flowers. When we came to visit we sat in the cool, dim living room, sometimes outside under the shade tree.

Based on descriptions like this, as well as her photographs, I've formed a picture of Mary on that first day of looking for participants: She's wearing a short-sleeved 1950s day dress, white flip-flop sandals, and no makeup. In her purse are a notepad, a pencil, and her camera. Her hair is up and away from her broad, high-cheekboned face. She wears glasses. She's hot as hell, but happy.

WHEN MARY ARRIVED in Uganda, she was forty-two years old. She had received her PhD rather late, having enlisted in the Canadian Women's Army Corps during World War II, so she was eager to get started on the academic career she had been working toward since she entered the University of Toronto at the young age of sixteen. But her husband, Len, had received a position at the University of East Africa, and she went with him.

She had spent the previous four years working with Dr. John Bowlby in London, another overseas stint she'd gone on because of Len, who had been completing his degree there. Bowlby was working out his theory that the love babies feel for their parents had evolved to keep them close and safe, like geese lined up behind their mother. This attachment, he believed, was at the root of the child-parent relationship, and stood in stark opposition to the prevailing theory of child-parent affection at the time, one that posited that babies love their mothers because their mothers feed them. If the so-called theory of "cupboard love" was correct, it wouldn't matter if a child was separated from a parent, as long as someone was there to boil the peas. Bowlby, who had been working with orphans and delinquents in post– World War II England, knew that was wrong. He saw firsthand how these separated children were, in fact, deeply mourning the loss of their parents.

Mary, like almost all the psychologists of her day, didn't buy Bowlby's theory at first. So she set out to see for herself.

IN THE 1940S and '50s, scientific understandings of the impact of parenting were fuzzy, even lacking what we might today consider common sense. B. F. Skinner, the behaviorist guru, championed the belief that our feelings and actions were simply robotically conditioned responses to stimuli. To prove his theory, he raised one of his daughters for the first eleven months of her life in a labor-saving "baby tender," a standard-size crib with removable safety glass and its own air circulation system, like a fully functional baby-scale house. No more pesky adjusting of nightclothes or bedding. No more midnight feedings. By simply keeping the baby in a clean diaper and adjusting the temperature of the baby tender, the Skinners found that their baby was very happy. So cheerful, in fact, that she was almost entirely silent. "During the past six months," Skinner writes, "she has not cried at all except for a moment or two when injured or sharply distressed." The proud Skinners found that the many hours they may have wasted in playing, touching, feeding, and comforting their baby were much better spent in some "welcome leisure." This was, as Skinner writes, a "brave new world which science is preparing for the housewife of the future."

As outrageous as the baby tender sounds, the idea that children are simply mechanical beings, reliant solely upon things like food and shelter in order to thrive, was pervasive. The behaviorists explicitly frowned upon showing children too much affection, as if loving attention would make babies "soft" and needy. Both the cupboard love theory and the behaviorists try to explain away an emotion as wild and inconvenient as the kind of love that parents and their babies have for each other.

I get it. Love has a way of taking over.

FOR A FEW very happy months, Mary traveled through the villages, observing the women, their children, and their world. Mary was with these families through their children's milestones, first-wife/second-wife dramas—there was a group of polygamous families in her sample—and one tragic death. She watched the mothers cradle their ill infants, sit them up for photographs, bathe them several times a day, carry them on their backs, and smile at them from across the room. She brought the children candy and relished watching them eat it, their little bodies sticky with sweetness. Mary's days were completely absorbed in her observing and her wondering, showering these unbelievably lucky families with her wise and loving attention.

As payment to the twenty-six families who finally agreed to be involved in the study, Mary offered to drive the women and their children to and from the clinic in nearby Kampala for their routine checkups and shots and whenever they were sick; it was a valuable service in a community where transportation was difficult and illness was common. Here she had a chance to sit with the babies in a new, strange, and slightly scary situation and to watch them be afraid and then be soothed by their mothers. Or not. Trying to distract them, she let the babies play with the pencil in her purse or watched them get momentarily distracted by her oddly white, sandaled feet. Then she'd watch them retreat from her, back onto their mother's lap, when they'd had enough of her games or were afraid.

What she learned in those hours of sitting with babies and their mothers in the hot waiting room planted the seeds for the development of what would come later—one of the most important laboratory procedures in the history of psychology.

INFANCY IN UGANDA, the book Mary published in 1967, is filled with intimate black-and-white photos she took of babies in strappy rompers or wearing little anklets and long, quaint dresses. It's filled with the affection she developed for the mothers and their gentle but confident child-rearing, undramatically raising their adorable and physically precocious children, who were "clearly accelerated in their rate of sensorimotor development" and thus walked, talked, and were potty-trained so far ahead of Western babies. Some babies had achieved "elimination control" by the age of four months, but almost all by the time they were a year old. She admired the way mothers so seamlessly offered their breast, and just as effortlessly tucked themselves back into their dresses, designed for easy nursing, when they or their babies were finished.

A rather proper Canadian lady of the 1950s, Mary was impressed by this culture of such fine manners, one in which "the children over two years of age (or thereabouts) sit politely with their feet tucked under them out of sight, listening to the talk of their elders." Mary seemed especially pleased by the way babies were considered such a blessing in this culture, and treated so tenderly. She writes, "The ladies sit chatting on mats on the floor. The youngest babies are held on laps and are passed around from one lap to another, for it is considered a pleasure and an honor to be given someone else's baby to hold for a while."

But these mothers were far from perfect, especially from a contemporary Western perspective, where we have some big assumptions about what it means to be a good mother. Some of Mary's favorite mothers did things like "beat" (that was the mothers' word; it was more like a little thump) their babies with a cupped hand for misbehaving. Not all of the mothers breastfed or slept with their babies. They potty-trained their young infants by holding them up and teaching them to squat over a hole, and, in the process, had to deal with a lot of accidents. Mary watched a baby or two have a bowel movement on their mother's lap or on the floor, which the mother cleaned up "without fuss."

Mary was completely taken with the Ganda women and their "dignified and graceful carriage," and it appears that the feeling was mutual. One family was so convinced that their beloved Paulo would have a better life with Mary in Canada that they asked her to take him home with her.

Because she was a particularly strange stranger—most of her subjects had never seen a white person—entering these babies' homes every couple of weeks or more and sitting down in the family's one chair to chat with their mothers for an hour or two, Mary repeatedly had the experience of watching babies who were shy and fearful sit gazing and smiling from their mothers' laps as they worked up the courage to walk across the room to her for a sweet or a cuddle. This back-and-forth between mother and her reminded her of what she had learned when she wrote her dissertation, which was about the way young adults use their parents as a "secure base" as they grow and differentiate from their families. She began to see the way these babies did this through what she and John Bowlby would later refer to as "attachment behaviors" like crying, following, climbing up the mother's body, or smiling in order to signal to their mother their need for comfort or attention. Some babies were able to get adequately reassured by the secure base of their mother to make it all the way to the other side of the room, where Mary sat invitingly. Others were more shy or hesitant, or just unable to settle. It became clear to Mary that what she was watching was more than just two people negotiating space and boundaries. It was a *relationship*. The idea that these babies cared about their mothers only because their mothers fed them was ridiculous. These babies and their mothers were *connected*.

Mary also began to see that the children who were very attentive to their mothers and who, in return, had attentive mothers were nearly giddy with delight much of the time, clapping their hands, returning to their mothers *even when they weren't hungry,* smiling from across the room for no good reason. They seemed to have a mutually pleasing, special relationship.

Through the home visits, clinic observations, and sharing of such cozy, intimate time with these twenty-six women and their children, Mary began to see Bowlby's budding theory of attachment come to life before her very eyes. Something was going on between these pairs that made them so tuned in to each other, and it was something much deeper and more subtle than physical hunger; it was more like an invisible force that made them move in tandem, as if reflections in a mirror. "It was," she says, "a sudden, total, and permanent change in perspective."

chapter five

When the Ainsworths left Uganda in 1955, Len got a job in the Baltimore area and Mary was eventually offered a position at Johns Hopkins, teaching psychology. In addition to settling into a new routine, she had another very big task ahead of her. Her visits in Uganda totaled hundreds of hours, and she had taken copious and continuous notes on everything from sleep practices, discipline, feeding, elimination, and other people in the family to clothing, home decor, and manners—basically everything she had observed. And now, from her desk in Baltimore, reading and rereading her handwritten notes, seeking both patterns and surprises, she had to find her way through it all.

She had started to sort the children and their mothers into three categories. Around 57 percent (sixteen pairs) were what she called "secure," meaning the children appeared to know how to use their mother as a secure base in their explorations of the world. And explore they did.

Juko (thirty and thirty-two weeks) did much cheerful exploring, even out the front door of the house. Especially at thirty-two weeks, he kept returning to his mother and seeking the breast before taking off on another jaunt.

Around 25 percent (seven pairs) were what she called "insecurely attached," meaning the babies found it difficult to relax into reliance on their mother, thus making it more difficult for them to experience the world with the zeal of the others.

Sulaimani (forty weeks) cried immediately when his mother put him down but stopped when she picked him up again. Again she tried to put him down; he screamed, and did not stop this time even when she took him up again. Later he permitted her to set him down on the floor but he played in a desultory way and protested whenever she moved away.

And just a handful (five pairs) were "not yet attached," meaning they didn't seem to have a "special" relationship with their mother at all, a phenomenon Ainsworth came to understand very differently later.

The twins manifested very little attachment behavior during the period of investigation. At twenty-three weeks they were described as lifting their heads up and vocalizing (as though they wanted to sit) in response to the approach of a person, but the response seemed quite non-differential . . . Neither baby cried when the mother left the room and both were described as behaving toward the mother no differently than they behaved toward others.

While we often think that babies not responding differentially to one special caregiver is a good thing, a sign of a certain degree of self-sufficiency, Mary began to believe that the opposite was true—that being able to discriminate one's attachment figure from all others is in fact the infant's first step in developing an attachment. While secure babies may well enjoy the affections of many people, attachment theory posits that children benefit from having one special relationship, even in cultures where children are cared for by many loving people. More and more, Mary saw that babies who didn't seem particularly affected, at age one, by an attachment figure's departure and return might actually be responding to various upsets and anxieties in their family's life that negatively impacted the attachment process, and she was very sympathetic about this.

Struck by the differences in attachment behavior she was seeing in her notes, Mary wondered why. Was there more going on than what she could see on the surface? Aside from the expected emotional ups and downs of family life, why would some relationships create a more secure feeling for babies than others?

As she searched her notebooks for clues, she noticed that there were "a few gaps in information." Even though she had made every effort to visit each family for roughly the same amount of time, she began to see that she had significantly less information about some babies than others. She realized that in some cases this was due to a "reluctance to cooperate," which made perfect sense: if a mother wasn't very forthcoming, then of course Mary wouldn't have a lot of data about that baby. But in other cases, the families had been visited with regularity and she was left *feeling* that the mothers were totally cooperating, so much so that Mary found it "unbelievable that the data could be incomplete."

She noticed that the babies about whom she had the least data were the ones she deemed insecure or "not yet attached." This was big—an observation that is at the root of all the attachment research that would come later.

Some of the mothers from her study were "very pleasant,

welcoming and cooperative" but didn't really have a lot of rich detail to share about their child, or were more interested in chatting about "things other than the baby," while other women, who were "equally hospitable . . . proved to be excellent informants." When asked about their babies, "they responded readily, volunteering relevant information and giving much spontaneous detail about the baby's behavior." Of the former group, she writes, "The phenomenon of finding incomplete data, despite numerous visits, highlighted the fact that these mothers *differed in their excellence as informants*" (italics mine).

Mary investigated further by looking back through the data and asking which mothers had the *most* insight into their children. And what did it mean, if anything?

What she found was that "mother's excellence as informant" was significantly correlated with babies being securely attached. This was a surprising finding that continues to unfold in contemporary attachment research. It points in an incredibly important direction—toward the *experience* of being a parent. Of the other possible factors she thought might be related to attachment security—warmth of mother, multiple caretakers, amount of care given by the mother, total amount of care, scheduled vs. self-demand feeding, mother's milk supply, mother's attitude toward breastfeeding—the only two that showed any connection at all were "mother's attitude toward breastfeeding" and "total amount of care." The latter, she believed, emerged as an important variable because the mother's availability, her "total amount of care," is simply a "necessary condition" for interaction. In other words, it's not so much the care itself that is associated with security, but the fact that the mother has to be there in order to be in a relationship with her child. "If the mother is elsewhere," Mary writes, "she obviously cannot respond to and interact with the baby, although her mere presence is no guarantee of sensitivity or interaction."

The fact that Mary even thought to ask these women whether or not they enjoyed breastfeeding, that she uncovered that it was the mothers' *feelings*—their pleasure, their delight—that mattered more than the nursing itself, is a major departure from the way mothers were viewed in the 1950s, and it still is.

In other words, while all the external, easily observed behaviors, like feeding and playing and cuddling and disciplining, were interesting to Mary, ultimately these actions were more like the bread crumbs leading back to what Mary found really mattered—a mother's "attitude." Excellent informants were mothers who were able, for some reason, to pay more attention to their children and, through their own awareness, to tell a compelling, detailed, vivid, and true enough story about them. And so it was that, by tracking the behaviors between mothers and their babies, she began to see that a woman's internal experience called for investigation.

Radical. A woman's feelings about her child are worthy of the scientific gaze.

Mary couldn't wait until she could do another study confirming what she saw in Uganda—that babies really do use their mother as a secure base, and that a parent's attention is like the sunlight that grows a secure attachment.

What Mary saw and what has been borne out in study after study since is that the way we *feel* about our relationships gets conveyed in the stories we tell—about our children and about ourselves—and the lives we live based upon these stories. And so it is through these narratives, made manifest in our lives, that our children tend to feel what we feel, and internalize it. This is how attachment is passed down through generations.

And this is the way we can transform those stories, those feelings, and our excellence as informants: simply—miraculously—by shedding our light upon them.

part iii

miracle

This internalized something that we call attachment has aspects of feelings, memories, wishes, expectancies, and intentions, all of which constitute an inner program acquired through experience and somehow built into a flexible yet retentive inner mechanism (which we identify with central nervous system functions) which serves as a kind of filter for the reception and interpretation of interpersonal experience and as a kind of template shaping the nature of outwardly observable response.

—Mary Ainsworth, *Infancy in Uganda*

chapter six

Never in a million years would I have guessed that I would end up living in a Zen monastery. I grew up in a Jewish household that was Christmas-tree- and bacon-free, but not particularly spiritual. In fact, I never thought of religion as having anything to do with me. While some children might lie in bed and pray to God or try to confess when they feel guilty for the sins they believe they've committed, I just looked out the window and stared into the trees and tried to accept the fact that I felt so strange. I felt confused and emotionally disjointed, like I had no business in this realm I'd found myself in, as if I were experiencing the spooky edges of someone else's dream.

And while some teenagers, college students, and young adults seek cool, dharma-bum spiritual answers to their coming-of-age questions, not me. I took refuge in Anne Sexton, the suicidal poet who wrote and talked in a scary-real voice about how she would

> walk in a yellow dress
> and a white pocketbook stuffed with cigarettes,

. . . .

I walk. I walk.

Eventually I also took to the beauty of dresses, cigarettes, and long walks. As a teenager, I slept around. I got high too often, and with the wrong crowds. I drank too much. And though I never once thought about religion, I was struck, all along, by the feeling that some miracle was keeping me safe.

Eventually, that same miracle helped me get to college, even though I had been a weak student, to say the least. And then to graduate school, where I studied poetry with Allen Ginsberg as my adviser. In my first poetry workshop with him, he had us write our "Top Ten Memories" as poems. He made it clear that this was not necessarily meant to be our earliest memories, just big ones, for whatever reason. As my number-one memory, I wrote:

> Sitting in the bathtub,
> Foil walls wink.
> Dad opens the door.
> *No, get Mom.*

There it was again. That bathtub memory.

After I graduated with my MFA, I got a real job teaching writing. Another miracle, given my poor employment record. And then I really put the miracle to the test.

I was living in Brooklyn with my college boyfriend. One day, on the subway home from work, a man—we'll call him Charles—sat down across from me. He wore a button-down white shirt and khakis, and the way he held himself with confidence, then crossed his legs, made him officially the sexiest man I had ever seen. Then he stared at me. And then I uncrossed my legs.

That weekend I saw him again, walking in our neighborhood as my boyfriend and I were taking a Saturday afternoon stroll. He was across the street. We waved to each other.

"Who was that?" my boyfriend asked.

"No one," I answered.

Soon after, I broke up with my boyfriend and chased the experience of Charles with everything I had. Charles was a lovely man in many ways, but jealous and explosive. After a year and a half of being dramatically and compulsively "together," my life was unraveling. My friends were losing their patience with my mood swings and long, weepy phone calls, not to mention the erratic and scary behavior I had come to accept—like the time Charles lunged at me on the street and some UPS guys came to my rescue. My work life suffered—who has time to mark up student papers when your boyfriend calls, then sends you away, then calls you back in the middle of the night to apologize and summon you again? I was so preoccupied with insecurity that my creativity came to a halt and I stopped writing poetry, then quit writing even in my journals. I was so consumed with my fear of his absence and the dry ache of never knowing where I stood with him that one damp winter day, as the 2 train came charging in, I saw myself lying in the tracks, obliterated, liberated from craving. I wanted to feel the contact of the train so badly that the bottoms of my feet tickled with the urge to jump.

But I stayed there in the silver puddle of my own boots.

And rather than get on the train and return to the small apartment where I would spend the evening in a treacherous cat-and-mouse game with Charles, a voice inside me told me to walk up the subway stairs and out into the damp Manhattan dusk, then a few blocks downtown to the neighborhood Barnes & Noble.

I went straight to the self-help section.

Riding the escalator up to the second floor, I thought, *This is what it feels like to hit bottom.* I had considered myself a feminist, an intellectual, a poet. But here I was, at the mercy of a man, with nowhere to turn, no more poems to write or read, looking for a savior like every other sorry sucker.

I had been working with a therapist named Grace, whom I loved. I'd sit in her cozy, dark, leathery, book-lined room and search her kind eyes.

"He threw his Kleenex on the floor," I cried, "and I knew that was me. I don't matter to him at all."

"That must have hurt terribly," she said.

But ultimately, even her loving gaze wasn't enough. When the fifty minutes were over, invariably I was back in a loop of obsession, the walls closing in. I needed more; I needed something else.

I stood there before the sea of pastel self-help-book spines. They all looked the same. And then I glanced to my left, to the "Eastern Thought" section. I saw one book that was face-out on the shelf. It was lovely—white, with purple flowers and ginkgo leaves, feminine but understated. My draw to the book was almost zombie-like, predetermined. When I reached it, I read its cover: *Nothing Special: Living Zen,* by Charlotte Joko Beck. I opened it and read the first chapter:

> We are rather like whirlpools in the river of life. In flowing forward, a river or stream may hit rocks, branches, or irregularities in the ground, causing whirlpools to spring up spontaneously here and there. Water entering one whirlpool quickly passes through and rejoins the river, eventually joining another whirlpool and moving on. Though for short periods it seems to be distinguishable as a separate event, the water in the whirlpools is just the river itself . . .

Ninety percent of a typical human life is spent trying to put boundaries around the whirlpool. We're constantly on guard: "He might hurt me." "This might go wrong." "I don't like him anyway." This is a complete misuse of our life function; yet we all do it to some degree.

Reading these words, I felt a rush of relief, as if my breath were getting knocked *into* me. I *was* that rushing, crazy, dangerous river. I experienced a brief flash of complete physical aliveness. And then it faded away and I was just me, sitting under fluorescent lights on a hard chair among people walking across the carpeted floor of a windowless room.

But I was no longer alone. I had a new book, a new idea, a new reality—a secure base—to check back with when the current of my obsession threatened to pull me under, as I knew it would. I couldn't stop thinking about this: *Being on guard is a misuse of my life function*. I wasn't sure what my life's function was, though I knew it had something to do with love.

chapter seven

One day not long before Charles finally left me, I tried zazen, the Japanese term for meditation, for the first time. Sitting on my bed in the middle of the day, legs folded, back straight, hands resting in what's called the "cosmic mudra," for the briefest moment I made contact with my very own breathing self. After so much scrambling to avoid the pain of my anguish, it was a relief. Seeing myself in the plain light of day wasn't nearly as bad as I had imagined.

In fact, I immediately saw—even in the state I was in—that being present was in some strange way delightful. It felt so good to let my guard down. What a surprise! This was, as Mary would say, "a sudden, total, and permanent change in perspective."

The zazen instructions are to count to ten with each inhalation and exhalation then notice when you've stopped counting and started thinking, which happened instantly. My mind immediately raced off into thoughts of Charles—Charles in our bed, Charles in a new bed with a new woman, Charles walking up the stairs to knock on my door, Charles breaking up with me, then wanting me back. The instruction is, once you notice that your mind has veered off, to let go of whatever you were thinking, gently and without judgment, and return to the number one. So that's what I did.

"One" became trusted ground.

My safe shore was close—very close.

As difficult as it was—the physical pain of sitting still, not to mention my incessant brain chatter and overwhelming emotions—I was hooked. Charles broke up with me for real, and for two years I lived alone and sat through the pain of letting go of him. And my life returned, bit by bit, like an IV drip.

I found myself so drawn to zazen that I started practicing at a city center, then at a beautiful bluestone monastery in the Catskills called Zen Mountain Monastery. The founder and abbot was an American named John Daido Loori, known for being a traditional Zen teacher, which he laughed about, saying that when Japanese monks came to visit, they called his thoroughly American teaching style "cowboy Zen." The first time I went to a retreat at the monastery, I didn't know who Daido was, but I couldn't miss him as he stood in the dining hall with students. He was tall, skinny, and a little hunched, smoking a cigarette and holding court. A faded Navy tattoo peeked out from his rolled-up shirtsleeve. When I saw him later in his monk's robe, sitting at the front of the meditation hall with his legs folded beneath him, I was impressed with his ability to transform himself. That was when I decided to ask him to become my teacher.

And then, one Tuesday morning in June, a few years after I discovered Zen in a Barnes & Noble, I packed a bag and rode the Trailways bus up the winding road to the Catskills to spend a month at the monastery. I had visited several times and was practicing at the city center fairly regularly, so I knew some of the monks. I had noticed an intense young guy with clear blue eyes during one of my early visits, while I was standing in line for lunch. He was talking to one of the men I knew and laughing.

Walking into the dining hall that day in June, I saw him again. It was Thayer standing at the bulletin board, alone this time, in his gray meditation robe and shearling slippers. He was young—just twenty-two; I was twenty-eight. He was a powerhouse of a guy, with a wide back and short, dark curls. The floor seemed to carry him when he walked. He was beautiful and deep and safe the way a mountain is safe. And I knew in that moment that I would marry him.

In a picture taken by one of the monks after a sesshin—a silent, weeklong meditation retreat—Thayer and I are sitting on the back steps of the monastery, both in short sleeves. Thayer is looking ahead, intently describing something, and my entire body is turned toward him. My face is so wide open, I look as if I am staring into the face of a golden Buddha, which was exactly how I felt.

Three years later, we got married in a Buddhist wedding in a hand-chiseled rock quarry. One of my vows was to "spend the rest of my life studying the question *What is love?*"

AFTER THE WEDDING, we lived together in New York City until Thayer received his master's in social work. Soon after, we tied our mattress to the top of our car and drove back to the monastery. We settled into a little cabin in the woods heated by a woodstove. We loved waking in silence at 3:00 A.M. and walking down the moonlit path to the stone building, where we sat in stillness for hours at a time, chanted, lived communally, cleaned toilets.

And as plodding as the days often felt, Thayer and I loved it, because we felt like we were doing something big, something important. And it was such a rush doing it together. We even

contemplated the possibility that we may want to be monks forever, shaving our heads, making a vow to serve this community
and these teachers for life. While practice centers vary on this
point, at Zen Mountain Monastery, committed relationships
are acceptable for monks, but having children is not, because
Daido, who had grown children of his own, believed that once
a person has children, those babies should become the top prior-
ity. Which was fine with us; it was depth that we craved, and we
weren't sure where else to find it, even though the rigor of the
life—the lack of sleep, the community living—was starting to
take a toll.

Near the end of our second year, I was tired all the time and
had developed a pervasive dizziness, throwing up at odd and
inopportune times. Finally, an ear, nose, and throat doctor diagnosed an inner ear infection gone haywire and handed me a
prescription for eight hours of sleep a night.

"Sleep," she said, "is the only thing that will heal you."

Getting a doctor's note put a fine point on what had been
dawning on me, sadly. As much as I loved the Zen teachings and
practice, I couldn't live a monastic life. I had seen it coming, but
I was disappointed. I could practice Zen outside of the monastery, as I have, but I'd been enamored with the idea of the sin-
gular and wholehearted spiritual commitment required by
monastic life. This was partly a reflection of my need to get to
the heart of this great matter of life and death, but it also
stemmed from my hope that if I was totally plugged into something other than myself, I might be able to gloss over the pain of
being me.

But no such luck. I was exhausted, and I didn't really want to
live the rest of my life doing everyone else's dishes.

After a couple of months of heart-wrenching conversation—
with the monks, with Daido, and with ourselves—we decided
it was time to leave. We both craved an intensity that our regu-

lar lives didn't seem to offer, but it had become clear that monastic life wasn't the answer, either. We knew we wanted to stay close to the monastery. And we knew that there was another path that called to us in our quest to understand what it means to be a human being, one that would surely keep us close to home. Very close.

Sitting in front of the wide soapstone Buddha in the pine forest cemetery up the hill one winter afternoon, Thayer told me about a dream he'd recently had, of being in a city with lights and children floating between buildings like souls. One of the children approached him. This was a sign. He felt like it was time to go.

"Are you sure?" I asked.

He looked at me.

"Okay," I said. "Let's have a baby instead."

chapter eight

The first time Thayer and I drove up Fawnview Acres Road, it was soon after our decision to leave the monastery. We saw an ad for a house in the local paper, then we made plans with the realtor to check it out.

Driving down the woodland road along a stream, crossing bridge after bridge, we felt as though we were driving deep into the wilderness. From the long and winding road, we turned right. And there, perched in front of a wide, sky-filling Catskills mountain ridge, was the red cabin with the big stone stoop that we both immediately knew would be our first real home and—we hoped—the home of our child.

It was nine months later that we made love in our tiny bedroom, just big enough for a bed, surrounded by the wood-paneled walls we had painted with three coats of white. The just-greening mountain rose above us. One small window opened onto the sounds of the river at the bottom of the hill. We got out of bed, showered together, dressed, and met some friends for dinner at a little tavern in the woods. I remember the white shirt I wore—fitted, with the Nehru collar—from my favorite thrift store in the city. Our friends said we both looked radiant.

Another nine months after that, on a cold, rainy day, we left the hospital, Azalea in my arms.

We carefully unfolded our daughter's little body into her first-day-of-real-life floral outfit, which a friend had given us, and then buckled her into the gigantic car seat, following the instructions the local police had given me when I went to the precinct to learn how to do it right. I sat in the back seat, looking back and forth between Azalea's sleepy face and the windshield. *Is she hot? Is she cold? Are we going to crash?*

Walking into our house on Fawnview, I noticed that it was a little musty from the rain and our absence. The cats looked up from their naps. And that was about all the world had to say. I felt like I was returning from a complete body and mind transfusion, barely recognizing a single thing about myself, and yet the walls just stood there, blankly holding up the roof, and the chairs relaxed their legs into the floor, passively collecting dust.

Azalea's little eyes were fluttering open, and she moved her mouth around—hungry—so I had to find a place to sit in my old house/new life, and remove my melon-size breast from the ugliest bra in the world in order to nurse.

The underwhelming silence of reality's non-greeting notwithstanding, the first few days of life with Azalea were lovely. People brought us food and wanted to stay and chat, but we shooed them away, too overwhelmed with nursing and diapering and keeping the cats away from the baby to socialize. Azalea slept in fits and starts in a Moses basket on our bed with us. We both carried her in matching slings and blasted Hawaiian music, which she showed us she liked by being quiet or, if she was really enthusiastic, by falling asleep. I sat down once an hour, at least, to nurse. I nursed like crazy, my tiny baby gulping milk from my breast. She looked at me. And I looked back. We looked at each other.

When Azalea was a tiny infant, it was fairly easy to respond to her every chirp with loving affection, even when I was exhausted. Thayer was home, for one thing, which meant that we shared chores, and we could tag-team the nights for diaper changes and for bringing our girl into the bed for nursing.

It was a new world, with our beautiful, perfect Azalea in it. While my approach to motherhood had been a bit detached, the moment I became pregnant, I was flooded with love and a need to protect the life inside me. And when we brought her home and I got to know all her constantly changing Azalea ways, I could feel a crazy mother love brewing in my heart. But soon enough, something else started to grow there, too—a dark seed of discontent, which would soon grow into despair.

I had been working as an adjunct at the nearby university but had taken six months off. Thayer was deep in his work as a hospice social worker, driving his tiny black Toyota from death to death. I was grateful to have the time off, and yet motherhood as an activity made no sense to me. I tried to get excited about cloth diapers and making baby food, but I found that my attention wandered. I went to a couple of mommy-baby gatherings but found the serious contemplation of nap timing and teething remedies painfully dull, and I left feeling lonelier than when I'd arrived, because I just wasn't into the whole *mommy thing*. The days were long. I counted the hours and minutes until Thayer came home, and then I was furious at him for having abandoned me.

It's like this: I was crazy for Azalea, the person. But loving my daughter and loving being a mother seemed like two entirely different things. I felt fatigued by being the one she looked to every time she blinked or cried or felt a pang of hunger. And

I didn't know what to do with her besides love her, which was not exactly something to *do,* or that could fill my days. So one morning I dressed her in one of the beautiful polka-dotted outfits a friend had given me and took a bunch of great pictures. This took all of fifteen minutes. Another time I placed her in a little bouncy chair and tried to ride the stationary bike. But she fussed instantly. Friends visited. I tried to pretend I was having a great time. I wasn't.

In a picture from those days, I'm sitting on the couch, tiny Azalea in one arm, faceup, asleep—big, fat Siamese Jimmy in the other, very much awake. I'm wearing blue sweatpants. My breasts are gigantic. I can hear Thayer now calling me by my nickname, *Betty,* from just over my shoulder, telling me to look in his direction. And there I am—head turned, face still, eyes open. Looking, but not seeing much of anything. Stricken.

The next part went something like this: The boredom turned to lethargy, which turned to resentment, which turned to flatness. Which turned to panic. I remember contemplating the coming moments, days, months, and years of my life, but this time that tiny twinkle that had always carried me from even my most harrowing suffering moment into the next—the very thing that had walked me from the subway to that Barnes & Noble years earlier—was gone. It was as if something so intrinsic I had never noticed it—something like blood or water—was being sucked out of my body.

Clearly, I was depressed.

And then one morning about six weeks later, I wasn't. It happened at a friend's house in New Hampshire. The day before, I had been faking having fun at the pool, faking enjoying grilled cheese sammies. Making some stupid dinner. But then, the next day, I opened my eyes onto the early-summer morning in this small antiquey guest room, saw Thayer lying alongside me, and heard the quiet of Azalea still sleeping in the pack 'n play next to us, and I realized the weight on my chest had lifted. Just like that.

Turns out it is not uncommon for postpartum depression to descend in the fourth or fifth month after giving birth, and to lift just as suddenly. My brief run-in has helped me appreciate what people go through with clinical depression, a nightmare I had never experienced before, and haven't since. Which was how I knew I wasn't depressed when my life as a mother continued to feel so bleak. Which was why I thought there must really be something wrong with me, to still feel so unhappy. I wasn't depressed anymore. And yet my restlessness, even when punctuated by the poetry of the world, or a wash of pleasure, was disturbing. Even after I went back to work part-time when Azalea was six months old.

Spring is a time of year that has always cut through even my biggest complaints or anxieties and softened me. And summer—forget it—nothing can stop me from smiling in the heat and hair-curling humidity. But this time around, I didn't look forward to anything; I didn't care about the sky or the trees or food or sultry nights. The fact that the earth's glory sprung up around me just made my smallness smaller and my sharpness sharper. I watched Azalea blossom, then looked back at myself and was disappointed in what I saw. I looked back and forth again.

I didn't understand that looking is a form of loving. Or at the very least, it's a step in the right direction.

chapter nine

When Azalea was six months old, she started drinking from a bottle, as well as nursing. She would lie in my arms and guzzle it down, making a little whistle sound through the rubber nipple, and then the sound would stop because she was asleep, bottle flopped next to her, daintily drooling. It was one of my favorite things, that whistling sound. Not only was it adorable, but it signaled some "me time."

And then Azalea would do something like wake up or spill something on me or distract me, and I'd open the door to her room too loudly or snatch a toy out of her little hand or glare at her. Once the anger passed, I was ashamed of the way my body lit up with hostility when all she was doing was having the big feelings of someone who can't talk or walk or control her bodily functions.

What kind of mother am I?

What kind of person?

Loving mothers don't feel annoyed if their toddler's face is red with tears after some minor food-dropping incident. Normal people are supposed to be triggered into *There, there, honey, it's okay* when a baby is crying because she feels alone and afraid.

A loving mother can put her own frustrations aside in order to tend to her baby. A good person doesn't feel cold. I felt as if the universe had made a terrible mistake in granting me the miracle of this child. I couldn't possibly be responsible for her. There was definitely something wrong with me.

During those wrenching early months and years, I thought a lot about my mom, comparing my wicked outbursts with her practical wisdom and even-steven temperament. I knew she never yelled at me, but I never really felt like she was *there* for me, either. I certainly didn't feel "felt." I was often frustrated by what I believed was her oversimplification of my complex emotional states, her cool distance when I described my pervasive childhood loneliness.

For instance, sometimes my mom asked if I was upset by her and my dad's divorce, which happened when I was thirteen, but she didn't press for details when I said, "Not really." Didn't she want to know me?

When Azalea was born, my mom was so excited, so happy that I had joined her in this experience of motherhood that she professed to love. She knew I was having a tough time with motherhood, though not the extent of it. She called me often to say things like "Oh, honey, I know it's hard sometimes, but can you even imagine your life without Azalea?"

The question annoyed me. *Yes, Mom,* I'd think, *I can imagine the way my life was six months ago.* The thing I couldn't imagine being without was this darkness, this feeling that there was something very wrong with me, that deep down I was broken. Maybe even sick.

Every now and then I checked back in with Dr. Sears and Martha and their attachment-parenting advice, as I was clearly drawn to something there and desperate for some understanding of the confusion I was moving in and out of. But then I read things like "The way baby and parents get started with one another often sets the tone of how this early attachment unfolds . . . The early weeks and months are a sensitive period when mother and baby need to be together," which terrified me. I wasn't really sure what this "attachment" was, but it seemed important, foundational even. Especially since, as they write, "we all mess up, but when attachment parents mess up, the effect is minimal because their basic relationship with their child is solid."

I worried about what was going to happen to Azalea when I "messed up," because surely I was a failed "attachment parent," and so our relationship could not be "solid." I wondered what happens when there's something wrong with the mother. Which I knew must be the case, because, according to Sears, "there is great comfort in feeling connected to your baby." I didn't feel comfort in being connected to my baby. For the first few years of Azalea's life, I felt angry about it.

Thank goodness even anger can be a window to see through.

WHEN AZALEA WAS three or four, I took her to Chinatown in New York City. Because I have always considered it my parental duty to encourage an appreciation of the finer things, I researched where to get the best dim sum. I thought she'd get a kick out of the food being brought around on a cart, and all the savory, chewy, pillowy steamed treasures inside. After much online perusing, I discovered a place that was reported to be a serious hole in the wall, but over-the-top delicious. Authentic.

After looping around and around a block, both of us getting a little hot and cranky, I finally found the place, wedged between a vegetable stand and a tourist mart, and we went in. The air-conditioning was on, but just barely. We were hit with that garlicky, fishy scent I love.

"It smells funny in here," Azalea said.

"It doesn't smell funny, it smells *good*!" I said, trying to sound cheerful as a familiar tightness began to settle around my eyes and mouth.

We were seated at a sticky table near the back, by the bathroom and the bin of dirty dishes. Azalea swung her legs under the table, chatting in her raspy voice, with her tiny front teeth and sausage curls in pigtails. I ordered a Diet Coke for myself and an apple juice for Azalea. When I realized there were no real dim sum carts—*only on weekends*—I was disappointed, but the show must go on. So I ordered fried dumplings, noodle soup with chunks of red-tinged pork swimming in glistening fat, and shrimp wontons stuffed with scallions. Azalea ate gingerly, looking worried.

"The soup tas-tes . . . funny." It was incredibly strong. And sour. Even for me. But I didn't want to hear it.

My jaw started to set as I thought about all my efforts clicking away at the computer, all my hard work that was so not appreciated. I felt that familiar chasm opening up, and scrambled to close the gap. I asked Azalea if she was okay. I wanted her to say, "Yes, Mommy, are you kidding? I'm having the time of my life!"

But she just nodded and gazed around the tiny restaurant. When she nervously spilled her apple juice and the waitress cleaned it up by smearing big gray rags all over our table, I started to free-fall away from myself. And her.

"Can I have another apple juice, Mommy?"

"Because I'm made of money?" I snapped, pushing the tumbler-size plastic cup of warm water toward her.

Sitting at the table, withdrawn, my face set in a cold and punishing mask, I couldn't see the small, *really trying* person sitting across from me anymore, the one I had dragged through the city streets to satisfy some dream I had. Azalea disappeared. She was over there. I, separate, was over here.

And then, for some mysterious reason, in that moment I was

able to see—in the very moment of my separation—that I was so desperate to be close with Azalea, I was willing to climb through the morass of myself to do it. I shook off the distance and came to. Azalea—soft face, blue eyes lined with feathery lashes, her little jeans and yellow shirt with white trim, her ears, her small chest rising as she pulled air in and out—was just sitting there. She was looking at me, sadly, around at the room, then back at me again.

The instant I let go of myself, I was able to see Azalea in all her little-kid glory. In fact, we arrived on the scene simultaneously. The waitresses' faces also softened, and the other diners looked a little more alive as they slurped their noodles. The place was filling up with spectacularly ordinary human beings.

It was a miracle.

I paid the check and we went straight to a Chinese bakery, where we bought sugary lemonade and a piece of toasted Wonder bread with margarine. We sat together in the dingy booth, watching people find their way through the crowds on the sidewalk, like a flock of birds moving across a cement sky.

part iv

birds of a feather

The sensitive mother . . . responds socially to [her baby's] attempts to initiate social interaction, playfully to his attempts to initiate play.

—Mary Ainsworth et al., *Patterns of Attachment*

chapter ten

In 1938, when John Bowlby was a young psychoanalyst, his supervisor, the famed Freudian analyst Melanie Klein, told him that mothers don't matter. As his first case, he was treating a young boy who was what we might now call hyperactive. The boy's mother seemed "an extremely anxious, distressed woman." When Bowlby wanted to talk to the mother, Klein said no, because she was irrelevant, and when the mother was hospitalized after a nervous breakdown, Klein's response was "What a nuisance." Since the mother would no longer be able to drive the child to his appointments, they would have to find a new family to study.

The classic Freudian stance of that time was that, while early relationships with, say, overinvolved or distant mothers and authoritarian or weak fathers were often seen as the reason for a patient's neurosis, the "treatment" was to work with the patient's internal drama, manifested as fantasies or dreams or compulsions, rather than to resolve a real, live relationship—past or present.

In fact, parental love was understood at that time to be so

insignificant that it was seen as a stand-in for the "primary drive" for food. Freudian analysts of the day believed that, as in some psychic shell game, physical fulfillment was simply masquerading as love. In other words, we love the hand that feeds us because it feeds us. Hence the cupboard love theory.

Though as a culture we tend to pooh-pooh these outdated notions, and we appreciate the power of relationships to impact our lives, when Azalea was born I was struck by the many voices I heard in the emerging "momosphere" at the time urging mothers like me not to worry too much—the whole "My parents neglected me and I turned out okay!" attitude. Looking back, I appreciate the wisdom in urging parents to take it easy on themselves, something I've had to learn how to do. However, just beneath the encouragement to be gentle to oneself is a belief that what we do as parents doesn't really matter . . . *that much*. Which I found unsettling.

When considering the question of parenting and the effect we have on our kids, it's only natural to ask: What about everything else? What about temperament and other inborn traits? How much responsibility do we take for our children's problems and, conversely, for their happiness? Mary Ainsworth put this false dichotomy to rest in an interview with Peter L. Rudnytsky in 1997, two years before she died.

PLR: So you are leaving some room for temperament?

MSA: Yes. But a mother can be appropriately responsive to a given baby even if she's had several babies who may differ quite a lot in their characteristics to start off, and she can be sensitive to each one in terms of his or her own leads.

PLR: So you're saying that there is something innate that each child brings?

MSA: Yes. Everybody knows that.

What Mary is saying is important. There are things that each child comes into life with, and they really matter. And there are varying degrees of sensitivity with which a caregiver can care for a child, no matter what his or her temperament, and the more sensitive and more attuned that care, the better. It's so painful to see our children suffer from all manner of human problems, and tempting to say that our love doesn't help. But it does. Regardless of what we face in adulthood, love in childhood will always make it easier to handle.

During the time of Bowlby's training, however, his supervisor believed that even though an individual's emotional pain may have been the result of an insensitive (or worse) caregiver, the importance of their *relationship* pales in comparison with an individual's very own interior, private psychic drama—the juicy stuff of on-the-couch, interpretation-of-dreams Freudian analysis. In other words, people were acknowledged as being part of a family archipelago, but ultimately considered distinctly separate and solitary within that string of isles. Individuals. And so it makes sense that when Bowlby, who was beginning to see just how impossible it is to extract someone from their relationships, wanted to work with the boy's mother, Klein actually forbade it. She believed that it was absurd to try to make an association between the mother's state of mind—and therefore her ability to be a sensitive caregiver—and the child's. Nor did she express concern for an already troubled child having to be separated from his mother, because to her, a mother was easily replaced.

I have often tried to imagine young Bowlby, who had devoted his life to boys like this one, scratching his head, maybe searching his soul over this heartbreaking failure, and trying to figure out how he could work within, then change, the system. Bowlby was an outlier in his field because he believed, as he put it, that "real-life events—the way parents treat a child—is of key importance in determining development." Even when a child's home life was investigated in a clinical case, which did happen occasionally, all the wrong things were looked at—the external factors of a child's life, like whether or not the parents kept a tidy house, drank, were divorced—instead of the nature of the child's relationships. Bowlby, on the other hand, believed that when it comes to a child's welfare, nothing matters more than a relationship with someone who cares about him or her. Love is the thing. He knew it. But because of the way he was trained, he wasn't sure why.

TWELVE YEARS LATER, in 1950, Bowlby was the deputy director of London's Tavistock Clinic. In response to the high numbers of orphaned and institutionalized children in post–World War II Europe, the World Health Organization commissioned him to write a report detailing the state of these homeless children and what could be learned from their plight. His research was published as a book in 1951 called *Maternal Care and Mental Health,* which sold 400,000 copies and was translated into fourteen languages.

What he found was that orphaned children deprived of a loving maternal substitute suffered terribly, and to the precise degree of their emotional desolation. In other words, children left with family members who cared for them fared worlds better than children left to decompensate in orphanages where they had no special other. These children's "adverse reactions" ranged from "diminished interest and reactivity" to "relative retardation" in language and motor skills. Using a perfect analogy, Bowlby writes, "maternal care in infancy and early childhood is essential for mental health. This is a discovery comparable in magnitude to that of the role of vitamins in physical health."

Through his research, Bowlby came to understand that mental health required that "the infant and young child should experience a warm, intimate, and continuous relationship with his mother (or permanent mother substitute) in which both find satisfaction and enjoyment." In the context of children fleeing murderous regimes, needing shelter when their parents are killed or taken away, Bowlby pointed to pleasant interaction as a must-have. Not only did he find that children needed to be in the mere presence of these parental substitutes, but he believed that "enjoyment," *delight,* was a requirement for healthy development. And because enjoyment does not happen in a vacuum, parents must be supported—economically and emotionally—by society. In the age of B. F. Skinner behaviorists and the cupboard love theory, this was a big deal. And it still is today.

After the publication of the book, Bowlby's investigations into maternal separations became so far-reaching and complex that he needed to hire more people to help him, so he placed an ad in the London classifieds.

When the Ainsworths arrived in London in late 1950, a friend showed Mary the job advertisement for a research position at the Tavistock Clinic for a project looking "into the effect on personality development of separation from the mother in early childhood." Mary and Bowlby met. It was the beginning of a lifelong friendship and one of the most important and productive partnerships in the history of science. Or, as Mary put it, "What can I say? . . . We liked each other!"

chapter eleven

In the summer of 1951, just as Mary was settling into her work at the clinic, and a few years before she and Len would travel to Uganda, a friend introduced John Bowlby to scientist Konrad Lorenz's work and the new field of ethology—the study of animal behavior. It didn't take long for Bowlby to realize that Lorenz's work had given rise to the theoretical construct he had been waiting for—the intellectual bridge to carry his beliefs about the importance of maternal relationships into the world.

"I mean talk about *eureka*," Bowlby wrote. "They were brilliant, first-class scientists, brilliant observers, and studying family relationships in other species—relationships which were obviously analogous with that of human beings—and doing it so frightfully well. We were fumbling around in the dark; they were already in brilliant sunshine."

The "other species" Bowlby was referring to were primarily waterfowl.

WHEN THE FUTURE Nobel Prize–winning scientist Konrad Lorenz was a young boy in Austria, his neighbor gave him a day-old duck. He was delighted to see that the duck seemed to treat him more like a parent than a member of a different species. As a boy, Lorenz didn't just love animals; he wanted to be one, and a greylag goose specifically.

Years later, in 1935, when Lorenz was a thirty-two-year-old physician, still obsessed with animals in general and birds in particular, he published his most famous paper: "Der Kumpan in der Umwelt des Vogels" (*The Companion in the Bird's World*). He had observed almost thirty species of birds living in and around his parents' Austrian estate and had cataloged their behaviors. Eventually he began raising some of their chicks. In the paper, he describes the experiment wherein he divided a clutch of goose eggs (seven to ten) into two batches—one to be raised by its mother in the usual fashion, the other to be raised by him as he mimicked the clucks and coos of the mother goose. He would call to his small flock with a nasal and slightly syncopated "CAW-caw-caw. CAW-caw-caw-caw-caw." They would run, and later fly, to his feet.

When goose chicks are born, they turn to the first moving creature they see for protection and care. This evolves into the chicks identifying that creature—whether goose or human—as their mother. They learn to track their mother by the sound of her voice. Which is how he discovered that the little goslings followed whomever they saw first—a genetic propensity that farmers had long noted but Lorenz actually named. He called it "imprinting." And he found that there was a period of twelve to seventeen hours after birth in which the gosling and many other birds would attach to whatever creature they saw first. It was love at first sight. And after about thirty-two hours, it was an endless love: regardless of who fed the little chicks, they would return to their original "mother." Food could be used to reward the birds and enhance the imprinting that had already occurred, but it was not the main motivator.

For thirty years Lorenz lived among the geese during what he called his "goose summers," imprinting goslings on himself, young graduate students, even objects: white balls, rubber boots of different designs—striped, zigzag, and polka-dotted. The little chicks followed whoever or whatever was first put in front of them.

In 1975, the National Geographic Society sent a film crew to the Max Planck Institute, where Lorenz was the director. The film (starring a young Leslie Nielsen as the narrator!) shows Lorenz's team of young German graduate students raising their own clutches of goslings. A young woman named Kristine demonstrates how the process starts before the chicks hatch. She gently plucks an egg from a tan ceramic incubator and holds it to her ear. "Vee-vee-vee-vee," she calls, her voice lilting up at the end as though asking the egg a question. The gosling answers from inside the egg with a high-pitched series of chirps.

By the middle of that summer, the gosling and his mates were plump adolescents with fawn-colored pinfeathers. They joined the other clutches of goslings in a grassy field. They found Kristine by her yellow-and-black-striped rubber boots; other goslings followed graduate students who wore polka-dotted boots or ones with zigzag designs.

Like one morning in Manhattan, when I was trailing behind a woman walking her three kids to school. Before crossing the street, the mom and the youngest girl turned left, but the other two—another girl and an older boy, morning-weary, headphones on—didn't notice and were about to walk into the crosswalk until they realized that their mother had changed course. And then they, too, wordlessly turned the corner.

It was like magic, that invisible something that kept those sleepy, tuned-out kids in tow, trailing after their mother, staying close.

. . .

IMPRINTING CHANGED EVERYTHING for Bowlby. The idea of an instinctive need to connect, attach, *imprint* a baby upon its caregiver helped him build a case for why those early relationships were not just some soft-focus happy place motivated by hunger, but a core aspect of the mechanics of our bodies and minds—an *imperative,* as critical to our way of being as following is to geese. Which would help explain why the consequences of early separation and deprivation could be so dire—it was the thwarting of a basic need.

One particular piece of Lorenz's work became especially important to Bowlby's idea of attachment, and that was the concept of "social releasers," the term Lorenz came up with to describe the instinctive back-and-forth he noticed between animals of the same species, but also between himself and his geese. This idea underlies the very concept of attachment—that innate call-and-response between babies and their caregivers, which leads to what he referred to then as mental health, or what he and Mary would soon call a "secure attachment."

The idea of social releasers is simple: the reaction in one body is triggered into being through the action of another, but it's one of those things that is so much a part of our everyday experience, it can be hard to notice. A social releaser is different from a reflex, which lies dormant until a stimulus arrives. In other words, it's our reflex to giggle or recoil when tickled, but there the reaction ends—in the person who's been tickled, as opposed to then triggering a chain reaction of tickling. And a social releaser is different from a physical need such as hunger, which exists autonomously within each of our bodies. Even if we were alone, we'd eat.

A social releaser releases something *social,* something that moves back and forth between socially engaged creatures. An easy-to-understand social releaser is the birdsong, which invites other birds to respond; we all know what that sounds like. But there is an infinite amount of social releasing happening every minute of every day in creatures great and small, including fish, reptiles, and insects, through cueing mechanisms like pheromones, feathers, dances, looks, physical touch, sounds, and smells. Even trees relate to each other, sending signals back and forth through their interdependent networks of roots. When someone smiles at us and we smile back, we're simply unlocking an expression that, viewed through a social-releasing perspective, belongs just as much to the person who released it in us as it does to us. Even our smiles don't ultimately belong to us. We think we are solo actors, just going about our business, but we're missing how totally connected we are.

Like when Azalea cried and my breasts tingled as they filled with milk.

WHILE WORKING WITH Bowlby on analyzing data from his postwar orphaned-child research, Mary was not impressed with this new theory. She later wrote that she was "so brainwashed" into believing in the cupboard love theory that she thought Bowlby was crazy, and told him so. When she found herself in Uganda after working with him, her goal was to see how mothers and babies *really* behave. Almost immediately she saw Bowlby's theory of attachment totally validated in the families she studied. She writes:

The transition I made from thinking in psychoanalytic terms to thinking in terms of ethology felt very much like what I later read Kuhn describe as a "paradigm shift." . . . In my many [later] disagreements with behaviorists . . . I really couldn't expect them to understand what I was talking about—and, although it made our quarrels useless, it did enable me to feel vastly superior!

In 1958, three years after Mary left Uganda, Bowlby's first paper on attachment, "The Nature of the Child's Tie to Its Mother," was published. It grabbed hold of the idea of imprinting and finally offered an alternative to the prevailing Freudian understanding of the parent-child relationship:

> It is my thesis that, as in the young of other species, there matures in the early months of life of the human infant a complex and nicely balanced equipment of instinctual responses, the function of which is to ensure that he obtains parental care sufficient for his survival.

He then goes on:

> To this end [i.e., infant survival] the equipment includes *responses* which promote his close proximity to a parent and *responses* that provoke parental activity [italics mine].

His colleagues were not ready for the idea that the "equipment" bestowed upon us through our evolution—both parents and children—is that fierce, *responsive,* and sometimes excruciating longing to be close to those we love. Or the idea that we "provoke" each other into "close proximity." This may not sound like much, but as attachment researcher Inge Bretherton put it, it was radical enough to raise "quite a storm at the British Psychoanalytic Society. Even Bowlby's own analyst, Joan Riviere, protested."

Bowlby was saying that love is more than a feeling. It's part of the whole behavioral system that, once activated, must reach its set goal in order to lie in wait once again.

The conditions that get the attachment system going in children are both internal and external. For instance, "illness, hunger, pain, cold, and the like" are internal, and "absence of or distance from [attachment] figures, the figure's departing or returning after an absence, rebuff by or lack of responsiveness of that figure or of others, and alarming events of all kinds, including unfamiliar situations and strangers," are external.

There are so many ways to feel vulnerable.

However, regardless of the source of our vulnerability—internal or external—the conditions that satisfy our attachment system's set goal are primarily *internal*. We have to *feel* felt. A parent handing a child a box of Kleenex to blow her own nose after she's thrown up isn't wrong, but it's a far cry from sitting next to her, putting a cold washcloth on her forehead, stroking her hair, and telling her you're sorry she feels so awful. And meaning it.

Hearing someone tell us they love us is nice; feeling loved is a state of bliss, setting us free to enjoy the world through *I'm loved* eyes. We humans, after all, know when someone is really there with us and when they're just phoning it in—especially our attachment figures, upon whom we so rely. We're so sensitive to the comings and goings of these important people—both physical and psychic comings and goings—it's as if we're one being.

And in fact, Bowlby describes the idea of social releasers as an operation between two bodies, in which each individual's instinct is not simply a lone lever, but so intrinsically connected to its releasing partner that these two ostensibly separate beings function as one, in an actual unit.

The basic model for instinctive behaviour which this work suggests is thus a unit comprising a species-specific behaviour pattern (or instinctive response) governed by two complex mechanisms, one controlling its activation and the other its termination.

For instance, a unit of birds, in response to one another:

> [A scientist] has observed that in early spring the mere presence of a female chaffinch leads to a reduction of the male's courtship behavior, such as singing and searching. When she is present he is quiet, when she is absent he becomes active.

The simple *appearance* of the female silences the male because his set goal—the proximity of a female to potentially mate with—has been achieved.

Bowlby's message is profound. At the root of who we are, the very thing that keeps us alive and procreating, is a someone else. We think we are individuals, but in fact we are thoroughly interdependent. We *are* a unit. We *are* a relationship.

Singing, searching, smiling, crying—the gosling following the mother goose, a baby and her mother smiling at each other across the dirt-floored room in Uganda, Azalea waiting for me to return from across the table in the Chinese restaurant—all the things we do completely, utterly, always together.

chapter twelve

After the Chinatown incident, I redoubled my efforts to be a good, loving mother. Though I've always loved to cook, I've never been a baker, because I can't follow a recipe to save my life, but I decided to bake some butter cookies for Azalea's first day of preschool. That early fall morning, I stood in the kitchen wrapping one in some waxed paper and drawing a heart on it, feeling pretty darn good about myself.

Imagining Azalea opening this up during her first real school lunch, I thought back to my own mom and the lunch she always packed for me—a sandwich with a thin piece of lunchmeat on white bread and a bag of Doritos, or potato chips, maybe. Our homemade dinners were always 1970s healthy, balanced, color-coordinated even, but looking back, I felt like they were a bit uninspired. Where my mom seemed to get excited was in the dessert department. We always had from-scratch cookies lying around, but I never really cared about sweets—yet another miss between us. My mom still has quite the sweet tooth; the minute we walk into her apartment in Michigan, Azalea goes right to the glass jar filled with peanut M&M's in my mom's spotless, totally organized cupboard. Though she lives alone, she cooks and even bakes for herself daily.

These days, when we visit, Azalea asks me why I can't be more like my mom.

Like a gong bringing me back from my reverie to the present moment, preschool Azalea strolled into the kitchen carrying her breakfast of miso soup and leaned against the fridge, staring up at me. "Mommy," she said, "I wish I could be just like you." *Awwww,* I thought. *My efforts are paying off! Look at me!* And then I asked, in an almost rhetorical way, "Why's that, honey?" To which Azalea replied, "Because then I could be angry all the time."

I was stunned.

"Do you really think I'm angry a lot?" I asked. *I mean, still?*

"Um-hmm," she answered, nodding confidently.

I asked, "What do I look like when I'm angry?"

"A mean animal."

"And what does the mean animal look like?"

She made a face. And there before me stood a perfect mirror.

THIS KIND OF thing happened all the time; just when I thought I had something more or less buttoned up, Azalea exposed the truth. It was kind of horrible when it happened, but I was fortunate enough to have a venue for writing about these moments and sharing them with people in a regular column on being a Buddhist mother that I had been invited to write for a regional magazine. I called it "Flowers Fall: Field Notes from a Buddhist Mother's Experimental Life." From midway through Azalea's first year until she was eight, I sat down every month to reckon with the conflicts I felt about my difficulties as her mother in the context of my Zen practice.

While my years of practicing Zen had taught me that the

way to relieve myself of my anguish was always by directing myself to my own mind, I was afraid that this practice was selfish. As a parent, was it wrong to focus on myself? Wasn't I supposed to be paying attention to *her*? Was I lying to myself by believing that I was becoming a better mother by studying myself in meditation? How did the awareness I was developing matter to her? Was it just an escape? I knew that the softening of my heart was a good thing all around, but I worried—as I am wont to do—and needed reassurance from trusted sources that I was on the right track.

So as Azalea grew up, I began interviewing all kinds of people for my work—not necessarily Buddhists, but writers, anthropologists, pediatricians, nutritionists, anyone who would talk to me. And I would ask them my burning questions about what it means to be a parent, and a person. *How do you do it?*

At the same time, I kept watching Azalea, like a barometer of my own heart, and she seemed to indicate reasonable levels of okayness. Which was a huge relief. She didn't *seem* totally messed up. Yet. She certainly never seemed so scared of me that she wouldn't speak her truth, which surely was a good thing.

In all my casting about to write my column and find some answers to my questions about parenting, about love, about myself as a mother, I started to notice the word "attachment" in articles, books, and interviews. This attachment business, however, seemed to be something distinct from Dr. Sears's lists and rules that I had read about as a young mother. And this was when I began seeing references to the Strange Situation, the odd experiment-type thing that involved babies and mothers and various kinds of attachment. Looking online, I saw pictures of babies with toys, of mothers in a chair, and pictures of an old-fashioned, grandmotherly-looking woman with cute teeth. Her name was Mary Ainsworth. She looked so serious and tickled at the same time that I wanted to know what she was thinking.

The Strange Situation seemed to me like half science, half dangerous parlor game for anxious, nerdy parents who wanted to find out if their kid was "secure" or "insecure," or "avoidant," or "ambivalent." How fun! How terrifying.

I started to watch all the videos of Strange Situations available online—babies and their mothers coming and going in the lab, babies crying, getting picked up, calming down. I would later learn that only footage of secure babies is shared publicly, though by no means did all the babies I saw look secure to me.

In one, a little girl named Caroline wears overalls. Her tall, gentle mother leaves her in the Strange Situation alone, and the girl cries her head off, going to the door, standing, waiting, weeping. Then the mom returns and picks Caroline up, shushing her, which calms her daughter down instantly.

"This baby appears secure," the researcher states. I didn't understand what he was seeing. Why would a "secure" baby wail when her mother left? I thought a "secure" baby was secure enough not to care about its mother's whereabouts? I was very taken by this real-time back-and-forth, but I think I was so preoccupied—a technical term, I would later learn—with worry about Azalea and myself that I could barely follow along. And I could not, for the life of me, imagine my mother and myself in a so-called Strange Situation.

Would I have cried when my mom left the room? Would she have noticed my tears when she returned, or would she tell me to "just ignore them"? Would she have picked me up? Dutifully, or with real affection? Would I care? Would she? What kind of pair were we?

ONE VIDEO IN particular really grabbed me, and I watched it a lot. It was called "Mary Ainsworth's Strange Situation: Attachment and the Growth of Love." It opens with the sound of *pat,*

pat, pat—a hand against a baby's back, then images of babies, little kids, parents and teens, adults—people in relationships. Then some sweet, simple guitar music begins and a man says, "Nothing in life is more precious than the intimate relationships we have with loved ones. Healthy love relationships delight us, give us confidence to take on challenges, and support us in difficult times. These emotional bonds, what we call love, were the focus of Mary Ainsworth's work, [which] can be described as the scientific study of love and how it develops."

This was a super-simple production. And I couldn't get enough of it. The "science of love"? While it seemed a little cheesy, I trusted this man and the images of the late Mary Ainsworth that flashed on the screen: her broad, open face, her 1950s formality. And for some reason, just watching the video again and again was helping me in my efforts to be kinder to Azalea.

My favorite scenes in the video were of this man, the narrator, in a family's home, watching and taking notes on a clipboard as the baby and its mother went about their day-to-day business. They said goodbye to Daddy, the baby was fed, the mother tidied up, the baby cried and got picked up. I wasn't sure what the narrator was looking for, what he was writing down, or what it had to do with attachment, but the way he watched these babies and their mothers with a kind but neutral smile on his face was soothing to me. As if by just observing these people in this unobtrusive but attentive way, he was loving them. And as I watched, I felt strangely loved as well.

IN 2016, WHEN Azalea was ten, I flew to Charlottesville, Virginia, and was met at the airport by Bob Marvin, the narrator with the clipboard and also Mary Ainsworth's protégé, dear friend, and executor. He is now white-haired. He drove me to my hotel in his tidy BMW, eager to share stories with me about his beloved Mary and to tell me about his many years of experience "at the foot of the master."

In the morning, I walked through beautiful old Charlottesville to the Ainsworth Attachment Clinic, founded and run by Marvin. He took me to the utility closet and we carried down twenty boxes filled with notes and papers from Ainsworth's study in Baltimore, including the hundreds of hours of meticulous home observation that she and her team, which included young Marvin, conducted, as well as onionskin coding sheets from the original Strange Situations and handwritten and typed-up research notes from Uganda.

I was the first to ever see the boxes. Because I was the first to ask.

That evening, he took me to his house and introduced me to his lovely wife, Cherri. He showed me Mary's mother's silver tea set, which he'd inherited, and a painting by her favorite artist, Herman Maril, of a boat in a Maryland harbor. Bob and Cherri took me out for dinner. We drank red wine and talked about Mary. Bob and I cried.

I STARTED TO see attachment everywhere. It kept showing up in articles that I thought were about something else and in books that had always been on my shelves. And I started to see it in the world—in the outstretched arms of a toddler looking for an uppie, in the way a baby's eyes rest on her papa on the subway, in a husband and wife searching each other's faces for comfort, in an otherwise distant kid wanting a cuddle when ill, in every Snapchat streak or FaceTime exchange. Every time I turned around, there were people being moved by a deep and physical need to be close to a special someone.

Bowlby put it this way: Young mammals and birds, when afraid, run to a place—a den, burrow, or nest. When we humans are afraid, we run to a person. As Bowlby wrote to his wife, Ursula, in a letter in 1958: "Most people think of fear as running away from something. But there is another side to it. We run TO someone, usually a person." Everywhere I looked, there it was again: someone running to someone, seeking comfort.

A baby rabbit hops to its mother when a hungry fox appears. A human baby is happily playing in a room when a stranger enters, then looks to her mother to confirm that all is well. An adult woman is thrown into total psychic shock when her own baby arrives. She scrambles and searches. She reads and wonders. She begins to *feel felt* by an idea.

chapter thirteen

On a weekend in December, some of our monastery friends—psychotherapists like Thayer—visited from Toronto. They were fans of Bowlby and Ainsworth and had just gone to a lecture by the well-known writer, neuroscientist, and attachment researcher Dr. Dan Siegel, and they had a whole other perspective on attachment, one I had not yet heard of.

After we got Azalea to sleep in a mountain of stuffed animals, we brought out the wine and cheese and sat in the dining nook of our now-blue house, ready for a serious catch-up. After delving into our personal details and family updates, they told us about an attachment research tool called the Adult Attachment Interview, which was basically a Strange Situation for adults. It was created by one of Mary Ainsworth's star pupils, for the purpose of revealing the "internal working model"—the mental representation—of an adult's attachment system.

The AAI is an interview of twenty questions about a person's early relationships. It is administered by researchers, then transcribed verbatim. Through his or her responses, an individual's attachment "type" is discerned, like the secure/insecure categories of babyhood, but for adults. The categories are "secure/autonomous," "insecure/dismissing," and "insecure/preoccupied."

Researchers have found that there is a massive 75 percent correlation* between an adult's attachment security as determined by the Adult Attachment Interview and the future Strange Situation results of their *unborn child*. In other words, you could predict the attachment security of your kid based on this test before he or she was even born. I was floored. Just what was it that was being measured?

As our friends explained that evening, the thing that is being looked at and what is being classified in the AAI isn't what *happened* to us as kids. It's the "mind in relation to attachment" that the AAI elicits—our present-day, very much alive *experience* of the past, not the past itself—which, of course, is long gone. Kind of, sort of.

Our friends explained that through our language—the words we use to tell the story of our first relationships—researchers claim to be able to track the way we think and feel about love. And that internal story develops into a way of being in our relationships, especially our most important attachment relationships. More than behaviors, it's that way of being we pass down, hence the 75 percent predictability.

Something clicked.

My life as a Zen student had taught me many things—how to be utterly still, how to clean a bathroom like I was tidying God's closet, and how to notice my mind as the source of my suffering—*and* my pleasure. Through many years of meditation, community living, and hard work, I had watched enough

---

* For a more nuanced conversation about this 75 percent correlation, please see the endnote.

knee pain disappear, frustration lead to softness, exhaustion turn to energy, and hopelessness morph into random moonlit bliss to know that my *feelings* functioned independently of what was going on around me. So it made perfect sense to me that the way I thought about my past was distinct from what had "actually" happened. In other words, there are the facts, and then there's the perception of the facts.

There's breastfeeding, and then there's a mother's attitude toward breastfeeding.

There's the observable world, and the internal state of being.

There's what happened to you, and how you feel about what happened to you, and the story you tell about it.

There's information, and there's *excellent* information.

I would later learn that in the AAI, a person's story is coded on the left for "probable experience," as in: What kind of parenting did the person experience? Was the parent loving, rejecting, interfering? And on the right, the person's story is coded for "coherence of mind," as in the *excellence* of their information. As in: How excellent is this informant, regardless of what they report happened to them?

One wow factor of the AAI is the lack of obvious connection between the right and left sides of a transcript. Someone can report abuse with great coherence and excellence, and be considered secure. Likewise, a person's happy tale of childhood won't lead to a secure score if the story is difficult to follow or lacking in detail—if he or she is not considered an excellent and reliable informant.

And it's the right side of the story—the coherence-of-mind side of the story—that gets transmitted to our children. It's the *interpretation* of events—what happens on the inside—that has the most lasting impact.

I considered this very good news. The other thing my Zen

practice had taught me was that if there is anything I have the power to truly transform, it's my mind—notwithstanding the Herculean effort involved.

SOON AFTER OUR friends' visit, I became completely obsessed with attachment and the Strange Situation. I started reading scientific studies like religious texts, seeking answers to what had become very personal and existential questions: How can I be so mean to the person I so love? What comes over me? What is love? What is "me"? And how on earth does this Strange Situation answer these questions? What kind of magic trick is happening in those twenty minutes?

I began looking at my whole life through the lens of attachment. And I was scared, haunted by the ideas behind the Adult Attachment Interview, worrying that some ugliness inside me would be passed down to Azalea. Because, of course, I couldn't see into the future, to Azalea as a preteen, on the brink of her own becoming. I couldn't see her still holding tightly to her beloved stuffed bunny as she falls into a solid stretch of sleep, her body and mind wiped clean from a hot summer day of swimming with her best friend. I couldn't see her delighting in tacos, or asking politely, "Mommy, can I have some privacy?" while she plays in my shoes in the yard. Or the gentleness of her hands as they hold a slice of nectarine in the morning or open a can of dog food.

I didn't understand that the love between us is ultimately not even a feeling, or anything to do, but a way of being. And that it gets passed down—not like a name, but more like a face, something you're born with but that changes over time.

part v

strange
situation

INSTRUCTIONS TO THE MOTHER

This is a set of instructions to explain what will happen from the moment you arrive at Room —— in ——. Here we will discuss any questions about the observation of the baby in the strange situation, and leave coats. When we are all ready to proceed, you will be shown the door of the observation room, then taken into the experimental room. You will stay with your baby in the experimental room until the end of Episode 3. Then you may go into the observation room to watch him/her through a one-way vision mirror.

We would like to stress an important aspect of your role in the strange situation: Try to be as natural in your responsiveness to the baby as you would generally be. Do not actively engage him in play with the toys in the first three episodes until we give you the signal to do so, but feel free to respond to his advances (smiling, approaching, etc.) as you ordinarily would at home. If the baby is distressed at any time while you are in the room, please feel free to react as you normally would in order to make him comfortable again. We want to watch the baby's spontaneous response to the toys and to the strangeness of the situation. For this reason we ask the mother not to intervene and attract her baby's attention. Yet we don't want the baby to feel that his mother is acting strangely.

Thus, yours is a delicate task of reassuring the baby of your support as you would normally do when he seems to need it, without interfering with his exploratory behavior.

—Mary Ainsworth et al., *Patterns of Attachment*

The first time I met Dr. Howard Steele, the co-director of the New School's Center for Attachment Research, it was the summer of 2014, when Azalea was eight. She was going into second grade, playing with My Little Ponies as she ate her breakfast, chatting away. It was around this time that she took to asking me, "Are you happy?"—an inquiry she especially liked to make after knocking over three glasses of juice in one morning. Her gaze into my face would sharpen, then she'd sing, "Mama, are you happy? Sad, angry, upset? Frustrated? Disappointed?" Nothing I said mattered, because she knew I was pissed.

I had written Dr. Steele and told him about the book I was writing about attachment—okay, it was really just an idea for a book—boldly asking him if I might ever be able to observe a Strange Situation in his lab, and he invited me to one that was happening the very next day. Dr. Steele and his wife, Miriam, both of whom worked with John Bowlby, are considered two of the world's experts in attachment, specifically adult attachment. They even met Mary at a drinks party at Bowlby's house when the two mavericks were given an award by London's Royal College of Psychiatrists, in the summer of 1989.

The Strange Situation I went to observe was being used, as it almost always is, as part of an attachment-promoting intervention that is a piece of a larger research project. Typically, the Strange Situation is introduced at the beginning of a study to establish a baseline of attachment security between an infant and his or her caregiver. The researchers then offer the mother and child some kind of attachment-promoting experience— like individual therapy or group support, for instance—over the course of several months, then they redo the Strange Situation to see if the attachment intervention worked, nudging the baby and his mother along in the desired direction: toward a relationship in which the caregiver functions more effectively for the baby as a secure base.

When I got off the elevator on the sixth floor, Dr. Steele— glasses, curly hair, a small but steady smile—met me there, shook my hand, and looked me square in the eye. As soon as he said hello, I heard his familiar Canadian accent. He led me down the hallway to a room where a one-way mirror looked onto another room with two chairs and some toys. He introduced me to the two young grad students who were running the study, one of whom was to play the "stranger." They seemed so young and so cheerful, I wondered what had inspired them to study attachment.

SINCE THAT EVENING with my friends from Toronto when I learned about the AAI, I had been trying to process my entire life through the lens of my still blurry understanding of attachment. Some things were making sense; other things were still opaque.

I had learned that 65 percent of people are considered "secure," which means that the rest of us are "insecure." What was it, I wondered, that 65 percent of people "had" that the rest of us didn't? Looking around at the world, I was surprised that the number of insecurely attached people wasn't higher. After all, I didn't know a single person who didn't struggle with self-esteem or feel unsure of himself or herself. "Security" seemed like a myth.

I also learned that securely attached kids do better in school, use drugs less frequently, and engage in less risky behavior. As Alan Sroufe, one of the world's leading attachment researchers and the co-author of an almost forty-year longitudinal study, writes, "Attachment history itself, while related to a range of teenage outcomes, was most clearly and strongly related to outcomes tapping intimacy and trust issues." It certainly seemed that I was a poster child for insecurity.

Insecure attachment in adulthood is also linked to a host of problems, from sleep disturbances, depression, and anxiety to a decreased concern with moral injustice and less likelihood of being seen as a natural leader. Insecure adults experience God as a more authoritarian God than "autonomous" adults do. But the biggest subfield of attachment research is concerned, not surprisingly, with adult attachment in romantic relationships. Can we express our needs? Do we believe that they will be met? Securely attached, autonomous adults are more likely to be satisfied in marriage, experience less conflict, and be more resistant to divorce.

While my young life seemed to be a checklist for insecurity, other than my difficulties with motherhood, my adulthood was quite the opposite. I was a great sleeper. I had been an activist, and sometimes even a leader. I had a strong, positive religious practice and moral compass. Yes, my early relationships had been tumultuous, which I had come to accept was likely due to some kind of neglect or even abuse I had yet to really understand. But I'm happily married now.

Where did that leave me?

As I was cataloging my own life in terms of attachment, I was also watching Azalea extra carefully, looking for signs of security and insecurity. And then I learned about something so basic, I couldn't believe it could be studied.

"Mentalization" is a Victorian term for the "effort the mind makes." Today, researchers define mentalization as "the ability to understand actions by other people and oneself in terms of thoughts, feelings, wishes, and desires . . . In essence, mentalizing is *seeing ourselves from the outside and others from the inside.*" This ability to mentalize comes directly out of the experience of being seen by—mirrored by—a sensitive other in infancy. We internalize that sensitive other's gaze and reflect it back. Back and forth, back and forth—the ability to see ourselves in another, and another in ourselves, is the gift of a loving relationship.

When we mentalize, we are recognizing that we have a mind, and that we are more than just our thoughts and feelings. This helps us recognize that others are more than their thoughts and feelings, too, which leads to empathy and the ability to imagine another's point of view.

It's like this: At the base of all attachment behavior is Bowlby's belief that, because babies can't handle their own fear, sadness, wet-diaper-ness, hunger, and the like, they need someone to handle it for them. This process begins with "co-regulation," meaning that the caregiver, through loving attention, helps the baby manage its difficult feelings. Parent and child regulate together. In the end, however, a solid dose of co-regulation ends with "the establishment of the self as the main executive agency of security-based strategies." In other words, children who are effectively soothed by their caregivers eventually learn how to do it for themselves, and then for others. But we need to be met in our dependence before we can be independent.

This was what Mary Ainsworth was seeing in Uganda with the babies at their homes—the ones who checked back in with their mothers the most were better able to venture away from them. Even Sears got this right when he wrote, "Studies have shown that infants who develop a secure attachment with their mothers during the first year are better able to tolerate separation from them when they are older," the line that struck me when I first read it. They cried the least, seemed happiest, and took pleasure in their relationships with their mothers.

WHEN AZALEA WAS a baby, I used to take her for walks in the jog stroller to help her take a nap. Once the motion started to quiet her, I knew it was time to veer the stroller onto the rocky side of the road so that the bumpiness would put her right to sleep.

When she cried, Thayer and I used to hold her in our arms and sway back and forth quite vigorously, patting her bottom with so much energy it made a thumping sound against the diaper. It was so loud it made people a little uncomfortable. But it worked.

I thought I was pretty good at helping my baby settle herself. Except when I wasn't.

I started thinking back to pictures of myself as an infant—actual 1969 Polaroids, as well as mental images. I wondered if my mom had been able to help me regulate myself when I was a baby. I remembered how, when Azalea was born and I struggled with keeping her little body occupied, my mom recalled, "Gosh, I used to just put you kids on the blanket with some toys." I didn't think that sounded like a very security-promoting strategy. I was probably an insecure infant, I thought, which was bad news for Azalea.

And yet the first time Azalea went to sleepaway camp, she wrote: "Last night I missed my own bed and my own house. I want to go home. I know today is just a bad day and things will get better tomorrow or even later today and I probably won't want to go home."

This is a perfect example of mentalizing. Azalea has always been able to watch her mind, as she did in the midst of her homesickness. Being present with her feelings, she has come to see for herself that they change—they are temporary—a big relief when she's flooded with sadness or loneliness.

But I couldn't imagine my mom, as she put me on the blanket, gazing into my face so deeply that I internalized it. So where did Azalea get it? She certainly has the capacity to see her own mind, and yet she grew up with me, who was sometimes harsh, insensitive, insecure. What was going on? Can attachment patterns change? Had mine changed in adulthood? Maybe it was all that Zen training I had clocked? Or therapy? What kind of miracle had protected Azalea from her insecure "mess" of a mother? And what would a totally contrived laboratory procedure have to do with it?

THROUGH THE OBSERVATION GLASS, Dr. Steele, the grad students, and I watched the silent, empty room. We would be watching a Strange Situation with one mother and her child, broken up, as all Strange Situations are, into eight episodes of coming and going, most lasting around three minutes. The whole thing would take around twenty minutes.

Two chairs awaited, along with a little table with some magazines on it, just like in a clinic in Uganda. There were some familiar blocks, a sorting box, a doll, and an egg carton for the babies to play with. And then in burst a little boy, with fast legs and sparkly eyes, and his mother, who beelined it to one of the chairs and picked up a magazine, as instructed by the grad student who accompanied her into the room and quickly left. That was Episode 1, and it lasted thirty seconds, give or take. The boy went for the sorting box and was having at it—trying to plug the star into the star-shaped hole with his little fingers. He was actually squealing with delight. "Unusually vocal," said Dr. Steele. Mother and baby alone is Episode 2.

In Episode 3, the grad student playing the stranger came in and sat with the mother. The boy looked up and said, "Uh-oh," but seemed pretty unimpressed with her presence. And then the stranger asked, "Can I play with you?" and "What's your name?" The boy ignored her. And Dr. Steele said, "The stranger is too chatty." He explained that the stranger's instruction is to never interfere, so that the child can act as naturally as possible, but she seemed like a babysitter trying to develop a rapport before the parents left.

In Episode 4, the mother left, the stranger stayed, and the boy cried. The stranger told him, "Mommy's going to be back." And then she was, and the stranger left. During Episode 5, the boy resumed playing, "certainly happier," as Dr. Steele noted, than when the mother was gone. Dr. Steele told me later that this was good news, because it showed that the boy was using his mother effectively as a secure base.

Episode 6 was when the mother left again, and this time the baby was alone. This episode can last up to three minutes, but no more than twenty seconds if the child is really upset. Because this boy was crying like crazy, the stranger came in early for Episode 7—and was of no use to the boy. I learned later this was more good news, because from an attachment point of view, a baby should show a "differential" (as in special) relationship to his mother and not be subject to being charmed (or not charmed) by just anyone, as was the case for Mary's twins in Uganda, who didn't seem to recognize their mother as someone special.

Things were looking good for this pair.

The boy was still inconsolable with the stranger, so the heavy artillery—the mother—was sent in.

For Episode 7, the mother came in and the boy stopped crying. *Phew!* I was relieved to see that the mother smiled and stooped down to give her son a kiss. I noticed the mother yawning. I could imagine she was kind of wiped out by this truly strange experience, and to me it seemed as though the boy was able to be soothed by her presence and return to his play, which is exactly what you want to happen—being able to be involved in exploration and play in the caregiver's presence is the hallmark of healthy, secure-base behavior.

But I watched Dr. Steele observe the boy, who did not actually go to his mother's arms or "seek proximity," not even a little. Alerted more to Dr. Steele's response than anything I saw happening, I asked what he thought was going on, because now the boy had this kind of heartbreaking, faraway look on his face as he stood frozen in front of his mother, who had returned to her magazine. The boy then started circling his mother, his face long and still, even as he wanly returned to the toys. Dr. Steele pointed out that even though the boy had stopped crying when his mother returned, he was sad. Then he added, "It's quite puzzling why he didn't go to his mother," noting that there were "some signs of disorganization." And I could tell from the way Dr. Steele said it that this did not bode well for the pair.

WHEN THE STRANGE Situation was over, Dr. Steele invited me back to his office. As we sat face-to-face, he offered me some more studies to read and asked me more questions about the book I had told him I was writing. Watching my first Strange

Situation had required such close attention that I was starting to space out and get a little foggy. I flashed on the mother walking in to see her wailing son, and on her yawn. I felt sleepy, too. I mentioned again that I was trying to understand myself by understanding attachment, and that I was writing about this in my book, but I knew I was just repeating what I had already said. I could feel myself losing touch with Dr. Steele, his office, the books on the wall.

"You know," he said, narrowing his eyes just a bit, "this might be a very difficult book to write."

"Oh?" I said, looking back at him, snapped back into attention.

"When our attachment systems are activated, like yours is in learning about this research, it can be difficult to also be creative. The basis of attachment is that we need to be secure in order to creatively explore."

Dr. Steele was suggesting that perhaps my own attachment system was too riled up for me to do the work I needed to do to actually learn about this complex, unwieldy academic field. My sleepiness seemed to prove his point.

As he walked me to the elevator, I was very much aware of how I felt: unnerved by the boldness of Dr. Steele's observation about my life, flattered that he cared, and more curious than ever.

chapter fifteen

The National Museum of Psychology is a modern four-story building located on the deserted outskirts of one of Akron, Ohio's fading pedestrian malls. In the lobby and throughout the museum are exhibits of photos and artifacts from some of the most famous studies in psychology—including Stanley Milgram's obedience studies and the Stanford Prison Experiment—as well as Freud's home movies. Visitors can even lie on Sigmund's couch.

For a week in the summer of 2015, I woke up in a little room I'd rented, then walked to the stop where I caught the local bus that delivered me to the museum and the archive where Mary Ainsworth's papers are housed. It had been a year since I met Dr. Steele and saw my first live Strange Situation. It was hot and humid outside but freezing in the archive, so I packed a sweater and a random lunch I had gathered up from a deli near the house. I felt a little ridiculous, making this huge effort in this unassuming town for a book I was not really writing yet about a topic I could barely comprehend. But every morning, as the librarian wheeled the cart labeled MARY AINSWORTH to my desk, I knew there was nowhere in the world I'd rather be.

. . .

MARY DINSMORE SALTER was born in 1913 in Glendale, Ohio. Soon she had two younger sisters. In what I later learned is a typically clinical Ainsworthian detail, she described her family as "close-knit . . . with a not unusual mixture of warmth and tensions and deficiencies." In 1918, the Salters moved to Toronto.

Although her mother was the primary caretaker, she felt closer to her father. She and her sisters were all expected to excel academically, and Mary did not disappoint. When she was just three years old, she learned to read sitting on her father's lap, figuring out the "squiggles" of his newspaper. She would spend the rest of her life recognizing and unlocking patterns.

One of the Salters' favorite family rituals was visiting the local library every week and taking out as many books as their five library cards would allow. When Mary was fifteen, about to graduate from high school early, she checked out a book called *Character and the Conduct of Life,* published in 1927 by psychologist William McDougall:

> Self-knowledge is only to be obtained by critical reflection about oneself, about other persons and about our relations to one another. Reflection about oneself is necessarily introspective; one has to look inwards and observe the movements of the mind, the impulses of the heart, the workings of conscience, the nature and direction of desires, the shrinkings and aversions and antipathies we discover; one has to learn not only to recognize these things for what they are, but also to value them, to estimate them as good, bad or indifferent, and to discover whether they are deeply rooted, pervasive and recurrent, or merely fleeting and incidental.

As Mary put it, "It had not previously occurred to me that one might look within oneself for some explanation of how one felt and behaved, rather than feeling entirely at the mercy of external forces." It was after she read this book that she decided to become a psychologist, devoting her life to "critical reflection" and "the impulses of the heart."

Years later, Mary wrote about the power of this one book to change her life: "What a vista it opened up!"

MARY'S FATHER THOUGHT it would be a good idea for her to become a stenographer before she married, but she was determined to follow her dream of becoming a psychologist. She graduated from high school early and entered the University of Toronto at sixteen, where she "gobbled everything up with great enjoyment," coming to believe that "the science of psychology was the touchstone for great improvements in the quality of life." At Toronto, she met Dr. William Blatz, whose "security theory" described the way children use their relationships with their parents to help them venture forth into the world. This was the first time Mary had come across a theory of personality development, which was, she wrote later, "what I had been waiting for!"

Upon Blatz's suggestion, she wrote her dissertation extending his work. Mary collected data by evaluating the secure-base behavior of a group of college students and their parents in a self-report assessment. She then checked and validated her classification of their behavior by using the same students' autobiographical essays for another class. She wrote, "It 'blew my mind' to find out how similar this material was for persons yielding the same pattern of scores on the two scales."

In other words, even as a graduate student, long before she met the mothers of Uganda or the AAI was developed, she saw a clear connection between the way these students told free-flowing stories about their lives and a more formal assessment.

Making this connection between a life story and scientific inquiry excited and inspired her. She would eventually call her method of investigation, combining naturalistic observation in the home with Strange Situations in the laboratory, "back-and-forthing."

When Canada declared war on Germany in 1939, as Mary put it later, "everyone's career plans were changed." Mary served as an enlisted major in the Canadian Women's Army Corps from 1942 to 1946. She eventually became "superintendent of women's rehabilitation," developing her expertise in history taking, diagnostic testing, and counseling.

In the winter of 1943–44, Mary was assigned a tour in England, where she met her British counterpart, Edith Mercer, who later showed Mary the listing for the job at Tavistock Clinic, where she met John Bowlby.

From 1946 to 1950, Ainsworth and Blatz directed a team of student researchers charged with developing scales for assessing security. One of the researchers was Len Ainsworth. Mary soon married him. Later she wrote that "the prospect of his continuing for a Ph.D. in the same department in which I had a faculty appointment seemed uncomfortable." So when Len was accepted to complete his studies in London, Mary went with him, with nothing lined up for herself until she got there and found her new job with Bowlby.

Photographs of Mary at this time show her as confident and composed, her eyes clear and bright. In one she wears her army uniform. I find her beautiful, though I can also imagine people of that time calling her "handsome."

She was, by all accounts, fastidiously studious and rigorously honest. She was known to have written down her students' ideas so she would never inadvertently claim them as her own. She was also incredibly kind and supportive, though "in some ways" she "was pretty dismissing." And "with respect to sex, Mary Ainsworth liked and enjoyed men, and appreciated male pulchritude."

And yet, while Mary was a serious feminist in many respects, she seems to have felt a need to temper her fierce intelligence, or at least keep a gendered peace. She was a maverick, and yet still a woman of her time. She said that when she was in high school, she "pretended to be indifferent to learning in order to ingratiate myself with my peers," but I wonder if she didn't really mean "ingratiate myself with the boys."

How times changed as Mary grew up. Among her claims to feminist fame is that she desegregated the Johns Hopkins faculty lunchroom by staging a one-woman sit-in, "wearing, as she later reported, her best suit and a rose corsage."

THE MARY AINSWORTH collection in the Archives of the History of American Psychology consists mostly of letters, some handwritten in Mary's tidy script, others typed; some are quite long, warm, and newsy, others are short and all business. In the 1970s, she wrote to John Bowlby, by then a dear friend, about the difficulty of quitting smoking, her own and her mother's health, and her divorce, and he wrote back in kind. The two friends made plans to visit each other, argued over authorship, and read each other's papers. In one letter, where she offers detailed notes on a book of his, she writes, "I am gratified that you find 'secure' and 'security' useful terms—since I've been using them since 1936!"

She wrote to other attachment researchers, students, and editors of journals, offering critiques, support, and laborious back-and-forth edits of complicated scholarly journal articles, the likes of which we, in our cut-and-paste world, have never seen. She saved her appointment letters, like the one from Johns Hopkins in 1961 offering her $9,500 per year for a teaching position, a rate she learned later was considerably lower than what her male counterparts were paid. She rectified the situation by confronting the dean directly.

I had only a few days at the archive, so I spent most of my time scanning her letters onto my hard drive so I could study them later. But it was hard not to linger over the details.

Ten years after she'd married Len, then traveled to London for his studies, and then reluctantly accompanied him to Uganda for his work, the marriage came to an end. The divorce, in 1960, came as a life-changing rupture for Mary, which she called a "personal disaster . . . culminat[ing] in an eight-year psychoanalysis experience." Later she wrote that psychoanalysis—the reflective experience of becoming present with her own state of mind—might have been "the most important positive influence on my career." As she wrote to her friend and colleague Chris Heinicke in a letter dated November 15, 1962:

> Briefly to bring you up to date about me. I've been in Baltimore since autumn 1955, and at Hopkins since spring of 1956. It is a good little department here . . . I have been given a 3-year grant from FFRP to undertake research on the development of infant-mother interaction during the first twelve months of life. I'll get started on this as soon as I have finished the first complete draft of my book on African babies. Personally, these last seven years have not been easy. The difficulties culminated in a divorce in the summer of 1960. My almost immediate response to this crisis was to enter analysis, which, I guess I had wanted to do for a long time anyhow. So I've joined the club, and things have been getting progressively better ever since.

The stories of Len are few and roundly unflattering. They include Mary saying, "Perhaps I could just say I was the *first* of *four* wives." And there is the story told by her student Mary Main of when Len "inexplicably disappeared at [a] dinner" he and Mary were having with "a very correct British gentleman"—Dr. John Bowlby—and how Len never returned, much to Bowlby's "dismay, distress and great embarrassment for his friend Mary."

But as difficult as the divorce was, Mary loved her psychoanalysis; she delighted in the experience of being with the difficulty, of getting to know herself in this new way. It seems as though it was a refuge for her, a time to see herself clearly and to let her guard down. As Main writes, "From the first weeks of analysis forward, she felt energized in her work, and began working daily (and into the night) with tremendous enthusiasm, leaving whatever troubles might otherwise have impeded her work to her daily hour with her analyst."

Main continues:

With respect to infancy, Ainsworth emphasized that a secure infant typically moves out from the parent to explore and play within the immediate environment, then returns to its "secure base" (often showing or emotionally sharing the results of its explorations), then moves out again, and then returns—a characteristic which is seen in happy adult relationships as well, in which the day is discussed, and its pleasures and unpleasures revealed to the partner, before a new day and a new temporary leave-taking takes place. It is evident enough here that Mary Ainsworth had the capacity to fully enjoy her days and nights of work immediately upon finding a daily source of security [her analyst] with whom to discuss it.

These were good years for Mary. She lived with her cat Nnyabo in half of a Victorian house on a hill, the work of her favorite artist, Herman Maril, on the walls—beautiful, bold, abstract scenes of boats in the harbor or gulls on the beach. Her piles of books and files and letters and papers sat in her study, behind the closed door. The rest of the house was pretty, decorated with rugs and comfortable silk-covered chairs and sofas, ready for entertaining grad students or colleagues, playing cards, or watching tennis on TV. Once or twice a week, she cooked chicken dinners for her student and eventual executor Bob Marvin, drinking bourbon, smoking Benson & Hedges, the two of them talking about attachment until 2:00 A.M. "She could talk attachment twenty-four seven," recalls Bob. Sometimes during a game of bridge she'd bark, "Come on, Bob!" when he took too long playing his next card.

Bob had met Mary in 1962, when he was a sophomore at Johns Hopkins and he took her Theories of Development class. Bob remembers those days well.

She'd walk in carrying her briefcase, and she had the same briefcase for decades. And it was beat up like crazy. But it was special. She would put it on the table and she would take out two or three manila envelopes with her notes, her cigarettes and her ashtray. People would watch her. She had this ritual and people would just watch her. You could tell she was nervous because she would get a cigarette when one was already lit. Sometimes there would be three lit cigarettes at once. Legend has it that she had six concurrently lit cigarettes at one time.

In those days, as Bob remembers, "You'd sit down and light up." Most people would ash their cigarettes on the floor and then, when they were done, stamp out the butt on the floor. But not Mary, who carried a brass ashtray with her everywhere she went.

As Bob says, "She was clearly refined."

IN JULY 1963, firmly ensconced now in her post-divorce life and work, Mary wrote to Bowlby about a new project she had been longing to begin since her return from Uganda. It was another longitudinal home study of babies and mothers, but this time from a mix of Catholic, Protestant, and Jewish working- and middle-class families in Baltimore.

> I began with a compulsive attempt to consider attachment behavior in detail—what the behavior patterns are, what their early non-differentiated prototypes are, what situations evoke these patterns, how they may be related to the infant's state, to other behavior and to methods of infant care, how the adult responds to them, and what chain of interaction may emerge . . . and how one might best observe all this.

In order to put her emerging hypothesis to the test, Mary sought a stark contrast to her first African sample. She wanted to see how white suburban American mothers and infants behaved in *their* everyday lives. So instead of moving to a distant village, learning a new language, and making inroads with tribal chiefs, she simply asked local pediatricians to help recruit twenty-six families, and they were happy to oblige. When doctors met families about to have a new baby, they described her project to them—a study of infant development, which is how she framed it in Uganda as well—and asked if they'd be interested, adding that her first study had been done in Africa, thinking that the potential subjects might find that intriguing. As Bob Marvin says, "You don't say no to Dr. Ainsworth, for two reasons: one, she just had an aura; and two, she could talk her way into and out of anything."

Mary would then call the family on the phone, which tended to have a good result.

She could even—posthumously—talk someone like me into her right mind.

chapter sixteen

When the selected babies were just three weeks old, observations for the historic Baltimore Study began. Though Mary didn't know it at the time, it was this revolutionary research in the homes of these families that would lead directly to the Strange Situation in the lab, and to attachment theory as we know it today.

It was 1964, the year my mom sat on her nubby brown couch watching *General Hospital,* burping Sam, her first baby, her hair up in a big French twist with perfectly tendriled curls hanging down along her ears. Behaviorism was on the decline, and Harry Harlow, at the University of Wisconsin, had completed his breakthrough study of monkeys, showing that the little primates preferred terry-cloth-covered wire mothers over the wire mothers who dispensed food. The cupboard love theory was dying. Dr. Benjamin Spock's book *Baby and Child Care,* with its message to mothers—"Trust yourself and your children"—was on its way to becoming one of the most popular books of the twentieth century.

Mary's team of four observers included her—referred to in the notes as Dr. A—and three students: Barbara Wittig, who shared authorship with Mary on many of her most influential early papers; George Allyn, a young man particularly interested in psychoanalysis; and Bob Marvin. While Mary's graduate student Sylvia Bell wasn't part of the official team, she was an unofficial fifth observer, appearing from time to time to engage with the babies for her own dissertation research on object permanency and attachment, and she played an integral role in helping Mary design the study and code the data. From the beginning, the Baltimore Study, just like Mary's research in Uganda, was grounded in genuine curiosity. As Sylvia told me, "We just wanted to know what mothers and babies did."

Observers visited the twenty-six homes every three weeks until the end of the baby's first year—approximately eighteen visits per home in all. Visits often began in the morning around 9:00 A.M. and ended around 1:00 P.M., which added up to seventy-two hours per family, or three full days. At the end of a four-hour visit, the observer dictated his or her notes into a tape recorder, then the tape was transcribed by an administrative assistant who would turn the notes into twenty or more pages of narrative that would then be coded by a "naïve" group of four trained coders who didn't know anything about the families. These coders combed through the transcripts picking out the attachment behaviors to be tallied.

Ten years before Mary died, in 1989, she gave these transcribed notes from the twenty-six home studies to a research library at Harvard. Today a copy sits on my desktop in a 7,744-page pdf.

THE IDEA OF the Baltimore Study was that the home visitors would be "participant observers," like Mary and Mrs. Kibuka had been in Uganda, chatting with families, getting to know them, offering occasional help. As Mary put it, "To have somebody there for an extended period of time, just watching and taking notes could be very tension-producing. Besides, I wanted to see whether the baby would smile at us . . . and how the baby would behave with us in comparison with the mother." While observers "assiduously avoided interfering, giving advice, or implying criticism," it was difficult to maintain too much distance in a house with a new mom and a baby. In one transcript, Dr. A takes a baby for a walk in a stroller, along with an older child. After all, the researchers did want to get a read on the babies' "cuddliness."

As Bob Marvin described it, the routine between him and the moms became pretty natural. M (the mother) might offer him some coffee when he arrived, but quickly get down to the business at hand of feeding, bathing, and playing with B (the baby), or at least going through the motions. Bob says that during his time with his three families, he felt like Jane Goodall watching chimps—just a quiet researcher standing in the doorway, watching and taking notes as a mom went into a darkened nursery to pick up her baby.

According to Sylvia, it was the observer's job to "notice everything." But Bob remembers that they were also taught to pay special attention to "critical situations" involving the attachment behavior Mary had seen in Uganda—comings and goings, smiles and cries, pickups and put-downs. In order to keep a running log, observers used a watch to cue themselves to take notes every five minutes, though Bob says it wasn't long before he didn't need the watch and just knew when five minutes had passed.

WHEN AZALEA WAS a baby, she was up early, then was often asleep again by 9:00 A.M. So if I were in the Baltimore Study, my observer probably would have come later instead of in the middle of B's nap time. Or maybe that would have been the perfect time to arrive in order to get some time with me at the table talking about B, then watching my reaction when she called out with a cry at 10:15 and observing as I walked into her room and smiled at her little "cry face," picked her up, and nursed her. Maybe on the third or fourth visit, after a long night, or with a stressful day ahead, I'd snap at B. And my observer would still be there, keeping a running log of our back-and-forth in five-minute intervals.

WHEN AZALEA WAS a few months old, Thayer and I sat with a stopwatch in the screened porch outside her room, taking notes on what we heard in five-minute intervals. We recorded every sniffle, every fuss, every wail, every "goat cry" (our term for the jittery little cry that came at the end of a throaty one), and every POS (period of silence), as instructed by our favorite parenting book. We were sleep-training our baby.

We didn't know it, but we were participant observers. Noticing everything. In this very critical situation.

The authors advised that we set a time, say night-night to our little darling, and then stick it out till morning—which we basically did. They also suggested that we take notes, scribbling down stretches of silence and types of cries, which I think might have been intended to be the equivalent of the old-school father being asked to boil water when the mother goes into labor—something to make him feel useful and keep him out of the way. It did help us feel useful, but, perhaps even more important, we felt connected to Azalea as she wailed; far from ignoring her cries, we were über-aware of them. And from an attachment perspective, that's a good thing.

After all, as Mary and Sylvia would later find:

Crying is the most conspicuous of early attachment behaviors. Unlike smiling, which gratifies a caretaker, crying arouses displeasure or alarm and elicits interventions aimed at terminating it and discouraging its recurrence. Herein lies the power of crying to promote proximity more effectively than other early signaling behavior.

The authors promoting this sleep-training method promised it would take only a few days if done at the right time and done well. And that our baby would be happier with a good night's sleep.

And they were right.

Azalea did sleep quite a bit every night before sleep training, but in fits and starts, with lots of nursing in between, which I enjoyed. But Thayer and I both believed she would be better off with a solid stretch of sleep. And I knew myself well enough to know that the challenges I was facing as a new mother were absolutely insurmountable without every possible resource at my disposal—especially a good night's sleep. After all, one of the reasons we'd left the monastery was my exhaustion. And I knew that my challenges were Azalea's challenges, and that she was even less equipped than I was to take them on.

So on May 8, 2006, Thayer and I changed her little diaper and laid her tiny body in her crib at 6:00 P.M., her usual bedtime. Then we sat together paying meticulous attention to what was happening in the dark chamber of her room, pens in hand.

6:30 L [loud cry]
6:35 M, G [medium, goat]
6:40: G, L, G, L
6:45 M
6:50 Dad goes in. She quiets down, then escalates.
6:55: M, L, M POS [period of silence]

7: More POS
7:05: M, Long POS
7:10: POS
7:15 L, POS, L, M
7:20: Silence
7:25 ☺
7:28: L
7:30–8:30 Silence

The rest of the night continued in this way, with a wake-up at 10:30 where "Dad soothed but no pick up," a whimper at 11:20, a nursing at 12:38 (I think we allowed for one nursing a night), another wake-up at 2:00, and then "sleep until 7:30 A.M."

The next night we put her down at 6:45 P.M. She woke up at 3:45 A.M., and "Mom feeds until 4 . . . Wake-up at 6:45 A.M." The next few nights were pretty similar—no goat cries at all, mostly silence. A smattering of "mom feed." But then on Friday, day five, there was "a little goat" and "some whimpering" around 10:30, and a note in my handwriting: "Mom going crazy."

Even though Azalea was settling down, it felt horrible to sit on the sidelines of her anguish, noting each and every subtle variation of her birdsong. When Mary listened to babies cry, she wasn't the one who was supposed to swoop in with a pickup, so I imagine that, though it was painful, she bore it for the greater good, for science. And in her listening she found, interestingly, that secure babies had the most varied cries and used the most distinct chirps and caws to communicate to their parents, who were able—for whatever reason—to listen and respond.

By 6:23 P.M. on Tuesday, day nine, it was "quiet." And at the bottom of the page is a random phone number. My sacred log had become scrap paper.

Sometimes I see a picture of Azalea at that age, with her wispy hair and toothless smile, her adorable, uncoordinated little fingers clumsily holding a toy, or I see a baby in a stroller or being buckled into a car seat, *so helpless,* and my heart sinks, thinking of those nights of onesie-soaking goat cries. I can't believe we did that, but I'm glad we did. A few nights of tears, I trusted, paled in comparison with what I knew Azalea was up against, and what she'd be up against even more if she and I were both exhausted: My impatience. My anger. Me.

After that first night of sleep training, I called my mom in the morning, crying, afraid I had damaged Azalea for life. She assured me it just could not be so, not in one, two, even three, four, or five nights. I asked her how she did it—how did she get me and Sam and Matt to sleep? She claimed not to remember. "That was a long time ago, honey," she said.

Years later, upon reflection, my mom remembered. Per Dr. Spock's suggestion, she let us cry for twenty minutes. And it worked.

chapter seventeen

On my last night in Akron, I woke up to the sound of a cry-ing baby. I had been up late, reading and writing in bed, the air almost fogged with humidity. I was hot and tired from my walks to and from the bus that took me to the archive, but I had been planning this trip for months and was determined to squeeze in as much as possible before heading back to the Catskills. Eventually I did fall asleep in the thick, summery si-lence, the bed covered in academic papers, my own early moth-erhood journals, and notes from the past few days.

That day I had been scanning Mary's letters to and from Syl-via onto my hard drive. They were in the midst of analyzing the voluminous data they were collecting, trying to see the big pic-ture of attachment forming through the very fiber of these mothers' and babies' daily lives.

Mary writes:

The newborn baby is not attached to his mother or anyone else. He may be taken from her and given to a foster mother without any apparent distress or disturbance. But in the course of the first year of life he forms an attachment to his mother, and after this attachment had developed he is distressed if he is separated from her and he protests the breach of ties. How does this attachment develop? What factors facilitate this development or delay or prevent it? What are the criteria which enable us to judge that an attachment has been formed?

As Bowlby puts it, "on this foundation, it seems, the rest of his emotional life is built."

Sylvia and Mary's letters involved a very detailed discussion about the babies' crying. They were searching for a method of statistical analysis that would make sense in the context of what they were seeing in the homes—that babies who cried the most had mothers who were less "responsive," and vice versa. Mary had first noticed this in Uganda in 1955, and so both B's tears and M's responses were being closely tallied as they watched for threads and themes. Eventually they found that more sensitive responsiveness to crying in the first six months of life actually led to less crying in the second six months. And while I was nervous for the mothers being watched, I was also touched by the way these gifted researchers, neither of whom had children, paid such close, professional, *formal* attention to the wails and whines of babies. This line of thinking, like all of Mary's work, transformed the private world of a caregiver (mostly women at that time) attending to (or not attending to) a baby's middle-of-the-night tears into something worthy of scientific understanding.

Crying is particularly important as a human phenomenon because of the way it is so intrinsic to attachment. Through our tears, we present an important opportunity to be soothed, or not. It was this tension between upset and stability that Dr. Steele was warning me about as I prepared to contemplate my own potentially disturbed attachment system and write about it at the same time, which requires a certain groundedness. In other words, as

Mary writes, "in general, distress behavior is incompatible with exploratory behavior."

One of my favorite metaphors for these behavioral systems at work is Mary's description of a bird at a birdfeeder being suddenly surprised by the appearance of a person in the window. In that moment, fluttering its wings, with seeds in its beak, the bird must decide whether to feed or flee, because it can't have two primary systems working at once. And neither can we. If we're scrambling for safety, we can't be creative. I can only imagine that by creatively studying the way this safety-seeking mechanism works, Mary herself was strengthening her own secure base. As have I, in studying her work.

The article that Sylvia and Mary eventually published— "Infant Crying and Maternal Responsiveness"—was a correction to what they saw as a stubborn behaviorist-informed misconception that picking up crying babies led to "spoiling." Their data clearly indicated the opposite—that is, how much better off everyone is when parents attune to a baby's requests for soothing, which actually leads to less crying, which is good news for babies and parents. And they described the evolutionary purpose of crying from an attachment point of view. As Bowlby puts it, "it is fortunate for their survival that babies are so designed by Nature that they beguile and enslave" parents. Indeed, unlike other primates, we humans are born so helpless we can't even cling to our mothers for dear life, so we have our work cut out for us, enticing our parents instead to cling to us. And how do we do it?

Mary and Sylvia write, "Because it is disagreeable to adults . . . crying is generally considered a changeworthy behavior." Or as Bowlby writes, "As a rule, crying leads a mother to take steps to arrest it."

Which is why I thought for sure I must be dreaming when I woke up that last night in Akron to the terrible sound of an infant's cries, then screams, then more cries, in a house down the street. I sat up in bed, turned on the light, and saw that it was 1:30 A.M. I opened the curtain and looked out at the darkened homes on the block, but I couldn't tell which house the sound was coming from. I waited for the wailing to stop. It didn't. I wanted to put my hands over my ears. But I couldn't.

Was this baby alone? Maybe her parents were in the other room, catching up on the news; maybe it only sounded treacherous from a distance. Maybe the baby was colicky and they had been soothing her all night long and were spent. Maybe they were drunk, passed out? Didn't care? Shooting up? Making love? Were they even in the house? Was the baby ill? Or just desperate?

The baby's cries shifted back and forth from anguish to rage, from throaty sadness to screeching. The only pauses were for some phlegmy coughing. At least that's how it sounded to me.

Maybe this was what our neighbors heard on the warm spring nights Thayer and I sleep-trained Azalea, my tiny diaper-wearing baby sending cries into the abyss that, could she have formed words, would have spelled my name—*Ma-ma!*

Listening to the baby down the street cry, I thought of all the times I had been unable to turn toward Azalea's tears because I was too busy or too nervous, or just couldn't muster the patience.

Sitting up in my bed, reviewing the past years with Azalea, I asked myself with no small amount of trepidation: Where does a baby's unshared heartbreak *go*?

And then I heard footsteps in the hall. It was Candy, the woman who owned the house, who apparently had been awakened as well. Wondering if it was all a dream, I went into the hallway and saw her standing there with the light of her room behind her. I asked if we should call the police. Instead, she put on her shoes and walked down the street to knock on the door! Nobody answered. So she called the cops. Who never came.

And the baby stopped crying. And I went back to sleep, missing my daughter like mad and hoping she was sleeping well without me. But not too well. When I arrived home, would she run to the door, hugging me, seeking proximity, telling me about everything she'd been up to? Or would she barely look up from her book, a little (or a lot) peeved that I had left?

THE NEXT MORNING, I packed up my room and Candy drove me to the airport. We talked about the spooky sadness of the previous night, lifted by the simple fact of daylight. She shared some of her story with me—a single mother, grown children, a career as a nurse. And then she asked me how the week had been. Had I found what I was looking for?

I said I wasn't sure, but that I felt like I was getting warmer.

As in: getting closer. But also as in: heart melting.

WHEN I FINALLY arrived home after a long day of travel, Azalea was standing at the dining room table, a pile of Barbies in front of her in various stages of undress, two in their pink Corvette. She looked up and said, "Hi, Mama!"

chapter eighteen

Case 18 is a family from the Baltimore Study with whom Mary became so involved that they wanted to amend their will to include Dr. A, giving her visitation rights and an "advisory capacity" in the case of their death, like Paulo's family in Uganda, who wanted her to take their precious son home with her to the States. In the notes, Mary writes, "I was really very touched by this and although it's a responsibility I do not particularly want to take on, I felt I should not refuse."

This family was resistant at first to the idea of being studied. M, the mother, was in therapy and preparing to go back to work as a teacher, which Mary was particularly intrigued by, wondering how attachment would change with a working mother. M wasn't sure Mary would want to talk to the babysitter, and wasn't sure the babysitter would want to talk to her, either. Turns out M was wrong. Mary loved talking to the babysitter, who was named Theresa, and it seemed the feeling was mutual. Mary writes,

> Theresa is a real gem. She is a middle-aged grandmother with six grown children of her own . . . I was pleased to see

that she gives B very much the same type of attention that M gives him . . . she certainly doesn't seem likely to neglect him while M isn't there. On the contrary, she responds to every little fuss . . . She is a good informant about B and gives information very readily . . . M was certainly lucky in finding Theresa, but then it perhaps was not mere luck because this was exactly the kind of person she was hunting for and she had the sense to recognize it when she met her.

Quite the opposite of a problem, Mary found that Theresa was a great addition to what the contemporary Canadian psychologist Gordon Neufeld calls the "attachment village."

B is perfectly content to be with Theresa and uses her as a secure base . . . I don't think there's much doubt that B is more attached to M than to Theresa but he is probably attached to both and probably to F as well.

Mary found that M's going back to work was not a negative influence on B in the least. Years later, in 1983, Mary wrote, "I would like to consider the relation of my research contribution to the women's movement. By some it has been viewed as a stroke against women's liberation . . . It has been assumed that I believe in full-time mothering during the child's earliest years . . . [but] I acknowledge that satisfactory supplementary mothering arrangements can and have been made by not an inconsiderable few." I'm sure Case 18 is one of those few.

Another reason M from Case 18 was uncomfortable with the idea of participating in the study was that, like my mom, M wanted to breastfeed, though it was unusual at the time and she wasn't comfortable doing it in front of anyone. And finally, F, the father, wasn't thrilled with the idea of being studied; it turned out he had taken classes from Mary years earlier and felt like a bit of an expert himself. All of these factors made the family think it might be best not to participate in the study. So Mary and George visited the family before B was born.

> The visit itself was a very intense one, pleasant in some ways, but full of strain . . . Every now and then either George or I would find ourselves trapped. We would mention something about the mother, and they would latch onto that, "Aha! It is not just the baby you are interested in but the mother too!"

Of course the family was correct. After much back-and-forth, M agreed, but only under the condition that Dr. A would be assigned as the home observer. When the baby was born, Mary sent flowers to the hospital, along with a card.

From the beginning, Dr. A and M had a deep connection, which developed, over the next twenty visits, into a friendship. In Visit 1, Dr. A kept her notes focused on the details of what she observed, though she also incorporated M's reflections into her own insights.

> Before B was born I think that M was very anxious and scared of having a baby . . . They did not even discuss what to name him. She refused to get anything in preparation for his arrival . . . Now that he has arrived she seems to have warmed up to him very much. She is beginning to understand his signals and certainly wants to respond to them appropriately. She is very gentle and tender and slow in her handling of B and there seems no awkwardness or tension which is surprising . . . She says that when he cries a hungry cry she begins to lactate, spots on her dress.

In Visit 1, M also shared her therapy with Dr. A, as well as her reasons for deciding to enter the study after much trepidation.

At the very end M told me that the thing that had decided her to participate was the second letter that I had written. The implication was that she felt that I cared about her as a person, which, of course, I do.

As the relationship developed, Dr. A came to respect M. Beginning around Visit 12 and continuing over the rest of the study, Dr. A took note of the way B responded to her as the unfamiliar person that she was—when he looked at her, smiled, played, laughed, and accepted a piece of cracker she offered. After Visit 17, she writes, "I don't believe I'm any longer really a stranger to B." Starting with Visit 7, Mary occasionally stayed late for drinks and dinner. They ate meals like steaks, seasoned rice with peaches, and a chef salad, over which she and F and M had "quite an intellectual conversation."

In the notes from Visit 15, Dr. A writes:

It must be quite apparent to both parents that I enjoy these visits, that I like them and am fond of B and their interest in his development. Both of them always make me feel very welcome and M again reiterated that she hoped that we would keep our relationship up after the year's research was ended. I, of course, would like to do this, but I know how difficult it [is].

The Baltimore Study was the first of its kind, and the last. While other studies of mothers and babies collected data points, this was no box-checking exercise. Mary and her team were looking at *relational events* noticed from within "critical situations," in the midst of having very real relationships with the subjects. Instead of counting and tallying, say, M's smiles and B's cries in Case 18, the way mothers and babies had been studied up until that point, Mary was watching the dyad—the unit—for four hours at a time, in their instinctive back-and-forth call-and-response, like birds singing to each other through the trees at dusk.

> M leaves the room, saying that she's going to "throw a meatloaf together." As soon as she leaves B lies quietly in a supine position with his finger in his mouth, vocalizing slightly. Again he didn't protest her departure nor did he follow her with his eyes but he has quieted down during her absence. M starts to make some rattling sounds with the pans in the kitchen. B hears this and becomes very quiet, listening and looking in her direction. Then he begins to vocalize "ah-ah-ah-ah-ah" again.

A study like this is incredibly time-consuming, expensive, and difficult to do—three good reasons why it's never been duplicated. As stated in the preface to the 2015 edition of the seminal book *Patterns of Attachment: A Psychological Study of the Strange Situation,* "the Baltimore study entailed a level of craftsmanship that does not easily scale to large samples." Thankfully, there's no need to do it again. The incredible profusion of data that poured out of those Baltimore homes is still very much alive. Those 1,872 hours of watching mothers and babies in the minutiae of their lives together, the 7,744 pages of observations, their millions of all-day, every-day subtle gestures of social releasing have been funneled into one twenty-minute crucible, brilliantly designed like an X-ray machine to reveal the bones of our relational future.

. . .

BACK IN HER office at Johns Hopkins, sifting through the piles of onionskin transcripts from all the observers' first year of visits, I can imagine that Mary was very pleased to see that most of the babies' attachment behaviors at home were exactly like those of the Ganda babies—the ways they cried, clung, clambered, and scrambled seemed to line up. Her dream had come true: with two samples about as different as she could find anywhere on earth, she had established that babies want to be close to their mothers, and that they will stop at nothing to get their attention. That's just what we human beings do—proximity-seek or bust.

But there was one thing that confused her. While the American babies did appear to use their mother as a secure base, it was less "conspicuous" with the Americans than with the Ganda babies. Looking through the transcripts and the coding, she could see the outline of the way they were returning to their mothers throughout the day, but it wasn't as marked as it had been in Uganda.

Mary believed one reason for this difference was that the Ganda babies were used to being with their mothers all the time, and less accustomed to being around strangers—especially scary "European" ones like her—than her American sample was. So it would stand to reason that the Ganda babies' attachment systems, which were under more stress with her around, were more visibly activated than the American babies' and thus easier for her to observe.

"All right," Mary said later in an interview. "If you don't see the secure-base phenomenon very clearly at home, that doesn't necessarily mean it doesn't exist . . . If I could bring the children into the university with their mothers, maybe I could see how they used the mother to explore."

In a letter to Bowlby, Mary writes:

I have been focusing my thoughts upon the way to devise little test situations that might yield nice, controlled, quantitative data, and lend an aura of scientific respectability.

To which Bowlby responded:

It is a great pity we cannot discuss this at leisure! In general I heartily endorse your line of thought. Studying the infant's response to pre-defined critical situations seems extremely promising.

So, in 1964, Mary began taking mothers and babies to the lab at Johns Hopkins to see how they responded in an unfamiliar environment, usually around Visit 18 to 20. Others before Mary had devised similar situations, so it was not, as Bob told me, a "de novo" idea to include a "strange" element in her study. However, the fact that this "little test situation" of hers was something she created after spending a year immersed in "what mothers and babies actually do" was what made the Strange Situation the powerful tool it is today.

As Mary describes it:

I thought, Well, let's work it all out: We'll have the mother and baby together in a strange environment with a lot of toys to invite exploration. Then we'll introduce a stranger when the mother's still there, and see how the baby responds. Then we'll have a separation situation where the mother leaves the baby with the stranger. How does the baby respond to the departure? And when the mother returns, how does the baby respond to the reunion? But since the stranger was in the room during the first departure, maybe we'd better have an episode in which the mother leaves the baby entirely alone. Then we could see whether the return of the stranger lessens whatever stress has occurred. Finally, we'll have another reunion with the mother. We devised this thing in half an hour.

As Bob Marvin remembers it, "It was an afterthought. The Strange Situation was an afterthought."

GENERALLY SPEAKING, babies behaved in the Strange Situation as Mary predicted. After all, by Visit 20, she knew them well, either because she herself was their observer or because she had read their lengthy transcripts.

When their mothers were nearby, the babies explored the toys that had been set out to entice them, but they did this less when the stranger appeared. The first time the mother left the room, 20 percent of the babies cried immediately, and only 49 percent cried at all. Some babies were "lured" back into playing by the stranger, and when the mother returned, most babies pulled out all the stops with attachment behaviors such as smiling, reaching, approaching. Half of the babies wanted physical contact upon the first reunion, and almost all of the mothers provided that contact within fifteen seconds.

When the mother left the room the second time and the baby was alone, most of the babies cried. The stranger, who returned in three minutes, usually had little success in comforting the babies. And when the mother returned the second time, more than twice as many babies made contact with their mother as in the first reunion, and 47 percent of the babies exhibited some form of actual avoidance of their mother—though ever so slight, not enough to get them classified as "avoidant," per se.

Mary Ainsworth's "afterthought" was initially developed as something to check and deepen the rich data that were coming out of the home visits—the thousands of pages of detailed reports about pickups, cries, feeding, bathing, and comings and goings between mothers and babies. But the Strange Situation itself turned out to be so elegant, so effective at compressing her team's thousands of hours of observation into one twenty-minute laser-like tool, that it soon became, much to Mary's chagrin, *the* thing—as it is today. And while some have criticized the procedure for being "artificial," not a realistic scenario in which to judge something as important and complex as a child's relationship to its parent, so, says attachment researcher Jay Belsky, is the treadmill—but it's still used to reveal the inner workings of the heart.

chapter nineteen

The more I learned about Mary and her Strange Situation, the more I realized I was missing a lot. Every time I watched one of the procedures online or read about it, some new subtlety appeared. I knew that in order to truly understand Mary's magic trick, I would need some real training.

The summer after my trip to Akron, I traveled to Minneapolis, where I met Dr. Alan Sroufe. For the past forty-five years, Sroufe, co-author of the Minnesota Longitudinal Study of Risk and Adaptation, a major study of attachment begun in 1975, has trained researchers, grad students, and clinicians to become reliable coders of the Strange Situation for research projects around the world. I had written to tell him about my book and asked if I could attend his annual training for attachment researchers. He had said yes.

Dr. Sroufe is a kind, warm, minister-like zealot who often referred to Mary Ainsworth as a genius as well as a wonderful, supportive person. Though he had led groups like ours through the Strange Situation minute by minute for decades, he still did it with stars in his eyes, like someone who had seen a miracle. Thrilled to be part of his congregation—which this week included people from Italy, Peru, New Zealand, Mexico, Israel, Japan, and Zambia—I arrived in the classroom early every day and sat in the front row praising the gospel. Every day I saw something new; every day I saw just a little more of the light.

THE STAGE IS set: a room with two chairs and some toys on the floor. A mother and her one-year-old baby enter and begin the Strange Situation. It doesn't take long to determine the baby's baseline temperament: Was the baby, for instance, physical, running to every corner of the room, or inquisitive, intently exploring and mouthing every block, or reserved, wistfully holding a wind-up toy. The mother is told to sit down and even read one of the provided magazines if she wishes, so as not to distract the baby from whatever he is naturally drawn to do. Then a stranger comes in and the baby's reaction is observed—is she afraid of the stranger, nonchalant, or drawn to her? This indicates the style of relating to people in general. By comparing this style with the way the baby relates to the mother—a relationship that ought to be special—we can see their "differential" relationship.

Next, the mother is instructed to exit the room, leaving her purse on the chair, a sign that she will return. Here we see how the baby responds to the experience of being left—does she howl and run to the door? Or does she stay put on the floor, in a mountain of toys? The stranger tries to soothe the baby if she is upset. Otherwise, she leaves her to keep exploring.

After a few minutes (cut short if the baby is truly under duress), the mother returns for Reunion 1. Because of the behavioral system that has evolved to keep infants close to their caregivers and safe from harm, all babies will be under stress when left alone. And in fact, heart rate and cortisol levels indicate that even babies who don't appear distressed still are; they look calm on the outside, but inside they are suppressing their feelings. So when the mother returns to the room, researchers are watching to see whether her presence works as it should, as a comfort to the baby. Does the reunion do its job of bringing the baby from a state of relative anxiety into a state of relative ease? In other words, is the child soothed by the mother?

If the baby was upset during separation but sits still as a stone when her mother returns, it's likely a sign of an insecure attachment. If the baby was relaxed when left alone and is nonplussed by reunion, that's less significant. If the baby hightails it toward her mother, then screeches mid-approach, indicating a change of heart, that's a worrisome sign, too.

But the most important moment is Reunion 2, after the mother leaves again and returns again. If a baby who was upset during separation *still* does nothing to acknowledge her mother's return, it's a sure sign that the baby, at only a year old, has already come to expect her advances to be rebuffed. If the baby reaches out for comfort but isn't able to settle down enough to receive it (or it's not offered), it's probably a reflection of an insecure relationship filled with mixed messages. And if the baby is wild with sadness, then jumps into the mother's arms and immediately stops crying, the baby is categorized as secure, coming from a relationship in which she expects her needs to be met. The same goes for a mellow baby whose cues are more subtle, who simply looks sad during separation, then moves closer to Mother upon reunion. In both cases, the relationship works.

Separate, connect. Separate, connect.

At the beginning of the training, even though it was all starting to make more sense to me, I still got distracted by the wrong details or hung up on my own reactions. Is it the whiny babies who are insecure, and the robust, easygoing ones who are secure? Not necessarily. Attachment is not about temperament. If a big crier is soothed by his mother's return, he is securely attached. If an anxious kid knows how to scramble for safety and "feel felt," it's another good sign. This is why the Strange Situation works so well—it highlights the relationship while controlling for almost everything else. Ainsworth really was a genius.

Eventually I learned how to read the cues, and I began to notice the quickest glance and connect it with the rest of the baby's behavior. I now knew the difference between a full-on, wrap-around-the-legs greeting and a limp request for contact, and the significance of each. I started to wonder about the baby who reached up to be held, was picked up, then kicked to be let down. And I began to worry about all those "good" babies who just sat there, moving shapes around the floor, unaffected by their lifeline's comings and goings. I was learning that babies who don't use their mothers to soothe themselves have trouble later on—as children *and* as adults.

ONCE MARY SAW the American babies in her study using their mother as a secure base, like the Ganda babies had at home, that could have been the end of the Strange Situation. She could have just said, *Okay, yes, this secure-base thing is real.* But the different ways babies responded in the Strange Situation was so, as one scholar put it, "especially striking" that another layer of the onion revealed itself.

After watching the babies move through the Strange Situation, Mary and her colleagues categorized their individual differences, according to an "ABC" system, which is still used around the world to classify patterns of infant attachment: A is insecure/avoidant; B is secure; C is insecure/resistant or insecure/ambivalent. These patterns are now completely embedded in our understandings of attachment, and are the basis upon which the idea of "attachment styles" was built.

Today, though different studies have slightly varying results, it is generally understood that global averages for security in infancy is at around 65 percent, not far off from what Mary found in Uganda and Baltimore in her small samples. At home and in the Strange Situation, "Group-B infants showed significantly less frequent distress when mother left the room than either A or C infants," whereas "Group-C babies showed the most separation distress both at home and in the strange situation." B babies responded the most positively when held at home and generally tended to seek contact and interaction with the mother in the Strange Situation. A (avoidant) babies showed the least disturbance in separation episodes and tended to avoid physical closeness with the mother. C (resistant) babies were upset upon separation and also angry upon reunion.

Tens of thousands of studies over the past sixty years have shown how our ABC classification in the Strange Situation is moderately stable across our life span—if it changes, it's most often due to negative experiences—and is connected to pretty much every single aspect of our lives, including the ways we approach adult relationships, with all their ups and downs. Out of the shorthand wisdom of the Strange Situation, what Mary and her team discovered in those early labs at Johns Hopkins was three universal attachment patterns, one of which—A, B, or C—has been etched into our very being since our first year of life and will inform our feelings about who we are in relation to others and how we behave toward them—with confidence, anger, or lack of trust. The Strange Situation shows us what a one-year-old has learned about her world.

As Mary wrote in a letter to a colleague in 1983, "There seems no doubt now that there is continuity, coherence, predictability or whatever you want to call it between early patterns of infant-parent attachment and a number of aspects of later development."

Attachment, in other words, is, as Mary said, "a robust phenomenon."

BECAUSE THE B (secure) babies were the most predictable and prevalent, they were the easiest to notice. Many cried upon separation, then were soothed by their mothers, just like the secure babies in Uganda. Those who did not cry but enthusiastically greeted their mothers and/or energetically initiated interaction with them upon their reunion were also found to be secure. And because Mary had these babies' home data and consistently compared them against the Strange Situation data, she could see that the secure babies, even those who cried mightily in the lab, were the ones who actually cried the least at home and were the most easygoing when left in ordinary circumstances, like when their mother had to go to the bathroom or tend to other children (or fetch an ashtray or a drink for an observer).

However, the babies who behaved less predictably in the Strange Situation kept her guessing. Some of these babies were completely undone by separation, and when Mother returned, they continued to cry, fuss, kick, and resist. Finally, this group was deemed insecure/resistant or insecure/ambivalent (C), in the sense that they expressed a desire for contact but were, at the same time, resistant to its effects, or ambivalent. And indeed, these were the babies who at home were the fussiest. Mary writes, "Crying in the home environment, including crying when the mother leaves the room, is most closely related to resistant behavior in the reunion episodes of the strange situation." The resistant babies cried more in the Strange Situation than the other two groups.

Another group of babies wasn't crying during separations. Mary thought they might just need a little more stress, so she reluctantly added another separation. Still nothing. And then, when she looked at the home data, she realized that these babies actually cried more than the secure babies, though less than the resistant, and had mothers who were more rejecting at home. The ones who sat still as a stone during the entire Strange Situation were often upset at home, especially when put down. In fact, the home observers had described these babies as the angriest of the bunch. This conundrum led to one of her biggest breakthroughs.

Contemplating this apparent contradiction, Mary thought of the early work of Jimmy Robertson, her colleague at Tavistock Clinic, the same one who inspired her work in Uganda. She remembered a little girl named Laura from his black-and-white film *A Two-Year-Old Goes to Hospital* and how, even though her parents visited her daily, Laura was so pissed off about being left, she totally withdrew, and even refused to hold her mother's hand when her parents took her home. And Mary wondered: Can one-year-olds, preverbal, some still not walking and, as far as Freud was concerned, still egoless, be *angry*? Is that even possible? Is a one-year-old actually *person* enough to have such a deeply *personal* response?

While the world's answer was no, Mary's answer, after much close and careful observation, was yes. Even her dear friend Bowlby, who had made it his life's work to expose the world to a child's grief from separation, had a hard time buying that these avoidant babies were expressing a defense, per se. But Mary insisted that these babies' refusal to cry or seek comfort was in fact a very real defense against the pain of knowing that their mothers might reject them.

In a discussion with Bowlby, Mary said:

As for looking-away behavior, I was not geared to note it when we began to observe infants in a strange situation. It first became obvious in its most conspicuous form where a child would start towards the mother, stop, turn and walk away, refusing to come back despite the mother's entreaties . . . It was not until a careful examination of the home-visit data that we were able to make hypotheses about what the baby might be defending against.

Eventually Bowlby came around, and in fact felt terrible for doubting Mary, though she "largely took his criticisms as friendly scientific cautions." She said, "I expected that some children were going to be more insecure than others, that they would cry harder, that they would cry more promptly, that they would cry longer, be harder to comfort, and that they would be angry [C babies]. The thing that blew my mind was the avoidant response [A babies]."

That avoidance response is now well documented. These are the babies who appear to be very together and well behaved in the Strange Situation, though the opposite is true at home. Because we Americans tend to feel pride when our babies don't appear to need us—we value an independent, "easy" disposition—what is in fact a fear of rejection in the Strange Situation is often misconstrued as admirable nonchalance. However, by tracking the heart rate, skin temperature, and cortisol levels, researchers like Alan Sroufe have found that these babies are far from relaxed; in fact, as the avoidant baby sits perfectly still, playing with blocks, his or her face placid, on the inside a physiological storm is raging. It was these avoidant babies that Mary initially and wrongly called "not yet attached," including the babies in Uganda who didn't seem to know their mother from a stranger.

Which is to say, these babies are inhibiting—pushing down, *avoiding*—their inborn urge to seek comfort when under stress.

They are cutting off their attachment behavior, which actually echoes what Bowlby had described six years earlier in his seminal 1958 paper: "When, however, the [attachment] response is not free to reach termination [i.e., is not responded to] . . . we experience tension, unease and anxiety."

In the end, Mary and her team in Baltimore divided their twenty-six cases into three classifications—56 percent were deemed secure, 26 percent were avoidant, and 17 percent were resistant. Her Uganda babies (twenty-eight individual infants, but twenty-six dyads because of the two sets of twins) were divided into almost exactly the same numbers for secure infants, but the insecure classifications needed refining: 57 percent (sixteen pairs) were what she called "secure," 25 percent (seven pairs) were what she called "insecurely attached," and 18 percent (five pairs) were "not yet attached," which correlate more closely with avoidant babies. Eventually her Baltimore team added five subgroups to the three classifications of A, B, and C. And, "to Ainsworth's amazement, these eight groupings she created would hold up for twenty years and thousands of children."

In the 1980s, after hundreds more Strange Situations had been done, Mary's student Mary Main noticed that there was a group of Strange Situations that didn't fall neatly into the eight classifications. These involved babies who, upon reunion, behaved in unusual, sometimes bizarre ways that didn't seem to be part of any of the three patterns of attachment organization. They remained perfectly still, appeared to zone out, looked at the wall, or sometimes crawled or walked in circles around the mother, like the boy in the first Strange Situation that I saw with Dr. Steele. Main would soon find that these behaviors—statistically speaking, and not on a case-by-case basis—sometimes appeared when children were maltreated and perhaps felt afraid of their attachment figure. Main's husband, Erik Hesse, and

Main call this dilemma "fright without solution." And from an attachment/behavioral system's standpoint, it makes sense that this fear is difficult to tolerate. Consider Mary's bird at the window, munching away when a person—a threat—appears on the other side of the glass. Suddenly torn between feeding and fleeing, little does the bird know, or care, that that scary person was the same one who filled up the feeder. But when a baby finds herself in such a situation, it's trouble.

In other words, if a baby's attachment figure is a source of both comfort and fear, the baby finds itself in a serious psychological and physiological dilemma when it instinctually wants to turn to its attachment figure for safety and solace—because that person is also dangerous. It's a truly lose-lose situation.

This "disorganization" of the attachment pattern can also appear in cases where the parent is dealing with unresolved grief or trauma to such a degree that he or she is intermittently completely unavailable to the child—as in cases of dissociated affect, in which a parent seems to mentally disappear or wander off into some other place. Over time, even subtle forms of unpredictability can affect a child's faith in her caregiver's ability to tune in to her.

While it would take some time for Mary to accept this new "D" category, accept it she would. Today, disorganization is usually considered an element of one of the other patterns, though it is possible for an attachment relationship to be considered disorganized (D) as a primary classification. In other words, as researcher Barry Coughlan and his colleagues put it in a recent article, "disorganized attachment behaviors are not necessarily pervasive and may only become apparent for brief moments during the [Strange Situation Procedure]. As a result, children who receive a 'disorganized' primary classification also receive, where possible, a secondary alternate 'organized' classification."

By the end of my week of Strange Situation training, I had

become pretty comfortable with the three main classifications, though training in the D category takes an entire week of separate training to master. I was even beginning to be able to discern the five subgroups, such as the so-called B4 subgroup of secure babies, who can be a little misleading because they express a lot, and can be a bit feisty, but know how to get what they need.

AS AINSWORTH FIRST noticed in Uganda, then more and more in Baltimore, the mothers who seemed best at the dance of co-regulation, and most attuned to their babies' signals—for food, for comfort, for play, for sleep—had the babies who were *most able to use their mothers* to help them regulate in a stressful, strange situation. This makes sense from an attachment, social-releasing model of relationships. If mothers and babies are indeed a pair, then attunement to each other is critical for achieving our set goal of felt security.

However, some of the most efficient, well-meaning, even friendly mothers in the Baltimore Study just weren't able to show up for their babies when the babies needed them. They let their babies cry for long periods, rebuffed the babies' requests for contact, or essentially ignored them by multitasking as they went about intimate care such as changing a diaper or feeding them. And because these observations happened over a full year of study, Mary was able to see deeply entrenched tendencies and not just isolated incidents.

After the first round of Strange Situations had been completed, Mary examined each baby's home transcripts in light of what happened in the lab, taking notes, "back-and-forthing." It was in this early mirroring exercise—lining up the way mothers behaved at home with what their babies did in the lab, noting that the secure babies' mothers seemed more "sensitive"—that she first took the intuitive idea of maternal sensitivity and formalized it in a way that only she could.

> The term "motherly care" is too unspecific . . . Sensitivity to signals tends to ensure that the care the mother gives the baby, including her playful interaction with him, is attuned to the baby's state and mood—at the baby's own timing, not the mother's timing.

It is sensitivity *to signals,* sensitivity to another's experience—as opposed to an overall experience of *being sensitive*—that leads to security.

In other words, Mary's original concept of "maternal sensitivity" is revolutionary because it does not examine behavior in "absolute terms," as Mary put it—there's no tallying of specific behaviors that need to occur a certain number of times per hour or day for every child, no matter his or her temperament. Instead, "the most important aspect of it, I repeat, was the mother's ability to gear her interactions to infant behavioral cues, so that despite inevitable constitutional differences among infants who later become securely attached, all had had experiences of a good 'mesh.'"

The sensitive caregiver picks the baby up "when he seems to wish it, and puts him down when he wants to explore . . . On the other hand, the mother who responds inappropriately tries to socialize with the infant when he is hungry, play with him when he is tired, or feed him when he is trying to initiate social interaction." What Mary was looking for was a parent's ability to tune in to his or her child, which led to the two of them acting—as Bowlby put it—like a unit.

But as Howard and Miriam Steele often say, even the most securely attached relationships are attuned only 50 percent of the time.

Which means there's a whole lot of room for so-called error. We're nonstop social-releasing creatures, after all. Nobody can be expected to catch them all. Instead, it was through the experience of day-in, day-out, for-the-most-part-attuned interaction that Mary believed a baby would "build up a set of expectancies about what his mother will do . . . He gradually builds up a working model of his mother, in representational terms . . . therein lies his feeling of security in his relations with her." And therein lies the reason the Strange Situation takes only twenty minutes or less: with the mere flush of stress, the baby's expectations appear. It's an entire year expressed in twenty minutes.

Within the parent-child interaction, she observed yet another telling detail, perhaps the most important (and my very favorite) index of a secure, well-functioning attachment relationship. It's an index that can be thought of as the question at the heart of all of Mary's studies and scales: *Do M and B express mutual delight?*

For Mary, the word "delight" is a technical term. Delight—simply defined as "a high degree of pleasure or enjoyment"—can't be playacted with cheery smiles and a happy voice; it has to be real. As one scholar puts it, "This delight can be tender and gentle, but is not necessarily intense. It emerges during situations and behavior specific to the baby, and should not be confused with pride. Delight may be present in some mothers from the beginning but may develop in others only gradually."

Delight doesn't follow any rules.

OF ALL THE Strange Situations we watched during our week of training, my favorite starred a B4 girl in a lavender dress. Sitting in the darkened classroom, I watched the baby toddle around in her little sneakers, bawling her head off when her mother—a thin, sad-seeming young woman in Reeboks, with hair that was short on top and longer in the back—left. But when the mother returned, the baby ran to her and was immediately picked up. The crying stopped. This was not one of those moms with tons of affect and big expressions of *There, there.* She did not seem in the least delighted. But when she picked her baby up, with no fanfare whatsoever, the baby molded right to her and put her head on her shoulder, then the mother and daughter patted each other's shoulders simultaneously, which Sroufe pointed out, with—I swear to God—a lump in his throat, was a beautiful example of co-regulation.

Then the baby got back on the floor to play.

I looked around at all the mothers and daughters and fathers and sons in the classroom, staring up at the big screen as this sad-looking mother and her big-feelings daughter showed us all how it's done.

chapter twenty

In the 1970s, just as Ainsworth's first Strange Situation results were being widely published and replicated, Sroufe and his colleagues began their landmark study of attachment. They gathered 180 children who had been born into "modest poverty" to study over the course of their lives. Each and every aspect of these children's development was observed—four times in the first year, every six months through age two and a half, then once a year through the third grade and every two or three years thereafter. As of this writing, the subjects are still being followed, though the study has evolved to focus almost exclusively on their health outcomes. One of the most compelling findings is that secure attachment is associated with long-term cardiac health.

Security is good for the heart.

From the start, these observations took place in a variety of contexts—at home, in the lab, in school, and among peer groups. Assessments were made regarding every area of these kids' lives—relationships with parents and friends, their temperament, intellectual capacities, and cognitive functioning, and "the interplay of all these factors age by age in detail, beginning at the beginning." The study also included ongoing check-ins about the family's life—their particular stresses, and disruptions and support to the family system.

Thirty years into this exhaustive study, the results were emphatic. A securely attached childhood led to the following outcomes:

A greater sense of self-agency
Better emotional regulation
Higher self-esteem
Better coping under stress
More positive engagement in the preschool peer group
Closer friendships in middle childhood
Better coordination of friendships and group functioning in adolescence
More trusting, non-hostile romantic relationships in adulthood
Greater social competence
More leadership qualities
Happier and better relationships with parents and siblings
Greater trust in life

Among the researchers' key claims, number one was: "Nothing is more important in the development of the child than the care received, including that in the early years." Another biggie was that "development is not linear; it is characterized by both continuity and change." In other words, childhood wounds and strengths, while powerful and impactful, are—like everything else in the human realm—never static. Our very nature is to be poised for transformation.

As Sroufe and his colleagues write in the book on their research, boldly named *The Development of the Person,* it was "a dream of developmental psychologists to know what children experience . . . and to watch them unfold." There was one girl from the study who everyone agreed was "so remarkable" at age ten that they wanted to make a video about her. At the Strange Situation training, Sroufe showed us the video, and offered copies for sale. Of course I bought one and brought it home with me. It's called *Missy: A Developmental Portrait*. Azalea was ten when I came home from Minnesota, and summer was upon us. When I wasn't hanging out with her—back-and-forthing from my study to the kitchen, to the car, to the deck—I managed to watch this video. A lot.

The video takes place during a four-week summer day camp that forty-seven of the children from the larger longitudinal study have been invited to attend so they can be observed in every part of their day, especially in their relationships. It opens with the sound of a guitar gently strumming, then shows images of 1980s kids playing kickball and yelling happily, and then a group of girls running across a playground. Then it cuts to kids swimming in an indoor pool, with its ricochet sound. Then we see young Missy sitting at a table, curly brown hair and braces. She's wearing big 1980s glasses and a funky top.

Off camera, we hear the interviewer say, "We're going to do this camp again next year, so we wanted to know the kind of stuff that you liked and what you didn't like so we can make it really good for other kids." And then we watch Missy listen, holding her chin in her hand, looking thoughtful. She says, "Mmmm," then bursts into a big, shiny, tinselly smile, moving back in her chair, folding up one leg. Still smiling, she explains in a Minnesota accent, "Well, at the overnight you couldn't run around and all, and the boys got to run around." After describing a mixed review of what she liked and didn't like (mostly what she liked), the narrator, young Alan Sroufe, chimes in:

This is a delightful ten-year-old child. She's self-confident, expressive, and appealing. Her enjoyment of life and engagement with her world of peers are obvious . . . She was a peer leader, who other children were happy to follow. She did her best in all activities and enjoyed them. She had a notable comfort with her body. Her relationship priorities were well ordered for a ten-year-old child. She got along well with counselors, but the business at hand was peers.

When the interviewer asks Missy, "How did you feel about the boys?" she answers with great enthusiasm and dramatic pause, all the while maintaining eye contact. First she's smiling, then looking serious. Then she's smiling again.

Well, sometimes Derrick and Akeem and Paul will tease me in the car about my braces, but Akeem won't tease me about my glasses. He wears glasses, too. But Paul and Derrick will. But I just ignore them and sometimes I get back at them . . . When they call me Train Tracks, I call them Plaque Mouth because they don't have to brush their teeth after every meal [the way I do]. Akeem and them would throw a towel at me and all, I'd get it from him, and Akeem would take the towel and hit my glasses with it, and then I'd scratch him with my nails.

Missy looks pleased with herself for fighting back. I can only imagine how good it would feel to stand up to harassing boys and to "scratch [them] with my nails."

While Missy looked just as I did at her age—the curly hair, the big, silly glasses, the lanky body—she *acted* much more like Azalea than like me. After all, I was sullen, shy, and not exactly popular. And Azalea, while not as extroverted as Missy, is certainly confident, well liked, and very "expressive." Which made me wonder how Azalea—with a mother like me—would end up like Missy.

Sroufe continues:

> In sum, Missy had a clear sense of herself and an infectious enthusiasm and joy in living that made her attractive to others. How did she get to be this way? How early would we see signs that she was developing to be this healthy and sociable child? And what form would these early signs of positive adaptation take? Fortunately, Missy was part of a longitudinal research project. As part of this study, children were filmed in each developmental period in a variety of situations, beginning in infancy. Because of these films, we're able to look back on Missy's early life.

As I watched Missy's young life unfold in the film, Azalea moving in and out of the house looking dreamy but determined, Sroufe's words echoed in my head: *How did she—Azalea—get to be this way?*

Flashing to black-and-white footage of Baby Missy, still stiff on her little legs, wearing a barrette in her fine baby hair, Sroufe narrates: "In infancy, Missy received care that was reliable and responsive to her needs and signals . . . She explores freely and happily in her mother's presence."

I remembered Azalea toddling back and forth across the study floor as I sat at my computer. She was transporting blocks from one container and roughly placing them in another. Then looking up at me.

Next we see one-year-old Missy in the Strange Situation. Her mother, a teenager with remarkable presence, has left her, as instructed, in a laboratory playroom. Missy sits in a diaper. It's Episode 3, Separation 1, and the stranger is sitting in her chair nearby. Missy is still; Sroufe narrates that she is "subdued."

She sits with a dead Slinky on her lap, her face quiet. You can almost feel her cry tingling behind her nose and in her throat.

And then, as her mother so much as *reaches* for the knob on the other side of the door, like a bird swooping onto a branch, Missy's face lights up and she giggles and squeals with delight. "This is clearly a special relationship," Sroufe says over the image of Missy toddling over to her incredibly groovy, short-shorts-and-platforms-wearing mom, who sings, "Mis-sy, Mis-sy! Hiiiii!" then picks her up.

I remembered coming home from work and seeing Azalea run toward me on her little legs, Thayer not far behind, then quickly returning to her doll in the high chair.

During Episode 6, when Missy is left totally alone, she "becomes quite upset," standing at the door, crying hard. Poor Missy howls and resists even the lovely stranger who enters for Episode 7 wearing a flowered sundress and matching kerchief over her hair. Sroufe comments, "A stranger cannot substitute for her mother." But when her mom appears in Episode 8, she runs over to her and grabs on for dear life, gets the pickup she needs, and is instantly quiet and relaxed against her mother's shoulder, at home in her arms.

The next shot is of Missy—happy again—with her mother on the floor, this time actually playing with the enlivened Slinky. Sroufe says, "We see confidence in her mother beginning to become confidence in herself."

The next clips show Missy moving through her childhood, problem-solving, figuring things out. For instance, in one experiment she's confronted with a "lever problem," in which, if she can only manage to lift the lever up, she will receive a treat. Her mother sits quietly, supportive and engaged, helping only after little Missy grabs her hand and leads her over, saying "Push" in her baby voice, to which her mother replies, "Show me how!" In another, Missy sees "attractive toys" in a Plexiglas box "that's virtually impossible to open." She looks around the box, shakes it, tries one thing, then another. Sroufe says, "One can see in a tangible way her inner belief in herself." At one point, she even takes a play break "with the less attractive toys," then returns to the task.

In preschool, we see Missy playing with her friends, working out the drama of who gets to drape the cloth over the castle as a roof, and then at a table with a group of other kids making crafts. At one point, Sroufe tells us that Missy is "asked to share a Play-Doh cookie, which is obviously hard." The camera zooms in on Missy, a tableful of Play-Doh in front of her as she momentarily stops talking, looks distant as if she is doing some important internal work, gently shakes her hair back, then returns to what she was doing. Sroufe tells us, "She is able to manage her feelings and stay engaged. By age four and a half, we see a child that is well-managed, confident and self-reliant."

She reminded me of Azalea sitting across from me in the Chinese restaurant, waiting for me to return, and so many other times, too, "managing" herself as the world swirled around her.

I began to wonder, thinking about the little I knew about Missy, and myself and Azalea, what is the thread that connects us?

UNLIKE MISSY, AZALEA certainly hasn't been born into poverty—modest or otherwise—but she *tends* to appreciate what she has. An only child, Azalea has never wanted a sibling, lest she'd have to share her American Girl dolls or Barbies or clothes or books. Or us. At the same time, during a recent vacation with another family of three boys, she was in heaven, loving having someone to play cards with and make a video with, to laugh with, to complain about the adults with. "It's so fun to feel like I'm in a big family!" she said.

When I asked her recently about her feelings about being an only child, she answered with her usual balance: "Well, there are pros and cons to both."

Azalea met her two best friends when they were all six months to a year old. Going into seventh grade, they are all still BFFs. She has attended the same school since kindergarten, getting a ride each day with the dad of one of her best friends, who teaches at the school. He recently sent me a video of the girls on their way to kindergarten. Azalea's long, curly hair is in pigtails, and she's wearing a red dress that she loved so much she wore it to her first day of first grade, too. Her front teeth are missing, and she and her besties are sitting in car seats, singing and throwing their little bodies around to a song on the radio as our friend videotapes them through the rearview mirror.

It's the kind of friendship I've dreamt of my whole life.

The school gives written comments instead of grades, so, while these reports are certainly no longitudinal study, I can see themes in the teachers' comments. Unlike her mother (but like Missy), Azalea has been doing well in academic subjects, and, even more unlike her mother (and like Missy), she always gets reports of "exceptional" social skills and emotional intelligence from her teachers.

Comments about Azalea's work ethic and ability to focus have appeared in every school report since kindergarten, something she certainly didn't inherit from me, seeing as I did poorly in school until college. Sroufe and his colleagues found that one of the most marked traits to come from a secure attachment in infancy is tenacity, an ability to believe in oneself, stay on task, and not get too easily frustrated. Missy also showed this trait again and again in the lab and in school. I've always wondered if this trait of Azalea's belonged to her alone, or perhaps is something she inherited from Thayer.

I don't know anything about Missy's father. But from the time Azalea was born and Thayer jiggled her in his sling to Hawaiian music until she fell asleep, and carried her in the hiking backpack through the woods, and rode her on his bike seat into town, the two of them have been—well—birds of a feather. Every year they go to Comic Con in New York City together, dressing up as their favorite superheroes while I stay home and read; they go on an annual canoe trip while I do a weeklong sesshin. These days, Thayer starts seeing patients early in the morning three days a week so he can pick her up from school and take her to the gym, where they train in Brazilian jiujitsu. Together.

And then there's my dad and I.

In April of our second year at the monastery, we were visiting Thayer's parents' house when my mom called to tell me that my dad had died.

He had had his first heart attack at forty, after a life of smoking and loving the toasty brown edge of fat along a steak, extra hollandaise for his eggs Benedict at Big Boy, and "hamburgs," as he called them. Right after his heart attack, his business went belly-up and we lost everything and moved from the house with the bathroom at the end of the hall. My parents divorced when I was thirteen, and he moved to Phoenix to start over. After he moved, he gave me a toll-free phone card to call him whenever I wanted, so when I had nothing else to do on a Sunday afternoon, sometimes I called him and we chatted awkwardly. "Hey, Boop," he'd say, using the name he called me when I was little. "What's goin' on?" He'd ask me about school and friends and try to explain his decision to leave us.

"I just had to get out of Michigan, Beth. And start over. Can you understand that?"

To which my adult self answers, *Well, yes and no.*

A few years later, he remarried. And then, many years later, after a straightforward, apparently minor car accident, blood spilled over onto his brain. Which ultimately killed him.

Back in the day, my dad was pretty cool. Posing in front of his MG in Germany, where he was stationed in the army, he looks like an Instagram star, all filtered out, wearing skinny chinos and dark-rimmed glasses. But when he died, he was living in a nursing home, paralyzed on the right side, easily frustrated and crying "Anxious, anxious, anxious" into the phone. And though he'd been a lifelong Beatles fanatic, he couldn't name a single one of their songs. He couldn't even smoke.

His ashes were scattered at the Las Vegas Motor Speedway, where he had started racing vintage Porsches. On a chilly spring day, Daido officiated a small funeral for him at the monastery. I stood there with my coat over my meditation robe, chanting along with the other residents, tears rolling down my face, crying over the loss of an idea.

Now I'll never have a dad, I thought.

AZALEA LOVES TO hear stories about my childhood. And she can listen to the same ones again and again, like the one about the time I was three years old and got "lost" on my tricycle at my cousins' house, even though I was just down the block. My mom's sister Aunt Jo loves to harass my mom about this, saying, "Lib, what were you thinking? Letting a three-year-old out of your sight?"

"I don't know, Jo," my mom snorts. "I guess I *wasn't* thinking!"

They both laugh and shake their heads and reach for another cigarette.

When Azalea asks me about my childhood, I'm always careful to edit so that I don't appear too glum or harassed or misbehaving. Just the other day, during a slow summer lunch, she said, "I wish I could go back in time and know you when you were my age."

"That's sweet, honey," I said.

"You were a lot shier than me, right?" she asked, looking into my eyes.

"Kind of." I nodded, keeping it simple.

"I'd be nice to you," she said.

And I'm sure she would. Just like Missy.

If there were a Venn diagram of overlapping circles showing Missy, Azalea, and me, where would we converge? What would the gray spot represent?

Sroufe writes, "Children with secure histories seem to believe that, as was true in infancy, they can get their needs met and achieve their goals through their own efforts and bids." These days we call this trait "grit," as defined by Angela Duckworth in her important book *Grit: The Power of Passion and Perseverance*. In an article looking at the connection between grit and attachment, Jaclyn Levy and Howard Steele define this trait as being "responsible for the presence of [the] individual's long-term drive and determination." So-called gritty individuals "view achievement as a long-term process; their lead is endurance, determination and stamina." Levy and Steele continue, summarizing Duckworth: "Disappointment and/or boredom may indicate to many that it is time to modify one's trajectory, whereas gritty persons continue on track." And while grit is usually understood to be the result of certain personality traits, after a study of the relationship between grit and attachment, "it was found that high grit scores were significantly linked to high past mother and father care . . . attachment anxiety and avoidance were negatively correlated" with grit.

Whether trying to get picked up as an infant or figure out how to get a Barbie shoe on a ridiculously shaped plastic foot, the secure child is imbued with an overall sense of agency. She believes in herself and her ability to accomplish difficult tasks. As Sroufe says of Missy after one of the videotaped assessments in which she worked hard to open the locked box with a stuffed bear inside, "She expects, if she tries hard, she will succeed . . . this shows up in her flexibility."

While I hadn't done well in school or seemed very driven to do much of anything (I can totally imagine myself as a kid saying "whatever" about the attractive toys, preferring to sit down and look out the window), the one thing that has always grabbed my attention is trying to understand what it means to be alive. Like Missy, who, "when one thing doesn't work, she tries something else," and like Azalea when she's cooking up an idea for something to play, all my life I've been on a gritty rampage to figure it out.

chapter twenty-one

That first time I entered the dining hall of the monastery, I was crying. For two years after Charles left, I cried all the time—at home, on the subway, over breakfast with friends, while meditating. Someone who was working on a video about the monastery during that time said that every bit of footage from the zendo had me in it, and I was always in tears. I was embarrassed, but *Hey,* I thought, *I'm working my stuff out!* As soon as I started doing zazen, sitting in total stillness, I had trusted that posture, that practice, to lead me to something that was buried beneath layers of longing. It was messy, but I trusted my trust.

I was seeking proximity to myself. And I found it.

One day a friend of mine from college who was kind of scared for me—first all the Charles drama, and now this? Zen? Sitting like a statue for hours?—asked, "Doesn't it *hurt?*" She looked serious. I think she was afraid that I was punishing myself somehow.

"Hurt?" I repeated.

"Yeah, doesn't it *hurt* to sit still like that?"

I had never really thought about it like that before.

"Well, sure," I said, "sometimes. But it's nothing compared with the agony of not sitting."

And it was true. When I sat still and became completely absorbed in the morass of my sad, clingy, lonely self, I finally felt like something was working. By learning to see and report all my own states of mind and developing my ability to stay in the present, I was learning how to pay attention to myself.

One of the most important Zen teachings, something that is mentioned in pretty much every public talk and private encounter, is that in order to see and truly understand—deeply and personally—the Buddhist teachings, or anything for that matter, we need to become *intimate* with it. That was Daido's word—*intimate*. "When faced with a barrier," he would roar, "*be the barrier!*" Whether it's a puzzling Zen koan—a teaching story—or a problem at work or a painful emotion, instead of fighting it, which just makes the pain of it more powerful, let it fill you. Soften the edges. Turn toward it. Be *intimate* with your life. One of Daido's favorite sayings was "No gap."

From the Buddhist point of view, there's no gap between oneself and another. We operate as one thing. Just like Bowlby said.

I remember one question-and-answer session where a student asked Daido, tears in her eyes, how to forgive someone you love. His answer blew my mind. He said, "Forgive yourself."

ON THE LAST morning of a weeklong silent retreat, people are invited to share their experience aloud with the group. On one of those mornings many years ago, before Azalea was born or conceived, I spoke out in the predawn stillness about my mom. I talked about how I had been thinking of her that week, and how I was thinking of her in that moment. I described how, as we all sat there on our cushions, my mom would be rising in the darkness of her small apartment in Michigan and walking in her robe to her coffeemaker, pouring herself a cup, making it light with Kroger-brand half-and-half, then heading back to bed to watch morning news programs, smoking as the sun rose. I talked about how sad I felt to see her like that, alone and so far away. I talked about how I was often irritated by her, or disappointed by her, and about how our lives were so different in every way that I just didn't feel *intimate* with her. After meditating for a week, though, I softened toward her and longed for more closeness.

After we all went down to the dining hall, one of the monks hugged me in the breakfast line and said, "It sure sounds like you're intimate with your mom," which left me scratching my head. What did she mean? *Me and my mom? Intimate?* I'd just been saying that I felt the exact opposite.

I had always thought of intimacy as the kind of personal closeness I had been seeking my whole life, that super-amped-up rush of connection that I had never felt with my family and had searched for through sex and love and drugs and, now, even zazen. While my meditation definitely brought about a lot of very subtle states of settling, which I appreciated and held dear, I kept pushing for more, thinking there had to be something else to it—some final frontier or über state of bliss.

Because I thought I knew what the word "intimate" meant—as in two ships reaching for each other in the night—I missed the point that true intimacy comes out of the experience of being one thing. Which sounds super "spiritual" and special, but really it's not. It's just the way we're built. People know it; poets talk about it. Pablo Neruda writes:

> so I love you because I know no other way
> than this: where I does not exist, nor you,
> so close that your hand on my chest is my hand,
> so close that your eyes close as I fall asleep.

So close that sitting on my cushion in the dark zendo, I was right there with my mom as she rose from her bed in Michigan. Neither one of us was alone.

But I hadn't seen it—how unremarkable true intimacy is, how sometimes love flows so easily we don't see it. Our pre-dawn birds-of-a-feather co-arising was no big deal. Like every other person on earth, holding someone else in mind, loving them, it was an entirely ordinary situation.

part vi

get mom

There is a time to nurture a tender attachment and there is a time to encourage self-reliance. If you ask whether this or that practice is a good thing, I could only answer, "It depends."

—Mary Ainsworth, *Infancy in Uganda*

chapter twenty-two

In the bathroom at the end of the hall, I sit naked in the tub. It's 1976, and I'm seven years old. As the warm water rises, I sink my shoulders down and stretch my legs in front of me, letting my whole body slide under. Leaning back, I dunk my head, ears submerged, humming along with the swishing sounds of rushing water. I sit up. I have the shower curtain pulled back so I can watch the steam rise up along the yellow-and-silver foil wallpaper, then land wet on the mirror.

My dad pokes his head in. "No. Get Mom."

This flash of a moment—so vivid and foggy at the same time—made such an impression on me that as I grew up and wondered why I did what I did, it became the answer to the riddle of my life.

While other kids were sitting in school, and I was walking up a dark staircase to where my much older boyfriend waited for me on a mattress on the floor, that was the scene that flashed through my mind—*No. Get Mom.* Opening the screen door onto my friends holding out a forty-ouncer of beer and other things, too, I'd remember the steam on the mirror and think, *Makes sense.* Sitting in the back of English class, overhearing kids talk about their college acceptances, then looking in my folder at all the Cs and Ds, I was right back in that tub, and I wondered if the reason I had called out for my mom was because I'd been abused. I didn't have anything but awkward discomfort with my dad to suggest he'd done anything like that, but the mysteriousness of our relationship, coupled with my own wildness, made me curious.

I thought maybe there was more to the distance between my father and me than the fact that we had so little in common—he being an auto-parts salesman, me a little girl. And maybe my mom was in denial, and that was why she vacuumed all the time.

Maybe that was why I loved my daughter like there was no tomorrow but still acted like a mean animal.

As I moved through my life, that bathtub memory kept rising up like a watery message from the Magic 8 Ball: *Outlook not so good.*

chapter twenty-three

Six years before he met Mary Ainsworth, John Bowlby published an article called "Forty-Four Juvenile Thieves: Their Characters and Home Life," based on the troubled kids he was working with at the London Child Guidance Clinic. Some say this was the very first empirical study of attachment.

This historic study was, admittedly, flawed. Bowlby writes, "The research presented here was very limited by lack of resources; it was very unplanned, the number of cases are few, the data was collected quite unsystematically and several practical issues arose from working in a busy clinic." And yet one simple observation from this messy study inspired the work that would follow and lead to Bowlby's groundbreaking work on attachment: "40% of the thieves had experienced prolonged separation from their mothers . . . compared with only 5% of the control subjects, a significant difference."

It was clear that there was something different about these boys. As Bowlby writes, "There can be no doubt that they are essentially *delinquent characters*."

And yet he also writes, "It can be concluded that, had it not been for certain factors inhibiting the development of the ability to form relationships, it is possible that these children would not have become offenders." If and how those "certain factors" are related to "maternal separation"—which would obviously have a profound effect on secure versus insecure attachment—was the question he would spend the rest of his life answering.

I'VE BEEN THINKING a lot about Bowlby's thieves. Especially the ones he called "affectionless," the "children who lack normal affection, shame, or sense of responsibility." I think about all the *oh well* moments of my adolescence, how relaxed I was in the face of serious risk and potential life-altering consequences.

Was I affectionless?

Actually, quite the opposite. I was nothing if not filled with feeling.

Azalea talks about the eighties being "old-fashioned." And I know what she means. It was 1982 when everything changed for my family. My dad lost his business and had to declare bankruptcy. He had also had a heart attack. We moved that summer to a rented duplex on the edge of the "bad" part of a new town. And then, near the end of August, over a family dinner—such a cozy name for such a consistently unpleasant meal—my parents announced their separation, though it would take some time for my dad to move. He was on his way out of our lives, bereft without his beloved Jaguar, though my mom got to keep the red Caprice Classic station wagon. And I began mourning my chances of ever getting a pair of Calvin Klein jeans.

During the summer leading up to the big announcement, my mom, who never went to college or worked much when we were little, began transforming herself into a modern woman, preparing, I suppose, to be the main breadwinner and parent of three kids, two of whom were big, unwieldy boy-men, the other a soon-to-be-spooky teenage girl. My parents and I each had our own room upstairs. Matt slept in the basement, in a bed next to the washer and dryer, where Sam joined him when he came back from college.

My mom had it rough back then, trying to keep it all together in the midst of her marriage falling apart and her lifestyle dissolving, while attempting to tame two teenage boys with little to no support from my dad. I was still young and awkward, identifying with, I'm sure, or maybe projecting, my mom's feeling of being an outsider in her own family. I remember one dinner during that ill-fated summer when my mom was trying to teach my brothers some kind of table-manners lesson and my dad laughed at her and said, *Oh, Lib, luzum gayen,* which means *let it go* in Yiddish. She—ever poised—seemed uncharacertistically hurt, and so when she got up to clear the table, I, like a little goose, followed her in and quietly stood near her, not sure what to say. Scraping a plate of food into the trash, she looked at me and said, "I'm okay, honey." And I believed her.

Then my dad left for Arizona.

A couple of months into eighth grade, I was home sick with a cold, lying on the couch-bed my mom had made for me, watching soaps and MTV, dozing in a pile of tissues. The rotary phone (with a long cord so my brothers and I could drag it around for privacy) sat on the floor, silent and still, calling absolutely no attention to itself. And then it rang. It was Kate, a cute tennis player with freckles who I had thought was one of my new friends.

Kate said, "I don't know if you should go to school tomorrow, Beth. Everyone's really mad at you."

A wave of terror shot through me.

"For what?" I asked.

"A bunch of things," she said.

I quickly realized that Kate had nothing helpful to say, so I hung up the phone. Then I lay back down on my couch-bed and cried.

After I told my mom about the call, she said I could stay home one more day to collect myself. Which I did, fidgeting and queasy from anxiety. The next day, she dropped me off in front of the school.

"Hold your head up," she said.

I stared at the school across the lawn.

"They don't even know you!" she reminded me.

True, I thought. *Or maybe they do.*

"And besides," she said, "they're obviously just really insecure themselves."

I opened the door of the station wagon, walked across the street, and entered the school building, head held high. When I opened the door to the loud cafeteria, where we hung around till classes started, I scanned the room. In a corner was a group of girls awaiting my arrival. As I walked toward them, they formed a line and, one by one, told me why they were mad at me. Other kids watched. Some of the boys even got in on the action, which struck me as remarkable, even then. I knew this kind of torment was common among girls, but boys?

It was pretty crazy to watch my biggest fear moving from an idea into reality, affirming what I had always guessed—there was just something so off about me. And I was terrified to look ahead at my future as an *official* loser, cut completely adrift from the social life I had always dreamed of, and right when it seemed as though it might have been within reach. The things the girls said were grounded in just enough truth to make that same part of me believe I deserved this treatment. They were right! I *had* talked about kids behind their backs, as a way of feeling cool and like I belonged. I could see why I had done all the things they accused me of. I was a desperate, uncouth, blabbermouth jerk. Guilty as charged. And willing, in my thirteen-year-old way, to own it.

Part of me believed I deserved it. But another part of me didn't buy it. Which might explain why, during that first pile-on in the cafeteria, after ten girls detailed their complaints about me, I yelled, "Fine! Fine! But you know what? I'm not a monster!"

In the face of every onslaught, some part of me knew I was a person.

MY MOM WAS RIGHT: bullies are officially insecure, and usually avoidant. And insecurely attached kids who are resistant or ambivalent are usually the victims of bullying. In other words, as researchers Neville and Eileen Baglin Jones write, "children with 'avoidant-insecure' attachment relationships lack trust and expect hostility, and may thus develop aggressive patterns of interaction with peers." They're the bullies. On the other hand, "children with 'ambivalent-insecure' attachment relationships with parents are likely to be getting haphazard care and doubt their own effectiveness in influencing the caregiver. While staying somewhat dependent, they lack self-esteem and confidence in their own worth; and are thus susceptible to being victimized by peers." They're the bullied.

By contrast, the research tells us, "children who had been securely attached were able to distance themselves and avoid bullying or being bullied."

Looking back at all the bullying that I was prey to—starting with my own brothers, then into grade school, then culminating in the middle school years—a case could certainly be made that I was insecure/ambivalent or insecure/resistant. But even though I had been bullied and couldn't really fight back physically against my brothers, I wasn't exactly a shrinking violet.

. . .

BEING SHUNNED IN eighth grade at a new school definitely falls under the category of things that—if they don't kill you—will make you stronger. By ninth grade I had learned to like being alone; I rode the bus by myself into town, where I'd take myself out to lunch or look in stores at things I enjoyed imagining myself owning someday. I decided I didn't need shitty friends and eventually made a couple of new—much cooler—ones. And then some of the girls from the bullying incident came around and even apologized, wanting to be my friend. Sometimes I said okay. Sometimes I made them wait for it.

By the beginning of tenth grade I was making a name for myself as a kind of funky "free spirit." On the first day of school I met my soon-to-be best friend Tabitha, who was new to town. Soon enough we were trading vintage clothes, smoking her mom's pot, and hanging out after school in her family's small apartment, talking about the sex we'd had and hoped to have.

The next year Tabitha and I started hanging out with another girl named Cindy, and the three of us skipped school and drove around in Cindy's car, listening to Led Zeppelin and getting high. Always on the lookout for sourcing advice, the three of us went to some of our older friends, including a bad-boy Eddie Haskell type named Scott. He was one of those guys who make you feel like you're the only person in the world when he looks at you, then gets your name wrong. Which must be why, though I was attracted to him, I actually refused him on several occasions. As much as I craved the attention, I was even hungrier, I think, for respect. I didn't just want someone to think I was doable; I wanted to be loved. And I wouldn't settle for less.

Although I rejected him sexually, I signed right up when he called me from jail and asked me to break into his parents' house to steal his younger brother Chris's birth certificate. He had been pulled over for something and, not wanting to get busted for other tickets (or crimes?), he lied, said he didn't have any ID, and that his name was Chris. He needed proof of identity, so he called me. And I said sure. He whispered the instructions to me over the phone; what a thrill to be the dependable go-to. Cindy and I drove to his parents' house, then she distracted them at the door as I snuck into their den through the garage and found the file labeled CHRIS, just as Scott had said I would. I could hear his mother talking to Cindy through the front door as I grabbed the file and walked out the way I'd come in.

All in a day's work of adolescent risk-taking.

Part of my willingness to do something so ridiculous was, I can only imagine, par for the course for a kid, or for a human being, for that matter, but I was always willing to put more on the line than other kids I knew. And I have always wondered why. I wasn't the only kid whose parents were divorced or who were downwardly mobile. It seemed like something else was going on, and, from an early age, I wanted to know what.

In high school, I was obnoxious and resistant, sometimes late, often absent. I remember one English teacher who seemed amused when I so confidently stood up in front of the class and gave a funny, passionate oral report on *Moll Flanders,* which I had clearly not read. He mercifully gave me a C, one of my higher grades.

As to my future, I figured that I would waitress full-time, write poetry, and maybe have a baby.

And then one day toward the end of senior year, a really smart kid who took a shine to me and sat with me in the back of social studies class asked me where I was going to go to college. And I said, "Nowhere," which was true. I hadn't applied to a single school. And he said, "You should try Antioch."

I asked what kind of place Antioch was, telling him I'd never get into a "real college."

"They'll love you," he said. "All you have to do is write an essay."

After I applied, my mom drove me to visit the Ohio campus for a weekend, and we stopped for eggs and extra-crispy hash browns at the kind of greasy spoon we both loved. I met with the admissions department for an interview. The woman told me that, yes, my academic record was pretty weak, but they were willing to take a chance on me because they were blown away by the essay I'd written. They accepted me on the spot.

The essay was about my mom and our relationship, and how, though I had been angry about so much—especially for the way she just didn't get me—I could also see how connected we were.

I think I even used the word "attached."

chapter twenty-four

Sometimes I hang out and chat with other moms, and I listen to them talk about their own childhoods or teenage years, and to their stories of sneaking out, getting caught, getting grounded, smoking, doing drugs. My friends all seem to wonder how far their kids will stray, to what lengths they will have to go to differentiate, to rebel, to find themselves. They expect a certain difficult or angry or combative teenage stage, much like what they put their own parents through. And they're afraid of their beloved children growing away from them.

I'm afraid, too.

But I worry more, and privately, about how closely Azalea will gravitate toward me, growing along some subterranean roots we share. Cuddling at night, watching *Shark Tank* on TV, she asks me to tickle her arm, and so I do, lightly, up and down, as she likes it. I look over at her relaxed face, watching some fumbling entrepreneur try to convince a cocky billionaire to take a chance. And I try to feel the way her heart beats. And breaks. She seems so together, so still. *Are you what you appear to be?* I silently ask her—the ups and downs, the tiny untruths revealed, the tears, the love of lemonade, the goofy spelling, the emergent edges.

What secrets are you keeping from me?

Ever since I discovered I was pregnant with Azalea, and I realized that I would be—already was—a mother, I have been afraid. Afraid of nausea, afraid of genetic deformities, afraid of giving birth, afraid of the next long, sleepless night, afraid of Azalea's soft head crashing against the stone around the woodstove, afraid of myself and of my own heart.

But my biggest fear has been that Azalea would turn out to be just like me. Not in terms of my hair or my eyes or my difficulty with math, but in terms of the way I felt, and the way I *was,* the way I didn't seem to value myself.

Or did I?

And in terms of the way I shut my mom out.

Or did I?

AS A TEENAGER determined to experiment with wholly illegal and dangerous things, I spent a lot of time lying to my mom and avoiding her. Years later, she commented on how I suddenly became "so modest" at sixteen, no longer wanting to change in front of her or jump in the shower, though we shared a bathroom. That was the year I got a homemade tattoo on my back.

As passionate as I was about my goings-on, I always felt bad about being dishonest with my mom and living a double life, especially since I knew she was working so hard to make ends meet and to support us all, and to make a nice home for my brothers and me.

When I was sixteen, I got caught stealing a carton of cigarettes. I walked through the aisles of a big-box store, grabbed the long carton, and put it in my coat. As I exited, a man in a blazer who had followed me out said, "Come with me, miss." From the office, where I cried fake tears, I called my mom's friend, who would know how to get in touch with my mom, who was at her favorite patio bar, where she loved to dance to the oldies. On the drive home, she mostly fumed silently, worried but at a loss, I could tell. Then she yelled, "You have to quit smoking!" We were both silent after that, which felt a little bit like we were laughing.

But she wasn't laughing when I was up all night throwing up from drinking a pint of peppermint schnapps. Instead, she was sitting with me, putting a cold washcloth on my forehead and not asking questions.

I felt particularly horrible about her taking care of me because not only had I drunk too much, but I'd lied through my teeth about where we got the alcohol. I was so brazen as a sixteen-year-old and . . . *developed,* shall we say, both physically and in the fine art of deception, that I used to be able to strut into a liquor store, take a couple of bottles to the register—or ask for something behind the counter—and pay up. The cashier may have had some doubt that I was twenty-one, but I *never* got carded, even though I moved around to different stores to keep it interesting.

But when my mom came home early one night when she was supposed to be out dancing, my friends and I got busted because we reeked of alcohol. My mom demanded to know where we'd gotten it; I didn't miss a beat. I told her a sob story about someone's older sister, and how we felt so much peer pressure to drink, even though we hated it. I cried, peppered in enough detail to make it all sound true, and my mom actually felt bad for me.

At least she convinced me that she did.

In January 2018, *The New York Times* published an article about a researcher who studies deception in children. She found that kids who are good liars score higher in "theory of mind," an ability to know oneself and read the feelings of others. Theory of mind is closely linked to mentalization. And it's a trait that is almost entirely associated with secure attachment.

THE REASON BOWLBY'S early forty-four-thieves paper is considered so historically significant is that it draws a straight line between a child's behavior and a parent's affection, pointing out that most of his delinquents had suffered from significant child-mother separations. In other words, even before Bowlby or Ainsworth or anyone else could say why, he saw that a substitute parent who merely fed these boys wasn't enough to raise them to be emotionally and mentally healthy. They were suffering from a wound that had nothing to do with feeding and everything to do with a lack of proximity to their attachment figures, or what Ainsworth would come to call "total amount of care," because, as Bowlby would soon discover, we are imprinted by our caregivers and wired to stay close to them. Bowlby's thieves were victims of traumatic separations from attachment figures, and no one had come to take these important people's places. The boys were half of a unit, undone by grief.

"Studies of nonclinical samples ['normal' kids] show that securely attached adolescents are less likely to engage in excessive drinking, drug use and risky sexual behavior," attachment researchers Marlene Moretti and Maya Peled write. Another shows that "insecure attachment is associated with suicidality, drug use, and aggressive and delinquent behavior." As another attachment researcher, Joseph P. Allen, and his colleagues put it, "In adolescence, attachment security has been positively linked to outcomes ranging from peer popularity to higher self-esteem and inversely related to outcomes ranging from depression to delinquency." I was not very popular, had pretty shitty self-esteem, and, while I wasn't exactly depressed, I was pretty darn delinquent, right?

But I was not separated from my mom, not physically, anyway.

Alan Sroufe and his colleagues have refined Bowlby's definition of the attachment system to include as its set goal not necessarily just a desire for physical proximity—think goslings trailing safely behind their mother—but a need for what they call "felt security." In other words, it's not enough to just be close. We have to *feel* it.

And so maybe my delinquency stemmed from an insecure attachment that resulted from a lack of "felt security"?

Maybe, but as I've learned, not all delinquency is created equal. "Antisocial" behavior is considered much more serious when it begins before adolescence than when it occurs later, as it did with me, as a teen. Young delinquents whose risk-taking ends in adolescence or just after, as mine did, are considered even less of a concern. And finally, late-blooming young delinquents are so benign that they're considered almost normal. "It has been proposed that most antisocial females follow an adolescence-limited trajectory . . . [and] these females are hypothesized: a) to have no childhood risk factors, b) to be exposed to social risk factors, such as affiliation to deviant peers, and c) to desist from their antisocial lifestyle as they transition to adulthood."

My delinquency, while certainly dangerous, falls firmly in the "just trying it on" type that stems from "no childhood risk factors."

So what was going on with me?

While it's true that on the outside I looked mighty insecure with all that delinquent behavior, it's also worth asking how all that behavior was organized on the inside. What was I trying to *accomplish* with all my acting out? Yes, part of me was trying to

go numb, be cool, and feel powerful, but another, core part of
me was utterly devoted to creating a feeling of connection in
my young life—a life that didn't seem to offer much delight or
connection at home. And, in fact, I was often pretty successful.
As Joseph Allen and his co-writers noted, "the secure adolescent
tends to create relationships characterized by a balance of autonomy
and relatedness—to create their own secure bases from which to
explore—and to do this across relationships."

Some of the girls who bullied me, and whom I managed to
distance myself from, became close friends of mine in high
school. Though I did have a lot of dangerous sex as a teen, I lost
my virginity to a boy I loved and who loved me. I did lots of
drugs, but always with a mind toward self-discovery, taking
long walks, reciting poetry, and exploring my own mind and
this crazy, beautiful, totally trippy world. And I eventually
stopped doing drugs because I hated the way they made me feel.
I enjoyed experimenting with edges and darkness, but ultimately I valued my own pleasure so much that when I stopped
enjoying things, I just let them go. Usually.

My addiction to Charles nearly killed me. But it didn't.

When my brothers were mean, though I was powerless to do
much in response, I knew they were wrong and that I was being
mistreated. When people disappointed me, I pushed back, or at
least I tried. I believed I deserved better.

Was something working?

It could all make a certain kind of sense. My not-happy childhood, my shit-show adolescence, my sex-and-love-addicted early
adulthood, my struggles as a parent—all these things pointed to
an insecure attachment when I was a baby. Even before I knew
about attachment, this was the story I was telling myself—that
there had to have been a reason for me to be this messed up, and
it must have started in my childhood. Cue the bathtub memory.
No. Get Mom. And then, when I learned about attachment, I

thought, *Maybe it's not an abuse thing, but an attachment thing. Maybe I wasn't securely attached, which maybe made me feel abused?*

I have also wondered, looking around at my pretty amazing life, how I managed to make it through all that rejection and acting out as well as I did. Was it luck? Am I making it all up? Maybe things weren't as bad as I think they were? There has to be a reason for me to be this *not* messed up. *Maybe it's an attachment thing.* After all, research shows that, yes, a secure attachment in childhood tends to protect us from all manner of risk and adverse experiences. But the real point here is that attachment security protects us. From whatever life presents us with, or what we choose to do.

Enter grit.

As Moretti and Peled write, "Parental attunement and appropriate responsiveness give rise to secure attachment, marked by a view of the self as worthy of care and competent in mastering the environment." As Sroufe and his colleagues write:

> In our view, the explanation for why some people thrive and others seriously falter during this challenging period [of adolescence] lies substantially in developmental history . . . A basic sense of inner worth, of connection with others, and of others as available and supportive remains critical.

In other words: *Get Mom.*

After all, I actually called out for my mom from the tub. I wanted her to help me, and I trusted she would come.

Was a secure attachment the miracle that kept me safe?

How could that be?

Was my relentless pursuit of connection—through drugs and sex and friendships—an indication that *something was working,* first between my mother and me, then between friends and me, and even between myself and me? Was my determination to feel connected, what Sroufe and his colleagues call a "developmental achievement," due to my secure enough relationship with my mom? Was that "something" the miracle that saved me from drowning all those years as a lonely kid, a troubled teen, a sex and love addict, and a desperate mother?

Maybe it's the very same thing that has protected Azalea from all my struggles as a mother, my moving in and out from the edge of my darkness, exploring the middle, checking out the deep end, working so hard to stay afloat, arms and legs splashing.

In a word—*swimming*.

chapter twenty-five

One night when Azalea was still sleeping in her crib, Thayer went to comfort her as she cried out. As I lay in bed listening over the monitor, I heard her cry, "Nooooo! Get Mommy!"

Which made me sit up. And wonder. About everything I thought I knew.

a thing to slip into

This woman won our unstinted admiration for the competence and serenity with which she dealt with her large and complicated household. She grew all of their food. She made many of her children's clothes and had recently acquired a sewing machine to help with this task . . . she treated each child as a person important in his own right . . . she had time to talk to us in an unhurried way.

—Mary Ainsworth, *Infancy in Uganda*

chapter twenty-six

The most important development in attachment research since Mary Ainsworth "came up with this thing," the Strange Situation, in 1964 is an article published in 1985 by her student Mary Main and attachment researchers Nancy Kaplan and Jude Cassidy. The article is called "Security in Infancy, Childhood, and Adulthood: A Move to the Level of Representation," and it was the world's introduction to the Adult Attachment Interview. This groundbreaking article marks the turning point for modern attachment research and has been cited in the scientific attachment literature nearly seven thousand times.

Up until this point, insight about one's attachment system—in itself an invisible, internal construct—could be inferred only from something observable on the outside—secure-base behavior, for instance, in the home, in the world, in the lab. With the advent of the Adult Attachment Interview (the AAI), the subject of Main's article, researchers had a way to illuminate the inside, where our inner informant—excellent or otherwise—lives.

Mary Main was one of Mary Ainsworth's graduate students at Johns Hopkins, and she, like her mentor, was gifted with language. At two years old, she "wrote down some especially interesting sentences." Her parents had introduced her to philosophy by the age of ten, and she attended St. John's College in Annapolis, Maryland, an iconic school that teaches with primary texts. For graduate school, Main considered attending conservatory for piano, but she was also interested in linguistics ever since she'd read the work of Noam Chomsky. Chomsky, born in 1928, fifteen years after Mary Ainsworth, is known for many things, including searing political and cultural critique, but in academic circles he is most famous for his revolutionary theory of universal grammar, the breakthrough insight that all human speech is governed by rules unbeknownst to most of us, that indeed most of us can't articulate—very much like patterns of attachment.

Main applied to the Johns Hopkins linguistics program, but since grades at St. John's were based on participation in class discussions, and Main had rarely talked in class, she was not accepted. There was one professor in the psychology department, however, on leave at Stanford at the time, who was interested in this bright student with the terrible grades and willing to take a chance on her.

Mary Ainsworth offered Main a spot in her department if she would consider doing her dissertation on attachment. Main found this offer "singularly uninteresting," but she accepted, taking the advice of her then husband, who suggested that she could approach the study of babies through any lens, including language. When Main met Ainsworth, she was unimpressed. "She was fifty-five, and reminded me of a high school principal." Main became Mary's second graduate student, Sylvia Bell being the first, and the two would become very close over the years.

Main's dissertation, completed in 1973, looked at fifty toddlers who had been through the Strange Situation at twelve months and found that "infants secure with their mothers were the most intensely and lengthily engaged in exploration, and showed the most 'game-like' spirit," a phrase Mary would throw back at Main when she became despondent in a marathon Scrabble game: "And may I ask whatever happened to your . . . your *Game-like Spirit!*" Ainsworth jabbed.

Fully committed by now to the study of attachment, after receiving her PhD at Johns Hopkins, Main accepted a position at UC Berkeley in the psychology department, where in 1979 she would begin what is known as the Berkeley Longitudinal Study. This study began by following a group of 189 Bay Area "low risk" families, beginning with infants in the Strange Situation. In the sixth year of the study, Main and her team took the six-year-olds into the playroom for an attachment assessment using stories about separations, and took their parents into a different room to ask them about their own childhoods. The *way* the parents talked about their early lives—distinct from what they reported happening to them—was then carefully coded, the researchers looking for things like the ability to tell a coherent story using freshness of speech and consistent, concrete details with just the right amount of juicy bits—not too many and not too few. Main also looked at parents' ability to identify with their own parents in a balanced way without getting sucked into past anger or resentment or avoiding the topic altogether.

Based on what was discovered, the parents' transcripts were then classified in adult attachment patterns very much like Ainsworth's infant patterns—secure/autonomous (like the secure infant), insecure/preoccupied (like the resistant infant), and insecure/dismissing (like the avoidant infant). The correlation between the parents' adult attachment classification and their infants' Strange Situation from six years prior was 75 percent.

Incredible.

That's the big number that blew my mind when I first heard

it, and had inspired the last decade of my own obsession. And it's a number that's been replicated again and again. Howard and Miriam Steele even found it to be predictive. In other words, before a baby is even born, one can predict with that same level of accuracy—75 percent—the attachment classification of that infant based on its primary caregiver's Adult Attachment Interview.

The fact that something so powerful and predictive appears when we talk about our attachments is downright magical. And it also happens to be what some researchers call "one of the most robust findings of attachment research." This intergenerational transmission has been replicated "in samples of middle class families . . . families with low socioeconomic status . . . adolescent mothers . . . and West European, Japanese, and Middle Eastern cultures." As Alan Sroufe and Dan Siegel put it in the title of an article they wrote together in 2011, "the verdict is in." The generational transmission of attachment—while never simple or deterministic—is real.

At their most basic levels, both the AAI and the Strange Situation point to the natural laws of cause and effect, or what the Buddha called karma. Karma is often misunderstood to be one's destiny or judge, as in "Karma's a bitch," meaning you'll get what you deserve. Sometimes we do, and sometimes we don't. It all depends on your point of view about what's "deserved." As Mary Ainsworth made clear through her research, one action can have a variety of effects, which is why she insisted that what matters is not the following of a checklist of specific behaviors by parents, but how attuned parents' actions are to their babies. For instance, take something like reading to a baby. Most of us would agree that this is a good thing to do, in an absolute sense. But from a more nuanced point of view, reading a book to a hungry baby as she cries is quite different from reading the very same book after the baby's feeding and nap, when she is rested and ready to hear it.

One action is soothing; the other is misattuned.

Here's the thing. Everything we do is our karma. And it is this succession of relational karmic moments that creates our patterns—of attachment and otherwise.

As one Tibetan Buddhist teacher, Traleg Rinpoche, put it:

Buddhism contains the idea of an accumulation of karmic imprints [!] and dispositions, a gathering of propensities throughout our lives—habit patterns are formed, and so forth . . . we are who we are because of our karmic inheritance. We would not be as we are without it, but this does not mean we have to remain this way.

Bowlby would agree. He said attachment patterns also take root early and are so powerful that they tend to remain the same: "All that can safely be said is that, as the years pass, lability [the likeliness to change] diminishes; whether it be favorable or unfavorable, whatever organization exists becomes progressively less easily changed."

Powerful positive or negative attachment-related experiences—a loving relationship, a traumatic event—can change one's early attachment orientation, but it's a heavy load to shift, and it just gets heavier as we age. As Sroufe and his colleagues write, "As always, adaptation is a product of cumulative history *and* current circumstances. Current challenges and supports impact functioning and may even transform established patterns of adaptation. At the same time, the impact of new experience is modulated by expectations and capacities based on history. Fundamental change is possible in new contexts, even though history is not erased."

Or, as Traleg Rinpoche put it, "Karmic theory is supposed to encourage us to think, 'I can become the person that I want to be and not dwell on what I already am.'" "Not dwelling," however, doesn't mean avoiding. In order to become the person "I want to be," we have to face "what I already am."

chapter twenty-seven

It had been a few years since Dr. Steele invited me to his lab to watch my very first live Strange Situation. This time I was visiting him to get my very own AAI done, and I had some extra time on my hands, so I stopped in for a bit of welcome air-conditioning in the vintage clothing shop a few doors down from the Center for Attachment Research, near Union Square.

My mom likes to tell the story of the time she took me shopping with her, and she caught me flipping through the ladies' rack "like a pro." I was around five. And for effect, my mom then *flip, flip, flips* her long hands in the air in front of her, laughing, adding something like "She was so serious!" It is a funny image, little me in front of the tall rack. Looking for a thing to slip into.

Because I have heard that story so often, I could actually feel the body of that girl as I lost myself in a rack of 1950s skirts more than forty years later. I found a couple of skirts I liked— mid-knee, plain, pretty. I stood in the aisle and held each one up against me, conjuring myself in it, imagining which shoes I might wear, how it might make me feel, and wondering if it would fit. The thing is, my waist is bigger than it used to be, bigger than I imagine in my mind, so I always choose the wrong size. So now, at forty-seven, I had to correct for an old way of seeing. And of being.

I walked over to the other side of the store and looked through the children's rack, wondering if Azalea would wear one of the beautiful embroidered blouses from South America that looked like her size. I was a little better at judging the silhouette of her little-girl body cut in space.

And then—I was late. So I put everything back where I found it and walked out onto the bright sidewalk of Fifth Avenue to find out what kind of mother I was.

WHEN I MET Dr. Steele at the elevator this time, I was a different person from the attachment-curious writer/observer I was when we first met. Since my last visit, I had been to Mary's archive in Charlottesville, where I met Bob Marvin, and completed my Strange Situation training in Minneapolis with Alan Sroufe. I had watched Missy's video dozens of times. My screen saver was, and still is, a grainy black-and-white photograph of Mary Ainsworth sitting on a porch in Uganda, two young girls in white collared dresses on the ground in front of her. Mary's wearing a dress with a rather ravishing décolletage. Her hair is pulled back, she's wearing her glasses, and her face is makeup-free, of course, in all that heat. Her purse—filled, I'm sure, with her camera, candy, and a notepad—is tucked beneath her arm.

Azalea was just entering sixth grade. We had moved through those rough early years, and she seemed, much to my relief and surprise—my delight!—like a truly happy kid. She loved school, loved all things Justice League, and still lost herself in imaginative play for hours at a time: action figures, the sky, a mirror—it didn't matter.

We still took Mommy-Azalea city trips, riding the train to-gether, and I still got frustrated sometimes when I felt like she wasn't as excited as I wanted her to be; her even-temperedness cuts both ways. When I picked her up from school, she would tell me all about her day, the intermittent (but always mild) drama, what people wore, how much of her lunch she ate, the way her teachers treated her and other kids in the class. During the day, I felt like I knew her well. But, cuddling up at night, her little hand on my leg, I still always wondered what lay be-neath the sweetness. And I worried.

Azalea has always been a bit fixated—dare I say preoccupied—with me. Azalea is also well known among her friends as a "push-over," always ready to make nice with them, which I can only imagine might come from growing up in a house where she was always trying to please a pretty intense mom.

As grumpy as she gets with me—and even Thayer, too, these days—she never wants to go too far from home, or for too long, which has, of course, from a secure base point of view, concerned me. But last summer she decided she was ready to go to sleepaway camp for the first time. And she chose a girls' camp for young writers. Clearly, there were traits being passed down through the generations, some more visible than others. I needed to know more about the ones I couldn't see.

WHEN DR. STEELE said it was time to go to the interview room, I was nervous. I was putting myself through this ordeal, after all, not only to understand myself better but to learn more about Azalea and about our relationship, to illuminate the edges beyond what I could comprehend. I hadn't even allowed myself to think about the implications of intergenerational transmis-sion in terms of my mom; Azalea did seem secure, but I couldn't imagine that I would be, and I definitely didn't think my mom was. And so, if attachment theory was correct, which I firmly believed was the case, and I was part of the 75 percent majority of predictable patterns, I may well soon discover that I was insecure, which would rock how I thought about Azalea.

There was a lot on the line.

I tried to comfort myself with the knowledge that attachment, like karma, can change—that an insecure attachment is not, by any means, a life sentence. Whatever I discovered about myself, I told myself, Azalea would be the same reasonably well-regulated and happy person. That wouldn't change. I wasn't sure what would.

I FOLLOWED DR. STEELE down the narrow halls to a little windowless room with two chairs and a box of Kleenex and sat down. I thanked him for being so willing to do this for me, and I told him I realized it was a bit unorthodox to offer an AAI as he was doing, and to give me my classification.

He smiled gently at me and set up his iPhone for recording, and we chatted a bit about how the day would unfold—how we would do the interview, and I would then leave for a few hours to give him time to transcribe and code it, and then I could come back for the results and some "confidential feedback," which I could take with me.

Because I had done so much reading about the AAI, I knew that as soon as we were finished with these preliminaries, he would ask me to describe the basic setup of my family, and then ask for five adjectives to describe my relationship with my mother, then my father. Following that, he would take me through the words I'd chosen and ask me to supply supporting details and evidence for each. I knew that my ability to back up my adjectives with solid, fluent, "fresh" (as opposed to canned), and consistent details would be at least part of what he would look for when he classified me later that day.

I also knew enough to know that, as prepared as I was to answer the questions, the AAI looks for patterns of language that stem from the unconscious, and it would be a waste of time to try to manipulate the test. I feared that if my results came back "preoccupied"—I doubted I was dismissive—I would feel totally embarrassed, as if my entire interest in attachment was proof of my preoccupied insecurity. But I trusted the process, and I wanted to know the truth.

Can you tell me a little bit about the people in your family growing up?

Sitting there in this New York City attachment lab, with Strange Situation rooms down the hall, I was finally part of the story I had been teaching myself. A second-generation descendant of Bowlby and Ainsworth's attachment family was interviewing me. In a very real sense, it could have been Dr. A herself, chain-smoking, asking me if I enjoyed breastfeeding, which I had, very much.

Sitting in that little room on a hot September day, I considered the twenty questions designed to reveal what Mary Ainsworth might have seen had she watched my mom and me navigate our separations and reunions in the Strange Situation in Baltimore, or anywhere else, more than forty years earlier. As Dr. Steele asked me the open-ended, slightly startling questions about my relationships in early childhood, I searched my memory for all the details. While lying to my mom was easy, telling the truth about her, I found, was harder.

But I tried my very best to be an excellent informant.

The questions began with general inquiries about the nature of my relationship with my parents, then drilled down a bit. Even though I knew the basic gist of the protocol, the questions still worked on me as they are supposed to, "requir[ing] a rapid succession of speech acts, giving speakers little time to prepare a response." Then came questions about how my parents responded to me in times of early separation, times of illness or loss, feelings of rejection, "setbacks"—which Dr. Steele followed up with questions like "You mentioned that you felt your mother was tender when you were ill. Can you think of a time when this was so?"

The couch-bed I was lying on when Kate called me in eighth grade. My mother appeared in my mind as the person who tucked the sheet into the cushions and laid the afghan over me. The hand around the ginger ale was hers—long, slender fingers, painted nails. And I thought of the card above my desk from Azalea that read, "Dear Mom, I love you so much you stayed up all night when I was sick I love you soooooooooo much!"

Occasionally Dr. Steele would smile, or raise his eyebrows and nod, but I was on my own, filling the room—the space, myself—with my story. There was no amount of mental rehearsing that could have prepared me for how it felt to describe my early life to him, even with all I thought I knew.

I talked about my brothers' rejection, my dad's aloofness, and how my mom was kind, though also distant. I described my feelings of loneliness, my growing rage and resentment, and my shame, which I thought was related to having been rejected by my very own brothers, and then not protected from them—a double whammy. I talked about my adolescent acting out—the sex, the drugs, the bad grades. Near the end of the interview, Dr. Steele asked me if I had a sense of why my parents parented the way they did, and of course I said yes—my mom's mom was cold, so as much as my mom tried to be warm, the coolness came through. My dad was a sad guy who had never quite measured up in his own family. His dad died when he was sixteen, and his mom, Grandma Beryl, was brilliant, but a mentally and emotionally unstable mother, going in and out of being hospitalized. My dad had no idea how to be a parent. It all made perfect sense.

When we were finished, Dr. Steele turned off the recorder and smiled. I walked back out into the bright Manhattan streets and looked into strangers' faces, searching for a clue about what it means to be a person. I got a cup of coffee and sat outside on a bench, watching cabs and people, families and students, lovers and friends, birds of a feather, filled with their own songs and cries, calls and responses—the sounds of seeking, and of sometimes finding.

chapter twenty-eight

Two years after I received my AAI classification from Dr. Steele, Azalea stayed with Thayer's parents so he and I could do a two-week AAI training with the Steeles. They had recently learned from Mary Main how to train AAI coders, and we were thrilled to be part of their first cohort. Every day for two weeks, we sat in a classroom at the New School with a group of graduate students and clinicians and learned Mary Main's incredibly intricate method of how to read and code these transcripts. The complexity of coding the AAI makes Mary Ainsworth's scales look broad and primitive, though in fact it is more correct to say they are foundational.

We looked as a group through transcripts, first by coding for what's called "probable experience," as in what the subject says happened, and then for "coherence of mind," as in the way the subject describes what happened. We were given a set of colored markers and we learned how to use them. There was a different color for all the experience scales on the left side of the page: loving, rejecting, role reversing, neglecting, and pressure to achieve. On the right side, a different set of colors was used to indicate coherence: consistency in time, tense and relevance, and fresh and insightful—excellent—storytelling.

I felt as if I had died and gone to heaven.

WHAT WE LEARNED is that secure adults are able to describe all experiences coherently, whether negative (due to parental rejection or overinvolvement, for instance) or positive. Dismissing adults tend to not remember much, or idealize their parents without being able to come up with any good examples for their overly positive adjectives. Preoccupied adults are still very much involved and preoccupied with their past attachment experiences, getting all wrapped up in past hurts during the interview itself. Dismissing and preoccupied adults are both considered insecure.

From the very beginning of a transcript, looking at the five adjectives a person gives to describe his or her relationship with a parent, one can get a feeling for what kind of transcript it will be. It reminded me of when I used to grade hundreds of student papers a semester. After grading for a few years, I could tell by the first line what grade I would give it. The mark of a secure adult is a mixed set of adjectives—not seethingly negative, which might indicate a level of preoccupation, and not overly positive, which might suggest a defense against the more painful aspects of the relationship, otherwise known as idealizing.

The AAI has been found to give a reliable attachment classification, regardless of the speaker's intelligence or verbal fluency and regardless of the interviewer. The most articulate, detail-oriented trial lawyer, ordinarily linguistically unflappable, may report that her mother was kind, loving, warm, and fun but have an inability to recall any details to support that story. She might repeat herself or give irrelevant details. This would indicate a possibly insecure/dismissing state of mind, suggesting that the lawyer may well raise an avoidant baby. As Mary Ainsworth discovered in Uganda, it's the parent's state of mind *in relation to her attachments* that determines her child's attachment security, which develops into that individual's adult state of mind, which affects his own children's security. And so on.

Erik Hesse, Mary Main's husband and an AAI expert, gives a great example in an article in the *Handbook of Attachment*. As evidence for the adjective "loving," he offers three different types of responses:

> Well, because she was caring and supportive . . . I guess like, well, you know, she drove me to school, and I was always really proud of her, I mean, she was really pretty, and she took a lot of care with her appearance . . .

> Loving . . . My mom would stick up for me to the teacher, or to a kid's parents, or . . . anybody, really. I could put it another way, too. I just knew where I stood with her, and that she'd be comforting if I was upset or something . . .

> Uh, yeah, sort of very loving at times, like people were in the old days—uh, my youth, lot of changes since then. I remember home, and home was good and that. And, uh, loving, my wife is loving with [child]—taking him out to the movies tonight, special thing he's been wanting to see all week, dadadada.

The first of these is from a dismissive interview. Instead of diving in and offering any real-life examples to flesh out the descriptive adjective of "loving," the speaker remains on the same superficial plane of description and repeats similar adjectives that mean the same thing as "loving"—"caring and supportive." Instead of being able to recall an example of when the mother acted in a loving manner, the speaker stays focused on external appearances—"she was really pretty"—instead of a more detailed and personal, internal experience. The description feels restricted and classic avoidant.

The second is from a very secure, fluent, expressive, and evidence-filled interview. You can feel the speaker's ability to freely associate regarding this attachment relationship. The speaker is able to capture a concrete example of when her mother was loving—"my mom would stick up for me"—and her language is more flowing and relaxed.

The final passage moves haphazardly in and out of tenses and time, using disorganized speech patterns and made-up words like "dadadada." One of Mary Main's many genius observations is the way preoccupied speech incorporates nonsense words. This passage also fails to supply concrete evidence for the adjective "loving" and gives one the sense that this speaker is so preoccupied by this past relationship that it is very much alive, though unprocessed.

When scanning for security, the best places to look for clues in any transcript are hints about whether or not a person *values attachment*. Avoidant people tend to be focused on external achievements, such as professional or intellectual accomplishments, or appearances, like a mother's prettiness, citing successes as indications of happiness and pride. Preoccupied people are actively angry and "derogating," a technical term meaning they consistently put down their attachment figures and attachment itself. They claim they don't care about people or relationships, yet underscore *how very much they care* in their passionate if chaotic insistence on past and present injuries and insults. Preoccupied adults might reject overtures of connection, saying that relationships, or the people close to them, don't matter. The implication being that they care so much they can't bear the thought of being hurt. Again.

Securely attached adults, on the other hand, even in the midst of rejection and neglect, come through it all with a coherent mind, knowing who they are and *valuing attachment*. These transcripts are simpler, easier to follow, light and balanced. Secure transcripts show an interest in relationships—even imperfect ones—and might reference holidays spent with family, positive ideas about what a relationship should be like (even if their own relationships were a disappointment), and a desire, however rebuffed, to be close to others. Secure transcripts exhibit a core belief that the speaker deserves love, that people belong together, and that attachment—though most people never use that word—is real.

This is the telltale heart of attachment. No matter what secure adults have been through, they are governed by a trust in the importance of love in their life. Even when it hurts.

chapter twenty-nine

To say I was delighted when I arrived back at the New School and Dr. Steele told me that my transcript appeared secure/ autonomous would be putting it mildly. I was in shock; I was actually shaking as he handed me a copy of his prepared notes.

From his own copy, he read aloud:

Mother, Father and two brothers, speaker is youngest of 3, moved once in 1st grade and another time going into 8th grade. The latter move was on account of the parents divorcing, and father (an auto-parts salesman) having gone aground, "lost his way financially."

Confesses to a feeling of guilt "because I didn't feel that I was feeling the feeling I was supposed to feel."

Mum was very good at immediate verbal assurances. "I felt like she really cared for me when I was sick."

Sibling relationships are a powerful theme.

Dr. Steele looked up. I didn't move. He continued.

My eyes started to burn and my throat tickle as he read, "As a child regarding upset a predictable cycle is described, brothers would upset her, she would run to her mother who seems not to have wanted to get involved, and so learned to 'turn to herself,' and to her 'inner world' which became richly developed (as appears to be the case for her daughter too in the next generation)."

I couldn't believe it when he described the way I locked myself in my room filled with "deep frustration and recrimination" as an "adaptive strategy!"

The tears slid down my face. I reached for a tissue as Dr. Steele continued: "Overall, the narrative is balanced, thoughtful, probing regarding her own mind, her own responses, and her own ongoing efforts to do right by her daughter (together with awareness of ways in which she has, as we all do, repeated aspects of the parenting she received). Some ongoing resentment and anger, but mostly awareness of past anger, and capacity for anger that requires an effort of self-control, is present."

I was listening to my life story as Mary might tell it.

And regarding what Dr. Steele said about my Number One Top Memory—"being in the bathtub and having father poke his head in and saying, 'Go away, I want mummy' "—he said something that blew my mind.

"An empowering memory. You were safe enough to say something."

An empowering memory?

Safe enough to say something?

Me?

Wow.

I had been telling myself the story of my victimhood for as long as I could remember—my brothers hated me; I may have been abused; I never fit in; nobody loved me. And that bathtub memory was the key to the whole story I had spun. So much had rested on being pitted against my father in that moment—

little me, defenseless, afraid of the world. To imagine myself reaching out to my mom because she felt good and safe rather than because I was afraid of a nefarious father changed everything. I knew, after all, that Azalea so often preferred me, even though she and Thayer were really close. Which is not to say that my dad was attuned like Thayer; far from it. But to imagine myself as empowered—not just not abused, but *empowered*—changed everything.

Oh, what a vista it opened up!

When Dr. Steele was finished reading his notes, I felt like I had awoken from a dream. I was happy, touched, and a little disoriented. I had been working up to this moment for years. And my mind was flipping through the implications like skirts on a rack.

ONCE I GOT my bearings, Dr. Steele and I talked a little about what to make of my acting out with Azalea when she was younger. He suggested that there might be a slight touch of disorganization mixed in with my basic attachment security, which may well have stemmed from a pretty serious trauma history on my dad's side, as well as a lack of affection between my brothers and me, which might account for some of my anger. And then he referred me to the literature on delinquency, which shows that when delinquent behavior begins and ends in adolescence, like mine did, it's very different, and much less worrisome, than when it continues, as it probably did with Bowlby's thieves.

I wasn't such a hotshot badass after all.

As I began to let it all settle, I asked him if he could imagine what kind of baby I was, and he answered, "Maybe a B1, basically secure but a little avoidant," which again made sense, considering the way I felt so physically uncomfortable with my mom. Avoidant parents are notably uncomfortable with physical affection, and even though I know my mom—with all her warm and welcoming words—tried to overcome her own mother's coolness, I still felt it.

I could have sat there all day and all night talking about attachment. But after an hour or so of chatting, I knew it was time to go. Before I left, though, I had to work up the courage to ask the question that had been driving my obsession since I saw my first video of a Strange Situation online seven years earlier.

I knew, of course, that the chances were good—75 percent good—that Azalea would have been a secure baby, but I had to ask. I wanted to test the theory I had come to trust, and see it all play out.

"If I were pregnant," I asked Dr. Steele, "what kind of infant do you think I would have?" He took the question seriously, which I appreciated. And he answered easily. "B4," he said. "B4," I repeated.

Secure, with an edge.

I thought back to my training in Minneapolis with Dr. Sroufe, sitting in the classroom looking up at the big screen and watching the sad mom and her feisty B4 daughter, who patted each other in Reunion 2, like a mirror image of each other, operating in unison as one perfect thing. The pair that made Dr. Sroufe cry.

I thought back to when Azalea was that age, wearing dresses with giant bows, walking on stiff legs, flyaway curls in pigtails—an adorable, willful, comfort-seeking missile. Then there was me, kind of unavailable, a little moody, and with a whole lot of gritty energy.

Holy shit, I realized. Azalea was the girl in the little sneakers, crying her head off. And I was the mom in the Reeboks with the eighties hair.

And we fit each other like the world's most perfect dress.

chapter thirty

After my AAI, things felt different. I began to grant myself permission, for the first time in my life, to just be the mess that I am and, at the same time, am not. The question that had always plagued me—was I broken and abused, or whole and happy enough?—seemed kind of irrelevant. I'm not perfect. My parents weren't perfect. Azalea's not perfect. But something seems to be working. I seem to be working. Miracle of miracles, like a scared but secure baby in Reunion 1, I was calming down enough to get back to the work at hand: growing up and raising Azalea.

Since my AAI, I had been getting pretty comfortable with—even prideful of—the fact that I was secure and that Azalea probably was, too, and I was coming to understand how my ability to mentalize—again, the capacity to see one's own mind, which helps us to see another's mind—had played out in my life of self-reflection.

The Steeles have spent their careers trying to understand how this ability to mentalize, which they call "reflective functioning" (RF), is related to attachment; they even score for RF when they classify AAI transcripts. They believe that RF may be enhanced or sharpened in "the individual [who] may urgently need to reflect upon the minds of sometimes—or frequently—malevolent caregivers, and challenging sibling relationships. Being able to predict forthcoming hostility directed at the self, to have a theory of the malevolent other's mind, may prove essential to survival."

And so it made perfect sense to me that my reflective functioning was pretty high.

However, there was one little loophole that was bugging me.

In the adult attachment literature, there is one type of secure adult—the F3B—who is considered "earned secure." This rare classification is reserved for a person who reports a lot of adversity in his or her childhood but is deemed secure now. The thinking is that this person was insecure as a baby and in childhood, but somewhere along the way—through therapy or a loving relationship or spiritual practice—had healed himself or herself into having a secure/autonomous internal working model. I wondered if this was me.

The problem with this "earned secure" category is that there are so few longitudinal studies that show a child's classification in the Strange Situation and also include their adult classification for comparison. And in the few that do exist, such cases are rare. Attachment tends to remain consistent, and negative events have more of an impact than positive ones, usually leading a person in a more insecure direction rather than a more secure one. But I wanted to be sure. Had my adult security been passed down to me, or had I earned it through all my hours on the meditation cushion, in therapy, in self-reflection? If the generational transmission of attachment is as robust as the field claims it is—75 percent!—then there was one way to be at least 75 percent sure. I wanted to triangulate my own data.

After Thayer and I had finished our two-week AAI training with the Steeles, my mom came to visit.

Dear reader, you know where this is headed.

My poor mom was reluctant to go through the Adult Attachment Interview, even with her beloved son-in-law, Thayer. She put on her game-like spirit, though, and said, "If it will help you with the book, I'll do it." But she was not happy. She was, understandably, like some of the mothers in Baltimore driving with their babies and Dr. A to the Strange Situation lab at Johns Hopkins, afraid of how she would "do," and I must say I was a little worried, too.

It was hard to imagine my mom being able to really share openly about her past, with fresh speech and spontaneous detail. My sense of her was that she was actually pretty resistant to going too deeply into things, which frustrated me to no end. Once she told me about a "wild dream" she'd had, and when I asked her what she thought it meant, she kind of shuddered and said, "I don't even want to know!" The more I learned about what it takes to be scored as an autonomous adult, the more I doubted my mom would make the cut.

If my mom turned out to be dismissing—I didn't think she'd be preoccupied—it might plant a seed of doubt about Azalea's and my classification. I wanted to hit an attachment home run.

On the day Thayer and my mom were set to do the AAI, they both seemed to be, well, *avoiding* the task at hand. Finally, after going back and forth about the best place in the house to do their interview, Thayer got them all set up downstairs on some couches, with his phone as the recorder and a white noise machine for an attempt at privacy.

When they got started on our lower level, I was in the kitchen, at the top of the stairs, puttering around trying to distract myself. I immediately realized that I could still hear Thayer's clinical voice from downstairs, asking my mom to describe the people in her family growing up. I didn't want to interrupt them, so I just went into my study to keep myself from eavesdropping. But then I had to "get a drink of water" and heard this:

THAYER: I'd like you to just try to describe your relationship with your parents as a young child. And if you could start from as far back as you can remember . . .

MOM: I remember my daughter [me!] asking me what was my first memory with my mother and it was I was very, very little and I'd been outside playing. And I came in and my mother—I—I must have been being trained, potty trained, 'cause she said, "Did you wet your pants?" And I said, "No." I said, "No." And she lifted me up on the kitchen table and I had wet my pants. And she, uh, she gave me a little spanking. And if I remember correctly, she explained that it was because I had lied to her, not that I had wet my pants, why she spanked me. But that was one of my earliest memories.

And, um, and I remember a nice memory of when my mother was baking and I was sitting up on the step stool at the counter and she played pat-a-cake with me. And I remember that vividly.

I couldn't believe my ears. My mom's an amazing informant! Such a free-flowing narrative, with that much vivid detail about her mom, before the adjectives even started. No stammering, no hesitation, totally fresh speech, a reference to intergenerational attachment ("I remember my daughter asking . . ."). I was stunned.

And I was right. As soon as they came upstairs, Thayer and I shared a surprised, very happy look. I immediately emailed the interview file to the Steeles to get it coded by an official "naïve" coder and received the classification in a few days.

Just as I suspected, my mom's transcript was solidly secure/autonomous, though a little bit on the avoidant side, which made perfect sense, considering the way she described her own mother, and the coolness I had felt from her.

Speaker is approximately a 75 y/o woman raised in the Great Lakes region by a reliable but emotionally distant mother and a more affectionate, alcoholic father . . .

The speaker provides a largely coherent account of her childhood experiences and current attachment relationships. She provides balanced views of herself and others as well as coherent passages that reveal a strong valuing of attachment that would be inconsistent with a dismissing state of mind with regards to attachment. Descriptors of her parents contain some incoherence, taking the form of modestly positive adjectives with poor support with specific memories. The speaker thus shows some characteristics of a dismissing speaker, defensively restricting her affective recall of early experiences with caregivers. However, the overall classification is best captured by F2 [slightly restricted secure/autonomous]. The speaker is a strong example of the F2 attachment profile.

And in an intriguing twist, my mom's score for reflective functioning was even higher than mine.

chapter thirty-one

On a night soon after my mom left, Azalea wept because, among other things, I refused to let her buy a pair of shoes from Zappos. At one point, I was in her room listening, trying to feel the anguish of being a tween, that cave of frustration and desire to fit in; I wanted to just be there for her. But the travails of a privileged kid going on and on about not getting what she wanted finally tipped me over the edge, and I told her to get over it and walked away. Which wasn't a terrible thing to *do,* but the mind with which I did it was cold, mean, and all about me and my irritation. Why couldn't I rise above it? It's not as if she melts down very often. Would it have killed me to sit there and absorb her tears?

As I left her room, she tearfully confirmed something I already knew—that I "just don't know how to deal with kids." I went into our bedroom and asked Thayer to go in, then I lay in bed, heart racing, pretending to read. As Thayer gently settled her down, I listened to her cry about how alone she feels, and how she thinks I "hate" her (ouch), and then she hiccupped between sobs, "I feel . . . like I don't even . . . mat-ter."

I get it.

All those times I sat in my room at her age, feeling numb and alone, I definitely didn't feel like I mattered. Maybe that feeling is just part of our human repertoire, or maybe it's something that's been passed down, especially between sensitive people who grow up in families that certainly aren't perfectly attuned but aren't, as Dr. Steele suggested at the end of my AAI, technically speaking anyway, "that bad."

Azalea slept in our room with us that night, on the futon we keep under our bed for just such occasions, cuddled on the floor with our dog, CC. In the morning I told her how sorry I was that the night before had been so hard, and how sad it was to hear that she felt like I hated her. "Do you really feel that way?" I asked. And she looked up from her scrambled eggs, all showered and back together, and said, "Sometimes."

"You know," she added, "I didn't ask to be born."

WHEN AZALEA WAS FOUR, just as my fascination with attachment began to bloom, I had the opportunity to interview Jon Kabat-Zinn for "Flowers Fall," my monthly column. Kabat-Zinn is a mindfulness and meditation expert who has written many books, including *Everyday Blessings: The Inner Work of Mindful Parenting*. Because he is a senior teacher in a tradition closely related to Zen and an expert in spiritual life, I was hoping an interview with him might serve as a sort of Buddhist confession for me. Things with Azalea were getting better, for sure, but I still struggled, and mightily at times. I imagined my interview with him might absolve me from the shame of what I believed was my maternal—*human*—failure. Maybe he would kindly encourage me to set down my burden of guilt, and maybe even offer a final answer, a godlike *Let it go*. And in my fantasy, I would actually be able to let it all go! I would be relieved of my discomfort, the gnawing feeling that I was messing Azalea up.

But that wasn't what happened.

We sat on the porch of the cabin he was staying in at a nearby retreat center and had a long and meaningful conversation about spiritual practice. And then I started asking him my real questions. And he gave me some real answers.

KABAT-ZINN: The meaning of being a parent is that you take responsibility for your child's life until they can take responsibility for their own life. That's it!

ME: That's a lot.

KABAT-ZINN: True, and it doesn't mean you can't get help. Turns out how you are as a parent makes a huge difference in the neural development of your child for the first four or five years.

ME: That is so frightening.

KABAT-ZINN: All that's required, though, is connection. That's all.

ME: But sometimes I want to be separate from my child; I don't want to be connected all the time.

KABAT-ZINN: I see. Well, everything has consequences. How old is your child?

ME: Four and a half.

KABAT-ZINN: Well, I gotta say, I have very strong feelings about that kind of thing. She didn't ask to be born.

She didn't ask to be born.

Nor did I.

Beneath my memories of swimming around my mother, darting in and out of her attention, I was a person looking for her place in the world, trying to get the person I loved most to see me. That's what children do—find themselves through their parents. It's what we all do—find ourselves in another, another in ourselves.

Since my mother was always fantastically busy—busy with the dishes, busy with vacuuming, busy with the busyness of being a wife, a homemaker, a mother of three—and I, on the other hand, was never busy, I often felt alone, untethered, disconnected.

And then once, when I was around nine or ten, Missy's perpetual age, my mother asked me to empty the dishwasher. I said, "Why should I? I never asked to be born."

Which was my way of asking: *What am I doing here? On this earth, in this family? Why am I suffering this life? Why do* anything?

Why live?

So when Kabat Zinn said those words—"She didn't ask to be born"—I knew he was right. None of us asks to be born. We called Azalea to us from our small room on Fawnview, with the river rushing at the bottom of the hill. She answered.

My parents called to me.

This is my answer.

Though I felt like I barely existed, hovering above or beneath it all—depending on the day and the direction of my hurt and fragile little-girl sense of self—I did exist. I was alive enough to ask my questions, to see the edges, to notice the cracks, and, most important, to feel my longing for more.

And then, as a new mother, I vowed to disrupt that flickering light of disconnection—*I never asked to be born*—that unnamed suffering that seemed to cast anxious shadows onto everything I did, including trying to love people.

And then, there it was.

Azalea: "I didn't ask to be born."

Generationally transmitted . . . what?

The ability to be honest, for one thing. And to ask impossible questions.

As Mary writes:

> We shall never know what the inner life of an infant truly is, for the infant cannot tell us about it and the person later remembers [her] infancy imperfectly, if at all. Another approach, the one I have adopted, is to observe the infant's behavior, which is undoubtedly related to [her] inner experience, although not a transparent communication thereof.

Our protests, our tears, our demands, our morning-after reflections over eggs—our "infant's behavior"—are, as the Zen saying goes, the finger pointing to the moon. The moon is our "inner experience although not a transparent communication thereof." The life we can see points us toward what matters more than anything: the life we cannot see. Because that's where our connections lie—deep within, transmitted generation after generation. The galaxy, after all, is 85 percent dark matter. And though there is no telescope powerful enough to see it, scientists know it's there because of the gravitational pull this invisible force has on what we can see, like stars flashing in the night sky, or the person we love more than life itself sitting across from us, pushing eggs around her plate.

I'M FORTUNATE THAT what I now see as my attachment security may well have protected me from a life of addiction—of the drug, sex, or love variety—and maybe from the kind of delinquency that lasts. And I know how things are not as they seem. But still, I don't want Azalea to have to suffer as I did, or at all—though I know that's impossible. And in the heat of a conflict or in a wave of dread, as I hear my beloved daughter repeat my own sad words—"I didn't ask to be born"—I still freeze in the kitchen, or I lash out, leaving her room as if I don't care. I lose myself. I lose my way. I lose touch with the meaning of my life, which is to be in relationship.

But then I do the only thing I know how to do, which is to return to myself, whether on the cushion in zazen or wherever I find myself. Maybe driving back from the morning drop-off, trying to stay with and move through the echo of some unfortunate words I just said—or the void left from kind words left unsaid—instead of turning away from it, because I know that is the only way to move through the shame.

In my mind, I repeat the Gatha of Atonement, chanted at Zen weddings and funerals. And newborn entering ceremonies:

> All evil karma ever committed by me since of old.
> On account of my beginningless greed, anger, and igno-
>   rance.
> Born of my body, mouth, and thought.
> Now I atone for it all.

In other words, karma—a pinwheel of cause and effect—turns in every direction. Just like attachment. There is no first or final source of it. No beginning and no end. And so it is with our suffering, and the pain we inflict on others. To atone—to heal—is to step in now and own it.

The problem is that we are often so worried that we're doing it wrong, like I was, that we even use something like mindfulness—or attachment—to beat ourselves up. In 2015, a group of researchers from Portugal studied the relationship between "self-compassion" and "parenting stress" by way of attachment. In the introduction to their paper, they write, "The way parents relate to themselves in times of failure or difficulty, such as with self-compassion or self-criticism, is strongly associated with their attachment histories and may be expected to affect their parenting behaviors and, consequently, their children's psychological well-being." And, not surprisingly, the researchers found that the mothers who were secure in their own attachment histories experienced more self-compassion, which mitigated their parenting stress. Which is good for their children.

The study ends with this clinical recommendation:

> Parents may learn how to reduce their self-criticism with regard to their parenting skills or their child's behaviors and needs and to accept themselves and their children as imperfect individuals who deserve compassion . . . Although for individuals with insecure attachment styles, self-compassionate exercises may be extremely useful, these exercises may initially be experienced as difficult and even unpleasant tasks.

Looking at ourselves—regardless of attachment history—can be incredibly unpleasant, especially when we don't know how, which makes us all the more frazzled and insecure. But it's worth it. It's tiring, sometimes, all this digging deep, all this back-and-forth, but what can we do? As Daido used to say, "Seven times knocked down, eight times up." I have to rely on that generationally transmitted grit to return to what I know—my body, the people I love, what I have come to trust as true. When I get all wound up and freaked out that I'm terrible or that Azalea is doomed, I return to what matters. Her life. Our relationship. And I take a very deep breath. And start again.

If, upon my return to his office on the day of my AAI, Dr. Steele had told me I was preoccupied or dismissing or primarily unresolved (disorganized) or unclassifiable (also an option, though unusual), I would have cried different tears as he walked me through my results. But after I'd recovered from disappointment, I, like the well-trained, gritty Zen student that I am, would have just had to get back to work, trying to inch myself and Azalea toward security. But how?

Though Dr. Sears might disagree, Alan Sroufe says, "Attachment is not a set of tricks." There is no checklist for "attaining" a secure attachment, any more than we can become enlightened by showing up in a zendo or reading about meditation. Sroufe explains that a mother could breastfeed in a mechanical way or a sensitive way, just as a parent can bottle-feed as an opportunity for sensitive interaction or prop a baby up with a bottle in a Skinnerian baby box and go about his or her business. As Mary saw in Uganda, plenty of women who nursed and co-slept had an insecure attachment with their babies. And plenty of women in Baltimore who bottle-fed and had their babies nap on a schedule in a crib had loving, attuned, secure attachments.

So if the Seven B's of attachment parenting aren't going to help us, how do we learn to develop what we need in order to foster secure attachments in our babies, regardless of our own history? In other words, if we suck at reading cues, how do we get better? Trying to line ourselves up with a list of to-dos is actually the opposite of the kind of fine attunement that Mary Ainsworth and so many others have pointed to as the path toward security. Sensitive caregiving depends on having a mind that is open and supple enough to read another's. But what exactly is our mind? And how do we "do" anything with it?

The capacity to see one's own mind—the ability to *mentalize*—is a very concrete and important matter, especially for parents. Because of the way every attachment pair—every parent and every child—operates as a unit, what happens within our own state of mind in relation to attachment *is* what happens in our children's. So when we see the value of our relationships clearly, our children will as well, illuminated in our reflection.

When we can't see what's happening in our own minds clearly, our kids are left guessing in our dimmed light. Of course we all want to model good behavior for our kids—hard work, good manners, healthy living—but what the attachment research makes clear is that it's the capacity for self-awareness of even our so-called failures that leads to self-compassion, which leads to a more relaxed attachment system, which leads to mutual delight, which leads to a secure pattern of attachment.

It really works.

The Steeles work extensively with vulnerable parents to help them develop their reflective functioning through a unique program that includes using video. While other video-based interventions exist, theirs is unique in that it works with multiple families at a time, and positions parents to help other parents, an approach they learned from John Bowlby. Their program, called GABI (Group Attachment–Based Intervention), gives parents a supportive opportunity to watch themselves interact with their babies, which can be an emotionally challenging but transformative experience. As they write, "the effects of the experience of watching oneself on video-film, especially when watching oneself interacting with one's child, can be startling and evocative in ways that promote change. Multiple sensations, emotions, beliefs and representations are aroused, often in unsettling ways, very likely activating the attachment system."

Though triggering, this experience, coupled with a supportive group presence, helps parents develop their reflective functioning. "Randomized controlled trials have shown that mothers whose attachment patterns were classified as insecure increased in maternal sensitivity following treatment . . . compared to a control group." And this maternal sensitivity comes out of their ability to mentalize.

The Steeles' GABI program has been shown to be significantly more effective than other treatment models in helping "at-risk" mothers—many of whom have serious trauma histories or mental health challenges and may have had their children removed—improve their relationships with their children, interrupting the cycle of serious maltreatment, which is, as Howard Steele wrote to me, "too familiar for too long." There's nothing abstract about that.

Bob Marvin told me about a very powerful intervention he does with video with teenage mothers at risk of losing their children, at his clinic in Charlottesville—the Ainsworth Attachment Clinic. He and his team get five to ten pairs of moms and babies together for a gathering and then videotape their interactions, which are not always the most sensitive, shall we say. The clinicians then study the footage and find even the tiniest blips of affection—the handing off of a balloon, a smile, a baby's laugh—then splice it all together into one happy story of mutual delight, with the song "You Are So Beautiful to Me" as the soundtrack. And then they show it to the group.

Bob told me about the power of watching these young moms, who certainly didn't receive much sensitive caregiving themselves—who might not even be sure what it looks like, let alone how it feels—watching themselves bask in the glory of the love that does indeed exist between themselves and their babies. These women get to see how much their babies love them, too, reflecting back what's best in them, bringing their attention to the moment, and beyond the moment, too.

Bob and the moms then talk together about the miraculous ties they have to their babies. And this loving back-and-forth about who the mothers are and the stories they tell will change the course of history.

chapter thirty-two

The friends who introduced me to the AAI recently visited with their two young children, who followed Azalea around the house—and CC, too, giving her treats, making her sit. Because the little ones were going to wake up in our home on St. Patrick's Day, Azalea stayed up late the night before, setting up a big surprise for them, including oddly misspelled notes from leprechauns, baby powder footprints, and chocolate gold coins left over from Hanukkah.

One afternoon, as the dads took the kids down to a nearby pond and my friend and I sat alone on the couch, I showed her the black-and-white photographs from *Infancy in Uganda*. She stopped at one, of a baby named Nabatanzi and her mother. "You can't fake that," she said, delighting in the quiet affection on the mother's face.

And she's right, of course; you can't fake that. As Mary writes, "Attachment is internal." It's "an internalized something," a something that wants to work.

We looked together at one of my favorite passages from *Infancy in Uganda*. It's got it all—the bells, the candy, the little red sunsuit, the photographs, the back-and-forth, the scrambles, the return, the leaning back into bliss.

Our last visit took place when Kasozi was sixty-four weeks old. He was wearing a scarlet sunsuit and had bells around his ankles. He sat close to his mother. When I held out a piece of candy to him he started across the room for it, then stopped in his tracks and looked at me as though wondering whether it was safe to come closer. Mrs. Kibuka took the candy and offered it to him; he came for it and got very sticky eating it, sucking it, taking it out of his mouth to look at it, making it last a long time. His mother rose and went out of the house for a moment. Kasozi broke into a howl, scrambled to his feet, and followed her. When we took photographs Kasozi was quiet with his mother close to him. Back in the house he leaned against his mother and made contented noises. He spent most of our visit lolling back against her.

What a truly excellent informant Mary Ainsworth was. And what an incredible mother she would have been.
She certainly mothered me.

THE NEXT WEEKEND, Thayer and Azalea went to his parents' house and I stayed home to work. After a long day at the computer, I watched the film *Lady Bird* as my evening reward. It's a coming-of-age story about a girl who named herself Lady Bird and who, though she has a spectacularly difficult relationship with her mother, spectacularly doesn't hate herself. Or her mother.

One of my favorite parts of the movie is a conversation between the head of Lady Bird's Catholic school, Sister Sarah Joan, and Lady Bird after she has written her college essay about Sacramento, the city she lives in and claims to hate.

SISTER SARAH JOAN: You clearly love Sacramento.

LADY BIRD: I do?

SISTER SARAH JOAN: You write about Sacramento so affectionately and with such care.

LADY BIRD: I was just describing it.

SISTER SARAH JOAN: Well, it comes across as love.

LADY BIRD: Sure, I guess I pay attention.

SISTER SARAH JOAN: Don't you think maybe they are the same thing? Love and attention?

As I lay in bed that night listening to the quiet of our house, and CC breathing on her bed on the floor, I thought of the movie and of Mary. I thought of how much fun it would have been to watch *Lady Bird* with her and then discuss it with her until late in the night. We'd talk about mothers and daughters, and maybe we'd even talk about the daughters and sons she longed for but never had. We'd definitely talk about the daughters and sons she did have—her students, her legacy. We could even gossip about them, because now I know them, too. I lay there alone, thinking of the power of paying attention, which was, after all, her genius, her brilliance, like a jewel that lived inside of her, and, as she taught me, inside all of us.

Mary spoke of being childless as "one of the great sorrows" of her life. Struck by this, I have searched through her papers and work over the past decade, looking for some language to describe this desire of hers to be a mother—what did she think motherhood promised? What was she looking for? What did she feel was missing?

All I have found is the very briefest of mentions—as quick as the time it takes for a drop of water on a hot pan to ball up and evaporate. The babies she never had are, simply, the "children for whom I vainly longed." The children Mary never had are like ghosts, a negative space.

As sad as I am for her, I must confess that I'm grateful, too. Had she been a mother herself, I doubt she would have had the heart to look so closely into the workings of maternal love. She would have, like the rest of us, wanted to turn away. Not necessarily because we're avoidant, exactly, but because the love we have for our children, passed down through a beginningless line of imperfect human beings, feels delicate. But it's not. We think love might get hurt if we include all the brokenness, when in fact it's trying to keep our fractured, hurt parts out of the whole that we are that breaks us.

In *Character and the Conduct of Life,* the book that inspired Mary to become a psychologist when she was fifteen years old— "What a vista it opened up!"—William McDougall writes, "Wisdom is of the heart no less than the head; and, though the principles of a science may be rapidly assimilated, the share of wisdom that comes from the heart comes only with much experience of joy and sorrow, hope, disappointment, effort, failure and success."

Forty years after reading this passage, Mary had assimilated these two sides of human experience—the head and the heart— into one room, a room with two chairs and some ordinary toys. While neither she nor John Bowlby discovered attachment, any more than the Buddha discovered karma, she did give birth to an empirical, replicable, robust science that can track and follow the non-dual nature of love and of being.

Through her brilliance, what we can all see now is that attachment is not the study of the head or the heart, of intelligence or passion, of the body or the mind, of the self or the other. Walking us through the apparent two sides of a koan, or any life dilemma in which we found ourselves—*Should I take this job or that job? Should I live in the mountains or near the river? Should I stay here flapping my wings at the feeder or get out of Dodge? Am I a good mother or a bad mother? A good person or a bad person?*—Daido used to say, "It's not one side or the other. Nor is it both. Nor is it neither."

It's right now, right here, I say. Me writing. You reading. Two hearts beating.

part viii

retelling

After the Strange Situation we all went over to Levering Hall. Sylvia, Bob, Ellie and I although George did not accompany us. B sat in M's lap and took sips of iced tea from her glass and ate some peanut butter cookies that I bought at the counter for him. He was very sociable and became more and more active. He began to stand on M's lap, leaning over the table, almost crawling over the table, touching the sugar dispenser, smiling at Ellie and Sylvia. Now he looks at Bob and his mouth opens in a silent "hi." . . .

Now B is looking around, smiling at everybody and M seems very relaxed now and there is a cheerful atmosphere at the table.

—Mary Ainsworth, Case 18

chapter thirty-three

The photographs of my childhood are few. After all, I'm the last of three kids, born in the 1960s, long before photos proliferated like pollen on a spring day. But lately, my mom has been sending me what she has. I've seen most of them before, having studied them over the course of my life, and I realize now just how much these images have become the storyboard to the tale I have been telling myself, the concrete evidence that my life was a certain way—sad, lonely, rejected. Separate.

Stitched into my story, these photos had become an explanation for all manner of suffering that came later, cinematic flashbacks in the drama of my life. As in there I am in the living room on Garside Drive, one year old, standing on wobbly legs in a short dress, alone. There I am again, sitting on the lawn in a poncho, alone. A blurry close-up of my face against the brick wall of my cousin's house, smiling. Alone.

And then there are the group shots. There's me in our back-yard pool, making a silly face in a Snoopy bathing suit, standing next to the neighbor whose crowded garage made me feel funny. There's me and Matt and Sam lined up on the floor, the classic on-the-belly, chin-in-hands pose, where we siblings pass for cute and regular, as if there is love flowing between us.

And maybe there was.

In the past few years, since Azalea was born, I have come to doubt so many of my assumptions, so why not that one, too? The belief that the present is an artifact of the past, and that by looking closely at what *is* I can understand what *was*—maybe that's also flawed. Even though my brothers and I rarely talk to one another now, and I can't seem to recall much but outright rejection, I suppose it's possible that there is a thread of something that holds us together that I just can't see.

After all, there's the picture my mom sent Azalea a few years ago of Matt and me in the bathtub, huge smiles on our faces. I look like I'm two or three, and Matt must be four or five. And we're so happy! The caption reads, "Your mom and Uncle Matt sharing bath time at Grandma Rebecca's." When I saw that picture sticking out of the envelope with my mom's handwriting on it, it felt so off-script, I actually wanted to throw it away. But there's another one, too, taken a couple of years later, of my cousin Sara and me standing nude in the tub of our house, toothlessly grinning. Matt's blurred in the corner of the photo, also smiling, his curly hair falling into his eyes, and looking appropriately embarrassed.

And there's the group shot of the first batch of us cousins having lunch at our round white table in the dining room, sitting in the groovy seventies chairs. Smiling over us are my mom in a bikini and Aunt Brenda, looking glamorous in her striped cover-up. I'm mostly hidden, but my eyes peek out over my cousin Kendra, who is looking at her little sister Amy in a high chair. Kelly, her other sister, is also looking toward the baby. And there's Sam, looking, as my mom always said, "pretty," with his wavy blond hair and fine features. Matt, on the other side of the table, is also peering over his chair to watch the littlest among us eat with her fingers. He looks fascinated, and his eyes are laughing.

Today, I see the photos differently. I was never actually alone. On the other side of the camera, there was always a watchful eye framing me in the Kodak viewfinder. And connected to that eye was a person who was tracking my wanderings, my smiles, my efforts and frustrations, someone who probably thought I looked cute and made a choice to push the button, committing to that version of me forever. A person who was seeing something through the lens. Maybe even herself.

THESE DAYS MY mom fields all my questions over the phone or email about our homes, cars, outfits, meals, names of people, places, things. I ask her about my childhood—nap times, schedules, breastfeeding. Her answer is always the same—"Oh, honey, that was a long time ago"—until she thinks about it for a while and then emails me something like this:

> You had a nap every afternoon and slept about 10-12 hours at night. I took you for lots of walks in the stroller. I do recall sitting on the couch in our first house on Lincoln in Bay City. I was nursing Matt on my right breast, Sam was sitting beside me on my left side, and he very unexpectedly latched onto my left breast. I remember naturally being surprised, and I think gently disengaging him. Sam would have been between 2 and 1/2 and 3 years old, maybe that explains why he bit Matt when Matt was an infant. I recall explaining that Matt, being a baby, wasn't able to bite him back, so I did, just enough for Sam to feel it. It never happened again. Oh man, I probably did so much wrong!!

My mom is a truly excellent informant. And subject, too.

And, being a securely attached, autonomous adult, she values attachment. So when I asked her if she'd like to read this manuscript before it was published, she cleared her calendar and read it three times straight through. Then she called excitedly and said, "I get it! It's a love story—of you learning to love yourself."

When I asked Sam the same question, he said he'd love to. He and I chatted for a while, and I gave him a sense of what he would find. I told him about attachment, and the Strange Situation, and how the book is me telling the story of my life as I have understood it in the context of attachment, and how that story has changed. I warned him that there was a lot about feeling sad and rejected in our childhood, so that's what he could expect to find. I told him about his saying, "Hey, Beth, you're ugly," and we both knew that was just one harsh comment among many, made all the more painful because they were said in such a void of affection—no shared sense of sibling closeness or we-have-to-stick-togetherness. He cringed on the other side of the phone. "I really had issues," he said. "I was bullied in school, and I took it out on you."

"It's okay," I said. "You were a kid!"

"It was different for me," he said, admitting that our childhood was really pretty good for him. "But I was older," he added. "It's your story, anyway, and whatever you say, I'm sure I won't be offended."

As we were getting off the phone, I told him about how the book gets kind of "out there," and how I get all wrapped up in things like how the present contains the past, so we can change the past by understanding the present in new ways. He said, "Got it. So, like, the past is real, but not destiny."

Yes, I said. Just like that.

When I talked to Matt, he said he doesn't buy it. "The past is over," he said, declining my offer to read the book.

WHEN MY DAD died, I stood in the pine forest cemetery where Thayer and I would later decide to become parents and cried over an idea. I thought, *Now I'll never have a dad.* I was wrong. History can be rewritten. Through the tendrils of attention, climbing forward and backward through space and time, relationships, even with dead people, can change.

Azalea, as she's finishing one meal, asks about the next, and I laugh and tell her the story again of my dad and the time he checked his Thanksgiving leftovers on the plane so he could have a turkey sandwich over the weekend when he was traveling, and how he stood there and counted coolers—one for turkey, another for stuffing, a little one for gravy and cranberry sauce, of course. Every year, my dad's wife Kathy, my stepmother, comes for Thanksgiving, and the Wednesday before, we go to a restaurant for Trivia Night, which he no doubt would have dominated. Our team's name is Jeffy, which is what the ladies at the grocery store called my dad as they bagged his groceries during his sometimes twice-a-day visits. This year we won first place.

The other day in the car, Azalea said, "I'm so sad that Grandpa Jeff died before I got to meet him." Instead of telling her he's very much alive, I stay quiet—my best parenting trick these days—and let her change the subject when she's ready.

DAIDO DIED IN 2009, when Azalea was three. At the very end of his life, sick with cancer, he found Azalea a soothing presence and used to call us to ask if she could visit. One day I took her over and then stood back in the kitchen, watching as she approached him in his chair, with all the tubes snaking in and out, and the pills, and the hovering, doting students. She offered him a cookie, which he took and tried to eat. He asked someone to bring him his ink and brush. With Azalea sitting there at his feet, he made his very last piece of Zen art, a simple series of brushstrokes, a person sitting in zazen. He asked Azalea if she knew what it was. In her tiniest voice, she said, "No."

"It's a bodhisattva," he said, referring to a person whose understanding of one-thing-ness is so deep that they won't rest until each and every one of us is liberated from suffering.

"That's what you are."

IN THE SUTRA of the Whole-Body Relic Treasure Chest Seal, the Buddha says:

> If an evil man . . . falls into hell, he must suffer uninterruptedly, not knowing when release will come. However, if his descendants say his name and then recite this spiritual mantra . . . the molten copper and burning iron in hell will suddenly change into pond water with the eight virtues. This man will have a lotus flower supporting his feet and a jeweled canopy over his head. The door of hell will break and the Bodhi Way will open. His lotus flower will fly him to the Land of Ultimate Bliss. There, his knowledge of all knowledge will spontaneously unfold. Delighting . . .

Back and forth, from the past to the present, I speak my ancestors' names, and the names of all whom I love, releasing them from the story I have told about them and the story I've told about us. *Mom, Dad, Sam, and Matt. Mom, Dad, Sam, and Matt. Daido. Mary.*

Thayer.

Azalea.

And in so doing, I'm becoming free, too.

Untelling, retelling. In and out of burning hell, seeking this knowledge of all knowledge, I'm overcome with the jeweled bliss of spontaneously unfolding delight.

Which is to say we're all birds of a feather—flocking, fleeing, hurting, healing—together.

A wondrously strange situation.

epilogue

One spring morning when Thayer and I lived at the monastery, I was sitting in the zendo during dawn zazen—that beautiful time of darkness lifting—and I heard birds, first gently pecking at the silence with their back-and-forthing whistles and chirps, then growing louder into a sky-filling song. At the end of the thirty-minute period of stillness, when Thayer and I met for breakfast downstairs, I said, "Did you hear all those birds? What the heck? They were *loud*!" And he, younger in years but more experienced in the dharma, looked at me, smiled, and said, "So cool. Your mind is quieting."

Learning to speak the language of attachment has been like this. Nothing has changed; everything is new.

What I've discovered is that by turning the mind toward love, we love. And are loved. It's not that it works both ways; it's that there's only one way.

It's like watching the sun rise after a long night of darkness, loneliness, even despair, after maybe we have begun to make our own awkward—strange—peace with darkness. And then, with one silent twist of light, day breaks.

On the inside.

afterword

where angels fear to tread: attachment today

Despite the alarming incidence of neurosis in this world, full as it is of uncertain or conflicting information, parents—both Ganda and non-Ganda—by and large do well.

—Mary Ainsworth's final words of *Infancy in Uganda*

When I started writing this book in earnest in 2015, I signed up for a Google Scholar alert to keep me up to speed on all the latest attachment research being published. I was expecting to receive an alert every now and then, maybe once a month, and I imagined that I would be able to weave what I was learning into the book as I wrote it.

Instead, I receive two or three Google Scholar alerts per week, with three to ten significant studies included in each. Between the challenges of getting my story straight, not to mention Mary's, and the vast amount of research being published, I soon realized that I would need to incorporate the new scholarship into an afterword.

In this essay I will share some of the ways new research has been integrated into Ainsworth and Bowlby's original findings to paint an ever more thrilling and nuanced portrait of the power of human relationships to shape our lives. While this is hardly an exhaustive summary, my hope is to help us all see (and remember) that, as difficult and subtle and complex as it is to raise our children well and, as Mary says, "despite the alarming incidence of neurosis in this world"—my own absolutely included—we've got this.

But first a story.

Before archiving my in-box alerts, I take a peek at them and read the irresistible ones. For some of the years working on this book, I was also working as a researcher and so had access to academic journals and could download and read anything that came along. But during the past couple of years I've gone without access, so I've started writing to the scholars directly, telling them about my book project and requesting copies of their articles.

In January 2019, one title really caught my eye: "Attachment in Adulthood: Recent Developments, Emerging Debates, and Future Directions," by a professor at the University of Illinois, Dr. Chris Fraley. I had read articles by him before and knew he was a trustworthy attachment researcher, so I was eager to read his sweeping-sounding summary. I immediately wrote him at the email address included in the article. I gave him my spiel and included a link to the *New York* magazine article I wrote in 2016, the precursor to this book.

Professor Fraley wrote me right back, saying, "Hi, Bethany. I've attached a copy. The first paragraph or two will be a shocker!"

A shocker?!

My immediate thought was that he had discovered some fatal flaw in the AAI, and that Mary Main and all the scholars who followed in her footsteps had gotten it wrong. Maybe the

2009 article "The First 10,000 Adult Attachment Interviews," considered *the proof* that the AAI was a reliable measure, was found incomplete, or misunderstood, and the whole field was collapsing. That would be a real shocker. And a huge problem for my book, not to mention my life.

But instead I read these opening paragraphs:

> In a popular essay recently published in the *New York Magazine,* writer Bethany Saltman confronts several challenging questions at the interface of personality development, parenting, and relationships. Specifically, she describes the struggles that she has faced over the course of her life, including recurring self-doubts, ambivalent relationships with parents and various boyfriends in adolescence, and the uncertainties she experiences as a parent. One of Saltman's concerns is that the insecurities that she harbors about her past may adversely and indirectly influence the way she relates to her daughter and husband.
>
> Saltman turns to attachment theory—a well-known theory of human relationships and personality development—to come to terms with these issues.

A shocker, indeed! But a very happy one. What a pleasure to be included in the thinking of this prominent attachment scholar. How . . . *intimate.*

Professor Fraley continued:

> Although theories in psychology tend to come and go, attachment theory has been an unusual exception. Since its inception over half a century ago, the theory has been a rallying point for popular discourse on relationships, personality development, psychotherapy, and parenting. Not only has it shaped the way numerous people, including Bethany

Saltman, make sense of themselves and their relationships, it has inspired thousands of studies in subfields of psychology as diverse as developmental psychology, animal behavior, social and personality psychology, neuroscience, and clinical science. Indeed, in many respects, attachment theory has emerged as one of the leading theoretical frameworks for broadly understanding interpersonal functioning, relationships, and personality development in social and personality psychology.

I was flattered, of course, but, more important, I felt validated. My interest in attachment is not just some wacky hobbyhorse of mine, but a legitimate curiosity about what is at the heart of human development. It felt good to know I wasn't the only one who found attachment theory exceptional.

ADULT ATTACHMENT AND FROM WHENCE IT COMES

The article that introduced the Adult Attachment Interview to the world—"Security in Infancy, Childhood, and Adulthood: A Move to the Level of Representation"—was published by Mary Main, Nancy Kaplan, and Jude Cassidy in 1985. Two years later, the article "Romantic Love Conceptualized as an Attachment Process" was published by Cindy Hazan and Phillip Shaver. Where Ainsworth, Main, and most other attachment researchers up until that point were developmental psychologists, Shaver and Hazan are social psychologists, so their focus is more on how attachment affects social life than how it develops.

Shaver and Hazan's important 1987 article marks the beginning of the subfield of attachment based on "attachment styles," which can be measured with a self-assessment quiz-style questionnaire, as opposed to the AAI. Adult attachment styles is an enormous area in and of itself, so I will leave that for readers to explore on their own. But the gist is that the *attachment styles* work simply extends and makes accessible the classic *patterns of attachment* work of Ainsworth and Bowlby. For instance, Fraley writes that, while babies and children rely solely on parents and caregivers as a secure base, which is of course Ainsworth's central concept, "by the time they reach adulthood, many people organize their attachment behavior around peers (e.g., friends and romantic partners) rather than parents," and "research has shown that people become more likely to use their romantic partners as attachment figures as the relationship persists." In other words, what Bowlby called our internal working model becomes an attachment "style" that reveals itself as we grow up and become more intimate with the people in our lives, including friends, co-workers, lovers, and life partners.

And just as is the case with attachment itself, Fraley says it's important to note that "one of the implications of these [recent] longitudinal findings is that, although adult attachment styles may have their origins, in part, in early experiences, those early experiences do not completely determine whether people become secure or insecure as adults."

The question of determination is very interesting to me. Particularly, what creates stability over time? *Why* do approximately 75 percent of us pass on to our children our state of mind regarding attachment? Fraley cites Alan Sroufe in his article, reminding us that "early experiences should be construed not as determinants of development, but rather as setting the stage for optimal psychological functioning." Fraley writes that this idea—though clear from the beginning of work like Sroufe et al.'s forty-year longitudinal study of Missy and her camp friends—is "a major departure from the stereotypical [I would call it misinformed] portrayal of attachment research, which holds that early experiences fully determine adult interpersonal functioning." When it comes to human beings, there is nothing that "fully determines" anything. Even sensitive parenting, which is widely understood to be a good way to promote secure attachment patterns and styles, can't account for security entirely.

This lack of certain predictability regarding the transmission of attachment states of mind or styles from one generation to the next is such a "thing" among researchers that it has a name—the "transmission gap." In a 2016 article called "Narrowing the Transmission Gap," the authors write, "A test of caregiver sensitivity as the mechanism behind this intergenerational transmission showed an intriguing 'transmission gap.'" While this so-called transmission gap refers to the field's inability to pinpoint with 100 percent accuracy how attachment patterns persist and shift from one generation to the next, thus creating a "gap" in knowledge of the process, scholars are fairly certain about what is *not* a significant factor.

In the beginning of the article, itself a massive meta-analysis of adult attachment studies, the authors state that there is "little evidence [that] supports genetic transmission" of generational attachment, or that attachment is something in the genes. Though twin studies and the like have ruled out purely molecular adaptations resulting in patterns of attachment or attachment styles, I will explore later the exciting field of epigenetics, which shows how environmental/ecological factors can and absolutely do intersect to impact our psychosocial development, including attachment.

Likewise, though "everyone knows," as Mary put it, that temperament is real, and that different children will present different challenges to the work of being a sensitive parent, the idea that temperament is the primary driver of attachment "has not been persuasively supported." But of course, when it comes to human life, nothing is simple. One recent study found that post-adoption children with the most "negative affect" (i.e., the crankiest or most "difficult") were the *most* affected by an increase in parents' emotional availability. And another found that infants who scored low on the "negative reactivity" scale (the least cranky, "easy" babies) appeared *less* affected by parental sensitivity. Again, this all makes sense. Attachment is not a mathematical equation ruling that X amount of sensitivity will result in Y amount of delight, and thus a particular pattern or style of attachment security. But these many years of research do suggest a very clear direction in which we can move our relationships in order to establish a secure pattern, regardless of temperament. How does individual temperament play out *exactly*? As Brian Vaughn and Kelly Bost write, "Answering this question will be an important task for the attachment research community over the coming years."

To shed a little more light on this important question—How does temperament affect attachment?, which happens to be the question I get asked more than any other—let's return to Mary. As scholars R. M. Pasco Fearon and Jay Belsky put it, "Ainsworth never expressed the belief that the development of the relationship between infant and caregiver was determined entirely by the caregiver." In other words, it's not as if a baby is a tabula rasa upon which the adult will simply etch a secure relationship. At the same time, "recognizing the greater maturity and power of the adult, Ainsworth attributed disproportionate influence to the adult caregiver." Which is to say, the infant comes to its attachment relationship with its own set of circumstances, or what scholars have called "differential susceptibility," but even from a purely practical point of view, it's the adult who has the agency (maybe not entirely, but always more than an infant) to create the relationship. As Howard Steele put it so succinctly in an email to me, "Indeed, adults have needs and responsibilities. Infants have only needs."

Despite the challenge of the parent's task, even the most

"difficult" infant will benefit from sensitive parenting, though—
and this is important!—there are certainly limits to a parent's
power to affect a child under certain circumstances. Children
on the autism spectrum, for instance, have been found to be between 47 and 53 percent secure, not so far from the 65 percent
global average, which is impressive, considering that autism
spectrum condition (ASC) is "a lifelong neurodevelopmental
condition which, at its core, is characterized by *atypical social
communication* and restricted and repetitive behavior across
different contexts" (italics mine). While the "atypical social
communication" that defines ASC clearly does not prevent attachment from occurring, the more severe the case, the less
likely the child will be considered secure. And, most important,
a 2018 study found that there was a "theoretically expectable
link between parental sensitivity and infant security . . . in samples of children with ASC," but when the children are coded as
disorganized, most likely the more severe cases of ASC, "there is
no relationship between parental sensitivity and the child's attachment classification."

What does it all mean? It means that since inborn traits such
as temperament, DNA, and physiology—or, as the Buddha
would say, causes and conditions—are real, obviously, but not
considered *primary* determinants of attachment, attachment research is rightly concerned with environmental influences.

The article on the transmission gap I refer to above looked at
attachment in light of environmental risk factors such as parental stress, maternal depression, and domestic violence, as well as
whether or not the child was a parent's biological offspring. The
authors found some subtle effects occurring in each of these
populations, skewing the otherwise significant association of
adult attachment representations with child attachment patterns,
which should not come as a surprise. Rather than showing how
environmental conditions (our lives) interrupt generationally

transmitted patterns of attachment that are otherwise predetermined, I see this as more evidence of what Sroufe and his colleagues found with Missy and her friends—"change, as well as continuity, in individual development is coherent and lawful." When ruptures occur, life follows suit. These "risk factors"— e.g., violence in the home, parental emotional instability—are karmic seeds, after all, which by their nature grow in strength as they persist. The longer we live with ourselves, the more entrenched our "self" becomes. As Sroufe et al. write, "since the child adapts actively, and the personality is more formed and more complex at each point, individuals are increasingly forces in their own development."

Yes, our childhood affects us, *and* as adults we are increasingly responsible for forging our own paths, and those of our children. Because the forces at play are so complex, though still, according to Sroufe, coherent or predictable to *some* degree, it's not always clear why one parent with a dismissing AAI and even psychopathology can raise a secure child, or why a secure/autonomous adult's child might be anxiously attached. Yes, we are connected to our parents' state of mind in relation to attachment *and* we become increasingly powerful agents in our own path, but as my brother Sam put it so well, none of this is to be confused with destiny.

The transmission gap persists. The authors of the 2016 meta-analysis end their article by saying, "Future studies should focus on the identification of underlying mechanisms that may explain discontinuity."

WITH THAT SAID—we don't always know precisely *why* attachment develops as it does over the course of each individual life—the research on adult attachment styles and developmental patterns adds color and dimension to the story of *how* one's internal working model works. Fraley's 2019 article discusses how attachment styles are—as Bowlby and Ainsworth said—differentiated and hierarchical. Not all attachment relationships are created equal, because our attachment relationships are exactly that: *relationship*-based and not something we carry with us and overlay onto every single interaction with everyone equally. Over our lifetimes, we develop internal "global representations of attachment," based on our earliest experiences. We also come to hold expectations "specific to certain relational categories (e.g., parental relationships, peer relationships) and, within that category, even more specific relationships (e.g., those pertaining to a specific individual)."

In other words, there may be a difference in the ways we relate to co-workers and romantic partners and family members, though "there should be some degree of coherence among them. In fact, people who are insecure in general are more likely than those who are secure in general to be insecure in specific relational contexts." And this is the case with me. While I may well have been more secure with my mother than I realized, and I feel fairly competent in my most intimate relationships, I get caught off guard by how dysregulated I can get in friendships (though they are generally plentiful and deeply satisfying), which is certainly due to my early years of painful insecurity in the friend department.

One of Fraley's discussions about hierarchical attachment that I think is especially compelling regards "consensual non-monogamy," or CNM, "defined as a relationship arrangement in which all partners involved agree to have more than one romantic or sexual relationship at the same time." While this type of relationship is not of particular interest to me (I think my days with Charles made me deeply appreciate the stability I have with Thayer!), I know this is something on people's minds. CNM can include polyamory—which involves more than one life partner at one time—open relationships, and swinging. CNM "appears to be common: Approximately one in five [single] US individuals have engaged in a CNM relationship at some point during their lifetime." As if that weren't surprising enough, "moreover, according to Conley et al., up to 5% of people in relationships report current involvement in one or more of these CNM relationships." CNM relationships present a real conundrum for attachment theory, insofar as we assume that the same kind of exclusive hierarchy—what Bowlby called monotropy—is optimal for adults.

Monotropy is the widely accepted idea underlying attachment theory that, while the young child can and may well benefit from many important relationships (and this includes good-quality daycare), when it comes to getting the benefits of attachment security, or when a baby is in what Ainsworth called "a crunch"—illness, discomfort, fear, anything that causes distress—there's no substitute for that *one* special other, who, by the way, does not (and this is big) have to be a biological parent. Infants and children form attachments with parents (male, female, hetero, gay, lesbian, or trans), grandparents, and foster or adopted parents. I will explore monotropy as it relates to fathers specifically in more detail below.

The findings about CNM have presented a bit of a puzzle, which yields a wonderful solution: In a sample of 1,281 adults, those with "favorable attitudes" toward CNM were found to be relatively avoidant in their adult attachment styles, but those who are actually in such relationships are relatively secure. Fascinating! In addition to a sampling bias that might explain some of this paradox (some participants were found in online CNM communities), another possibility comes from the heart of attachment theory: "Given the stigma against CNM arrangements, those who are relatively secure may be most comfortable going against the prevailing social norms."

I love that. Attachment security helps us fight all kinds of power, including entrenched narratives about who and how we should love.

ANOTHER FASCINATING SPIN on attachment outlined by Fraley is related to the very basis of our attachment system, which of course is evolution. As he explains, "when Bowlby was writing about the evolutionary function of attachment in infancy, he proposed that attachment behaviors, such as calling out to and searching for a missing attachment figure, were adaptive. Specifically, he argued that such behaviors facilitated proximity between an infant and its attachment figure, thereby decreasing the chances that the child will be preyed upon, abused, or left behind." And so it would make sense that a secure attachment—one that leads to more effective secure-base back-and-forthing—is evolutionarily advantageous. What some researchers have been asking is this: Why, then, are so many of us insecure? What a great question!

One potential answer that I find particularly useful comes from what's called social defense theory (SDT). SDT assumes that our evolution is influenced not just by our individual needs (for security, among other things) but by the need to protect one's tribe or group. "Highly anxious people, for example, tend to be vigilant to threats, allowing them to more quickly detect environmental signs of danger. Although this comes with a potential psychological cost (e.g., greater anxiety and depression), when these threats are accurately detected and communicated to the group, they can facilitate group survival." Great news for anxiety; it's not for naught!

Likewise, "Highly avoidant people, in contrast, tend to be more self-reliant. Thus, when faced with an environmental danger, they will likely focus on self-protection. In some cases, this may involve eliminating the threat (e.g., putting out a fire), and in others, it may involve identifying an appropriate escape route that others can then also use. Researchers Ein-Dor & Hirschberger refer to this as a rapid fight-or-flight response, and it has the potential to benefit not only the self, but also others." Avoidant people see other people as a threat, which is not a very satisfying way of being in a relationship, but having such an inbuilt rapid response can come in handy for firefighters and other first responders.

This wonderful twist on how attachment insecurity has a role to play in the tribe is particularly resonant with recent research in companies and organizations showing just how much more effective diverse teams are. As Professor Fraley writes, "According to SDT, groups that are more diverse with respect to the attachment patterns of the individuals of which they are composed are more likely to be resilient to environmental threats than those that are more homogenous with respect to attachment." In other words, it's certainly more than diversity of race and gender that creates a truly powerful team effort. We might include a variety of education types, temperament (introvert or extrovert), and attachment style.

Finally, Fraley concludes his article by pointing to a relatively new area of adult attachment, which one researcher has named "thriving through relationships." He writes, "Attachment theorists emphasize that, when people feel stressed, scared, or uncertain, they turn to their attachment figures for safe haven functions: support, comfort, and assistance . . . Relationships serve to support thriving in the face of adversity not only by buffering people from the negative effects of stress, but also by helping people to emerge stronger from the process."

While the idea of our attachments being good for us is nothing new, the research into adult attachment via the AAI, as well as vis-à-vis "attachment styles," is adding depth and detail to this certain truth. Security in childhood doesn't just protect us from potential harm, but gives us a step up in making the best of whatever we're faced with, including our own demons.

SOME OTHER OBJECT: FATHERS AND ATTACHMENT

As I stated in an endnote to an early chapter of the book, since women were considered children's primary caregivers when Bowlby and Ainsworth began their work (though it's worth noting that two of the three women in my story—both Ainsworth and my mom—report having warmer feelings toward their fathers than their mothers), attachment theory came into being with mothers in mind.

In this section I will share some of the research about fathers and attachment. But first allow me to build the case that, regardless of our own conditions—say I'm a dad with little caregiving experience who wants to be more sensitive, but I don't know how, especially considering my own childhood, not to mention cultural messages about how incompetent and unnecessary fathers are—attachment security is available. *The secure autonomous adult values attachment.* All we have to do is turn toward attachment. And I'll get to the more specific studies about fathers shortly.

The fact is, as early as Uganda, Ainsworth made mention of children who were attached to their fathers, as well as to other caregivers, including aunts and sisters. Sarah Hrdy, a well-known primatologist, writes that it was Mary who influenced Bowlby to broaden his attachment-figure horizons:

> Bowlby assumed that the mother was the primary, typically exclusive, caretaker . . . [Later,] Bowlby (influenced by Ainsworth and others) mentioned the possibility of multiple caretakers, but he nevertheless continued to center his model

on a Victorian division of labor within a pair bond where a sexually monandrous mother nurtured offspring provisioned by their father.

Bowlby's Victorian ways run through his description of monotropy, which, as promised, I will describe, as it's key to understanding the way fathers have been understood in the history of attachment theory. I'll quote from Bowlby's revolutionary 1958 paper—the same one that introduced the concept of social releasers—as he waxes poetic and loyal to the maternal queen and her rather unglamorous substitutes—a bottle, a rag. A baby tender? A father?

Although I have described these five responses [attachment behaviors] as mother-oriented, it is evident that at first this is so only potentially. From what we know of other species it seems probable that each one of them has the potential to become focused on *some other object* [italics mine]. The clearest examples of this in real life are where sucking becomes directed towards a bottle and not to the mother's breast, and clinging is directed to a rag and not to the mother's body . . . No matter for what reason he is crying—cold, hunger, fear, or plain loneliness—his crying is usually terminated through the agency of the mother. Again, when he wants to cling or follow or to find a haven of safety when he is frightened, she is the figure who commonly provides the needed object. It is for this reason that the mother becomes so central a figure in the infant's life. For in healthy development it is towards her that each of the several responses becomes directed, much as each of the subjects of the realm comes to direct his loyalty towards the Queen; and it is in relation to the mother that the several responses become integrated into the complex behaviour which I have termed "attachment behaviour," much as it is in relation to the Sovereign that the components of our constitution become integrated into a working whole . . .

Good mothering from any kind woman ceases to satisfy him—only his own mother will do . . .

Naturally such a general statement needs amplification and qualification, but the tendency for instinctual responses to be directed towards a particular individual or group of individuals and not promiscuously towards many is one which I believe to be so important and so neglected that it deserves a special term. I propose to call it "monotropy."

At the heart of this quaint, culturally specific, and pretty outrageous description is a concept central to attachment. To update the language: Good *caretaking* from any kind *person* ceases to satisfy *the infant*—only his own *primary caregiver* will do. This is that mutual delight between the baby and her special other that Ainsworth first saw in Uganda—so intrinsic to patterns of security, and developed only through intimate contact.

At first blush, this notion sounds like a prison sentence for parents, especially mothers, à la Dr. Sears. However, this idea that nobody else "will do" doesn't mean that we shouldn't enlist the help of others; it's just to say that we do get attached to one person and come to depend upon contact with him or her, as Mary made clear with Theresa and M in Case 18. This is what Kabat-Zinn was telling me when he reminded me that Azalea didn't ask to be born. All we have to do is stay connected.

But that's a lot, I said.

And it is.

At the same time, since Bowlby's first formulation, recent studies on a variety of relationship types have been instrumental in showing just how flexible monotropy is. Over time, children—even those who have been exposed to painfully insensitive parenting, neglect, and abuse—can and absolutely do form secure attachments with new special others. The best pathway for raising a child with a secure attachment is simply to provide him or her with a sensitive caregiver. And remember, as Mary found early on and as thousands of studies since have affirmed and validated, this sensitivity is a state of mind that can *always* be accessed by anyone—regardless of wealth, race, ethnicity, sexuality, or how much time our kids spend in daycare.

Attachment security is a state of mind.

Mary Main has a phrase that I love and think about all the time: "attentional flexibility." This is the term she uses to describe the ability of the infant in the Strange Situation to move her attention from the parent to her toys, and back again, as her attachment system is aroused and soothed by her caregiver's presence. An avoidant baby can't as readily move between parent and separation, sticking to toys even when afraid or uncomfortable in the episodes of separation, instead of going to the door and wailing as many secure babies do. It's as if, as early as one year old, the avoidant baby has a plan for how to deal with her disappointment—and she's sticking to it. The resistant baby chaotically moves back and forth without ever settling. The attachment relationship isn't doing its job of bringing the baby back to homeostasis.

Likewise, Main found that the adult in the AAI expresses this same quality of attentional flexibility in the ability to move back and forth (or not) between describing experiences (what happened) and evaluating those experiences from the present state of mind—two different types of cognitive tasks. The resonance between what the adult reports as having happened and the way those events are evaluated indicates the adult's state of mind in relation to attachment. Is there a fluid back-and-forth that makes sense, that is clear and concise and relatively supported by a reasonable level of detail? Not so much as to overwhelm and get the adult mired, and not so little as to not reveal anything significant? Is he or she (or they) an "excellent informant"? Or is the person's attention stuck somewhere like a branch in the river of life, to use the metaphor I read the first time I picked up Joko Beck's book *Nothing Special* in the Barnes & Noble? This lack of flexibility gets in the way of manifesting our life's function, whatever that may be.

Attentional flexibility is a way of understanding Missy's ability to manage herself in the Play-Doh-cookie-sharing incident. She was obviously upset, so she took herself away from the action and then, once she'd settled herself, was able to return. This aspect of experience is called "emotional regulation." The capacity to self-regulate is strongly associated with attachment security, and it is *the thing,* in my opinion—the holy grail of human experience. Why? Because being able to regulate our emotions and physiological responses allows us to be present—in the moment—which, after all, from a Buddhist point of view, is where life really happens.

The popular Buddhist teacher Pema Chödrön writes, "To the degree that we're willing to see our enmeshment or grasping and our repressing [our avoidance and preoccupation] clearly, they begin to wear themselves out . . . That's what we're doing in meditation: Up come all these thoughts, but rather than squelch them or obsess about them [because we have attentional flexibility and we don't get stuck], we acknowledge them and let them fade." It's not surprising that many studies have found a direct correlation between mindfulness and attachment security, and that the capacity to self-regulate is considered *the* mediating factor connecting those dots.

Which is why it seems to me that if we want our children to take full advantage of the lives we work so hard to offer them, a good way to do that is to help them build the type of mind that can take it all in.

And how do we do *that*?

Regardless of who we are, or our bio-or-otherwise connection to the child we hope to raise well, we nurture secure children by becoming secure in ourselves, by becoming more supple and receptive and flexible in our own minds. As I've shared here, through work like the Steeles' and Bob Marvin's, it's never too late, even for parents whose own upbringing was far from ideal.

One powerful example of attachment training, if you will, is from the Minding the Baby program out of the Yale Child Study Center, directed by Professor Arietta Slade. This intervention has been found to help parents (in this case mothers) be more sensitive by increasing their reflective functioning (RF), which is very much like mentalization and—readers may recall—is what my mother scored so highly on in her AAI. Slade and her fellow authors define RF as "the ability to imagine or envision the baby's thoughts and feelings, as well as to understand the child's behavior as a function of underlying subjective experience." As Mary put it, the sensitive parent is able "to see things from B's point of view."

The nurses and social workers foster RF in a variety of ways. While providing basic concrete support for physical and social well-being, they also support the developing relationship between mother and baby by offering the mother therapy to work through her own history, by helping the mother "scaffold" (i.e., build) a sensitive relationship with her baby, and by fostering a trusting relationship—which can take time—with the mother herself. "MTB is a relationship-based program, meaning that the delivery of the intervention depends upon the quality of the relationship home visitors establish with mothers and their families." The authors refer to this approach as "psychotherapy in the kitchen," which is not unlike what Mary was doing in Baltimore with mothers like the one in Case 18. When a parent feels loved, he or she is in a much better position to love.

Based on what we know from a number of assessment instruments, including, of course, the Strange Situation, it should come as no surprise that an influx of relationship valuing would increase attachment security for the mother-child dyads being studied. When the mother's guard goes down, she is more sensitive to herself and her baby. "Results indicate that MTB mothers' levels of reflective functioning was [sic] more likely to increase over the course of the intervention than were those of control group mothers. Likewise, infants in the MTB group were significantly more likely to be securely attached, and significantly less likely to be disorganized, than infants in the control group."

The importance of this work and other programs like it lies not in the gender of the parent but in the indisputable power of loving attention to shift a parent's mind of attachment. By simply becoming aware of attachment (as is certainly happening if you've read this far!), we're moving in the right direction, because, again, the securely autonomous adult simply *values attachment* more than external achievement, or appearances—in fact, more than anything at all. Noticing all the ways we don't value our relationships—whether we're moms or dads—helps, too.

BACK TO DADS. Because of the prevalence of mothers as primary caregivers, fathers have unfortunately been most often discussed in attachment research as part of a group of "other" attachment figures and all things not-mother, including bottles, rags, and babysitters. The fact that as late as 2014, journalist Paul Raeburn wrote a book called *Do Fathers Matter? What Science Is Telling Us About the Parent We've Overlooked* says it all. Spoiler alert: Yes. Fathers matter.

I'll return to fathers with a wonderful footnote from Mary Main's loving tribute to her mentor, offering proof of how Ainsworth didn't discriminate in her expectations of parents.

As an aside I remark here that although her ability to set the Ganda mothers of insecure infants in context underscores her general attempt towards understanding the parent's own difficulties, she did not always do this, and in the moment could be impatient with parental insensitivity. Watching a videotape I showed her of one father who looked straight ahead in apparent disinterest as his terrified baby crawled under an empty chair to cry, for example, she asked no deep questions regarding the father's own troubles, but rather leaned forward towards the video monitor, and bellowed, "Do something, you big boob!"

Though, generally speaking, Mary took great pains to appreciate what parents were going through in their own lives, she could be just as frustrated by an insensitive father as an unattuned mother. And coming from Mary, that's a show of respect.

One of the most important voices in the role of fathers in child development, and attachment specifically, is Michael Lamb, a British man who traveled to Baltimore to work with Mary Ainsworth as a master's-level student at Johns Hopkins in 1973–74.

In one epistolary exchange between Lamb and Ainsworth from 1974, the by-then-ex-student has requested feedback on his research on fathers in the Strange Situation, which he believed showed that babies exhibited no preference for mothers *or* fathers. In the letter he received in response, Mary responds not so much to his results as to his process, giving the young scholar a bit of a lashing for being impetuous and careless. She takes him to task for lacking nuance in his reading of both Bowlby and her, being dead wrong about things she has written, as well in the way he interprets his own data. However, being a secure/ autonomous who always values attachment, Ainsworth ends her seven-page typed, single-spaced takedown by saying, "Forgive the avuncular (or perhaps it is maternal) tone of all of this . . . With my very best wishes to you and Jamie [presumably Lamb's partner at the time]."

Ainsworth's beefs with Lamb's paper are of course deeply personal. And yet, her critique is significant in that it offers a clear explanation of her understanding of the role of fathers, a position that—almost fifty years and tens of thousands of studies later—still holds true, not just for the role of fathers in attachment, but about critiques of attachment theory on the whole. This letter could be sent to many a critic today.

> The introduction rubbed me the wrong way. It seemed to me belligerent and contentious. It gives the impression that you are wholly critical of attachment theory and attachment research to date, whereas I know full well that you intend only to take issue with specific points in attachment theory that you either feel have been erroneous (or perhaps overstated) while at the same time you are generally working with the same framework.

> If you read Bowlby really carefully it should prove a salutary lesson—as indeed it has to me. You should note . . . that he tends to be modest, hypothetical, reasoned, and tentative in most of his statements and arguments . . .

> I think you have overstated the "claim" for fathers. I think your findings speak for themselves. I don't think you have to denigrate people who have (often for purely practical reasons) focused on mothers in order to point out that fathers have been neglected. Often an understatement is more effective than an overstatement . . .

Now the next thing I would like to discuss is the notion of "monotropy," which you correctly interpret as the notion that it implies that one figure usually the mother is the principal (and/or primary) attachment figure, rather than that this figure is the sole attachment figure . . . Time and time again in clinical studies one runs across evidence that in the "crunch" one attachment figure (nearly always the mother figure) is the figure the child most wants . . .

Personally, as a daughter who found her father more nurturant (as well as more interesting to interact with) than her mother, I can acknowledge that in some cases it might be the father rather than the mother who is wanted even in a "crunch." But evidence to date, even though of an anecdotal sort, suggests that for most babies and young children it is the mother—not because she is the natural mother, but because she has been the principal caregiver . . .

If you read *Infancy in Uganda* carefully, you will see that I certainly drew attention to babies' attachment to fathers. I expressed amazement that fathers, who having been absent for months, could return home and so quickly establish an attachment relationship . . .

Now let us suppose! Suppose that a baby had no principal caregiver—no mother figure. Could a father, returning home after a long absence, establish within a few days an attachment relationship that was the *first* that a baby had experienced? I don't really know the answer to that. However, my hypothesis is that a baby first establishes an attachment relationship with the figure with whom he has the most and the most satisfactory interaction.

After several pages of line-by-line, very concrete critique, Mary writes:

Finally, please don't think I am knocking this research project, or that I am opposing research on fathers. Research on fathers is long overdue, and I have freely said so over the years.

And then she can't help herself:

Incidentally, you skipped a step if you want to do naturalistic research. You insisted that both parents be present the whole time, and of course that is one way of getting at it differentially. But, strictly speaking you should visit at all kinds of times when father is home, and tell the family to go about their usual way of doing things.

Michael Lamb went on to become a celebrated scholar and important advocate for children and families, moving the dial on fathers in deep and subtle ways; I'm sure Mary would approve. Thanks to Lamb, now a professor of psychology at Cambridge University, today research on fathers demonstrates that, in addition to the primary caregiving/attachment figure role of fathers in some families, dads have a significant role to play in children's lives—and indeed, much attention has been given to play itself. While mothers often put in more playtime with babies in absolute terms (because of the higher "total amount of care" they put in, as Mary expressed it) "particularly boisterous, stimulating, emotionally arousing play" between fathers and children is thought to "increase fathers' influence more than would be expected based on the amount of time they spend with their children."

In the first chapter of the fifth edition of Lamb's anthology *The Role of the Father in Child Development,* he writes, "First, fathers and mothers seem to influence their children in similar rather than dissimilar ways. Contrary to the expectations of many developmental psychologists, the differences between mothers and fathers appear much less important than the similarities." As should be expected, "parental warmth, nurturance, and closeness are associated with positive child outcomes regardless of whether the parent involved is a mother or father. The important dimensions of parental influence are those that have to do with parental characteristics rather than gender-related characteristics." With that said, Lamb states the heart of the matter, the ultimate Ainsworthian takeaway: "The characteristics of individual fathers—such as their masculinity, intellect, and even their warmth—are much less important, formatively speaking, than are the characteristics of the *relationships* that they have established with their children" [italics mine].

As far as actual studies of attachment and the Strange Situation with fathers are concerned, one meta-analysis of the research indicates that the link between quality of paternal care and attachment security, "though robust, is clearly smaller than that generally found for mothers," but the source of this disparity is unclear. Some have suggested that because of the way the Strange Situation is set up, it favors a certain type of care, one that privileges maternal comfort over paternal activation. An alternative procedure was even developed: the Risky Situation, by researchers Daniel Paquette and Marc Bigras. They found:

> By having the same parent–child dyads participate in the Strange Situation (SS) and in the RS, researchers were able to demonstrate that the RS appears to evoke specific relationship patterns. Moreover, parental stimulation of risk-taking, the central construct of the RS, was shown to play a significant role after controlling for child characteristics (sex and temperament). These results suggested that the RS has the potential to make a significant contribution to the study of the human relationship.

Other recent studies delving into the specifics of how fathers and children develop their attachments have shown that, for instance, fathers' pathways to attachment security—play and caregiving—were mitigated by something as simple as whether or not it was a weekend or a workday. And another tracked the testosterone (T) in fathers in the Strange Situation. The researchers found that, while men's T did decline more when their children were distressed in the Strange Situation than when faced with a "teaching task," which suggests that T is linked with caretaking, this physiological response occurred within a host of other factors, such as the father's empathy score, his marital feelings, and his infant's reactivity. The authors also found that "fathers of daughters were more sensitively engaged than fathers of sons, consistent with previous research comparing fathers' sensitivity during interactions with toddler girls and boys."

What a tangled web of biological interdependence we weave.

And while the research on attachment has not yet ventured into the variety of family constellations people create today—two fathers, two mothers, an extended mix of bio and adopted parents—study after study assessing the outcomes of children raised in gay and lesbian families have come to the same conclusion: these children are thriving, sometimes even more than children from hetero families. So even though we don't have the attachment studies to prove it, I think it's fair to extrapolate that sexuality and family structure are in no way factors in attachment.

The same goes for the cross-cultural assessment of attachment. While different cultures skew differently in terms of the patterns that are likely to appear (for instance, in some African cultures, the avoidant patterns appear to be nonexistent), and attachment behaviors themselves are context-specific (for instance, babies and parents in Uganda don't kiss like Westerners do), the verdict is indeed in: attachment is real, and it is influenced by sensitive parenting, which occurs within an infinitely complex web of culturally specific causes and conditions.

What's more, attachment patterns in individuals have been found to affect our conditions, for instance, our health, the onset of puberty, and our brains—big-time. This line of ever-refining is still a matter of exploring the ways our environment (how we were raised, aka "nurture") affects the individual's body and mind (our nature). The recent documentary *Three Identical Strangers* brilliantly explored this question through the harrowing story of identical triplets separated at birth by asking us to choose a side: Why were these triplets who spent their lives apart so much alike? Was it a matter of nature or nurture? In the end, we see that in some important ways they weren't so much alike after all, and we were asking the wrong question all along.

Interestingly, this film draws our attention to the importance of a child's relationships with his or her parents in their development. Though the filmmakers don't use the word "attachment," we can understand it that way; I certainly did! And, even better, the focus in this film was on the relationship between three sons and their adoptive fathers. The mothers were in the background.

NATURE/NURTURE IS NOT A THING: ATTACHMENT AND EPIGENETICS

Some of the most stunning research to come out of the twenty-first century has been in the field of epigenetics, the study of the role the environment plays on our genes. Even the most basic reading of epigenetics reveals the fact that nature and nurture are, in fact, *not* two distinct forces but instead always intersecting. Epigenetics helps us understand attachment ever more deeply.

When Dr. Nadine Burke Harris finished her residency in pediatrics at the University of California, Davis, she wanted to work somewhere where she could really feel like she was making a difference. So when, in 2007, she was recruited by the California Pacific Medical Center to create a clinic in a "high risk" area of San Francisco, a neighborhood called Bayview–Hunter's Point, she was thrilled. In her book *The Deepest Well: Healing the Long-Term Effects of Childhood Adversity,* she writes about how, as soon as she started her work there, she began to see that "something medical was happening with my patients that I couldn't quite understand."

It started with the proliferation of diagnoses of ADHD and asthma, which at first appeared to be pretty typical childhood ailments, but were appearing in large numbers. But it wasn't long before "day after day I saw infants who were listless and had strange rashes. I saw kindergartners whose hair was falling out . . . Kids just entering middle school had depression." And in some cases, as with her young seven-year-old patient Diego, kids had stopped growing. When Diego's mom brought him to Dr. Burke Harris, he had asthma and eczema, was suspected of having ADHD, and was in the fiftieth percentile of height—among four-year-olds.

Burke Harris was struck by the sheer number of serious health concerns her young patients faced, and, at the same time, the violence and harshness they were exposed to. When Burke Harris asked one of her young patients' mothers if she had noticed any triggers for her asthma (pet dander and cockroaches being the usual suspects), her mother answered, "Well, her asthma does seem to get worse whenever her dad punches a hole in the wall." And this young girl was not alone.

Burke Harris's young patients were dealing with a litany of traumas—"parental incarcerations, multiple foster-care placements, suspected physical abuse, documented abuse, and family legacies of mental illness and substance abuse." Diego, the boy who inspired her book, had been sexually abused when he was four—the same year he stopped growing—a terrible event for the whole family that led to a cascade of unfortunate responses, including his father's guilty feelings and subsequent abuse of alcohol. Burke Harris writes, "For a long time the possibility of an actual biological link between childhood adversity and damaged health came to me as a question that lingered for only a moment before it was gone." But then she learned about the ACE study.

ACE is an acronym developed by a team from the Kaiser Permanente group in Southern California. It stands for adverse childhood event. The way an ACE score is tabulated is simple: Ask yourself these questions, on behalf of yourself or your child, and for each yes, you get one point. The total number of yeses is your ACE score.

Prior to your 18th birthday:

1. Did a parent or other adult in the household often or very often . . . swear at you, insult you, put you down, or humiliate you? Or act in a way that made you afraid that you might be physically hurt?
2. Did a parent or other adult in the household often or very often . . . push, grab, slap, or throw something at you? Or ever hit you so hard that you had marks or were injured?
3. Did an adult or person at least 5 years older than you ever . . . touch or fondle you or have you touch their body in a sexual way? Or attempt or actually have oral, anal, or vaginal intercourse with you?
4. Did you often or very often feel that . . . no one in your family loved you or thought you were important or special? Or your family didn't look out for

each other, feel close to each other, or support each other?

5. Did you often or very often feel that . . . you didn't have enough to eat, had to wear dirty clothes, and had no one to protect you? Or your parents were too drunk or high to take care of you or take you to the doctor if you needed it?

6. Were your parents ever separated or divorced?

7. Was your mother or stepmother often or very often pushed, grabbed, slapped, or had something thrown at her? Or sometimes, often, or very often kicked, bitten, hit with a fist, or hit with something hard? Or ever repeatedly hit over at least a few minutes or threatened with a gun or knife?

8. Did you live with anyone who was a problem drinker or alcoholic, or who used street drugs?

9. Was a household member depressed or mentally ill, or did a household member attempt suicide?

10. Did a household member go to prison?

One day, the psychotherapist who worked on Burke Harris's cases with her showed her a well-known 1998 article called "Relationship of Childhood Abuse and Household Dysfunction to Many of the Leading Causes of Death in Adults: The Adverse Childhood Experiences (ACE) Study." Burke Harris writes, "Before he could even shut the door I was halfway through the abstract. I was only partway through the first page when I experienced a jolt of recognition. Here it was. The final puzzle piece . . ."

Before becoming a physician, Burke Harris earned a degree in public health. She talks about one of the parables in that field, taken from the nineteenth-century cholera epidemic, which was finally traced to a well. This was long before we knew about the presence of germs. For her, the point she took from the story was this: "If one hundred people all drink from the same well and ninety-eight of them develop diarrhea, I can write prescription after prescription for antibiotics, or I can stop and ask, 'What the hell is in that well?'"

In the case of these terrible symptoms appearing in so many of her traumatized families, she started to wonder: What was in the "deepest well"?

What the ACE study found was that, first of all, ACEs are incredibly common. The authors surveyed more than seventeen thousand people—30 percent were people of color, and 70 percent were college-educated. In this population, 67 percent had scored one ACE, and 12.6 percent had four or more. Even more remarkable, the authors found that the higher one's ACE count, the worse his or her health will be. Specifically, "the more ACEs a child is exposed to, the higher the risk of developing chronic illnesses. In children, exposure to ACEs can increase likelihood of chronic diseases such as asthma. In adults, exposure to ACEs dramatically increases the likelihood of 7 out of 10 leading adult causes of death including heart disease and cancer." What she was seeing in her exam room was making sense. She came to believe that the underlying condition of many of her patients, including Diego, the toxin to which so many were being exposed, was adversity. They were drinking what is now known as "toxic stress" from the well.

As Burke Harris continued her work with patients, reading, studying, trying to understand everything she could about the way toxic stress was affecting the kids in her practice, she began to notice how common intergenerational toxicity was among her families. A depressed mother gave birth to a child who soon got diagnosed with "failure to thrive," a medical term that describes the forlorn infants left in orphanages—sad, withdrawn, not growing. ACEs galore. A great-grandmother brought in her granddaughter's child. His mother was in jail, many in the family struggled with substance abuse, and now the boy, named Tiny, was in trouble at school, acting out.

Burke Harris asked herself, "How is it that ACEs are handed down so reliably from generation to generation? For many families, it seemed that toxic stress was more consistently transmitted from parent to child than any genetic disease I had seen."

Burke Harris, in her ruminations, stumbled upon another study that helped her understand what she calls "multigenerational ACEs," but the study speaks to multigenerational love, too.

And delight.

FROM THE 1950S, when rat studies became popular among behaviorists like Skinner, researchers noticed that rats that were handled by humans for as little as five to fifteen minutes per day in the first three weeks of life became calmer, less reactive adult rats. While this was often considered the result of simply being touched by the human researchers, a young neurobiologist named Michael Meaney found that something else was at play. All that human handling rattled the little rat pups so much that it encouraged the mother rats to lick and groom their babies more, and "to engage more often in a behavior called arched-back nursing, in which the mother gives the pups extra room to suckle against her underside."

This human interference was like a Strange Situation for rats, stressing the little pups just enough to see what would happen.

What happened was that Dr. Meaney noticed that not all rat moms' grooming repertoires were the same—some licked more and some licked less; among rat-soothing relationships there are, just as in human attachment relationships, "individual differences." It should come as no surprise that the high-licking moms had more relaxed pups. And low-licking moms had more stressed-out pups. But that's not all.

Meaney and his colleague found that the grooming the mothers did in the pups' first ten days of life predicted what the babies' stress response would be throughout life, and beyond, into the next generation. High-licker female rats *gave birth* to high-licker females, who were then high lickers with their own pups. The degree to which one gave her babies affection became part of the rats' physiological makeup.

A pattern was emerging. The rat pups' parents' behavior—the pups' environment, their nurturing—was affecting their very nature.

In order to make sure it was the actual behavior of the parents that *became* part of the genetic code, and not something permanently inborn, Meaney switched pups at birth and had them raised by a different kind of licker, and lo and behold, pups conformed to the kind of care they received from their foster parents, even carrying their newly taught high- or low-licking responses to their pups when they had them.

IN A 2019 editorial called "Healthy Parenting in the Age of the Genome: Nature or Nurture?" Saoud Sultan explains that environment does not change DNA; rather, "epigenetics refers to the role of environmental factors on gene activation or silencing, without changing the DNA nucleotide sequence." He adds, "Maternal behavior is also considered to be transmitted in this manner across generations."

How does this happen? Through a complex interplay of our environment and our bodies:

Studies in both animals and humans have shown that the quality of parenting is affected in mothers who had received poor care during childhood. Hormones play a significant role in maternal behavior. However, for example, levels of oxytocin, which stimulates and maintains maternal behavior, have been found to be lower in mothers with insecure attachment after interaction with their infants than mothers with secure attachment. In addition, adverse parenting received during the early years of life negatively influences women's brain morphology, such as the hippocampus, as well as maternal brain activations to child stimuli, such as in the hippocampus, nigrostriatal pathways and insula.

While wise scientists (and writers about science) usually resist the urge to make connections between, say, rats and people, animal studies can serve as windows into an aspect of our own behavior, if not exact replicas. As Swiss scientist Marialuigia Spinelli wrote in 2017, "Intriguingly the results of Mean[e]y's [rat] experiment appear very similar to John Bowlby's ethological theory of attachment." She goes on to describe the social-releasing, back-and-forth process of a sensitive caregiver attuning to an infant's signals as "the basis on which the child develops . . . a set of [attachment] behaviors that help keep the caregiver nearby in order to be protected and supported while exploring the environment." In other words, the co-regulation that happens between baby and caregiver is like the grooming and licking that helps cue attachment epigenetically, i.e., through the impact environment has on genes.

Spinelli goes on: "It can be argued that this spectrum of [secure-base] behaviors descripted by Bowlby [and Ainsworth!] is the consequence of the epigenetic footprint provided by mother [caregiver] to offspring," which means that we learn how to be sensitive not just by way of the gaze we receive when our parents look at us, but because it becomes expressed through our genes.

While epigenetic experiments are tricky to perform on people, in that they require shifts in environment radical enough to test the impact on one's genetics, there is a naturally occurring "experiment of opportunity" that has been studied by attachment researchers: foster care, the common practice of children being raised by people other than their biological parents. And indeed, the latest research on foster parents found that the correlation between a foster infant's Strange Situation and the foster parent's state of mind was 72 percent, almost exactly what is found in biological families. The authors of the study believe that "these data argue for a nongenetic mechanism for the intergenerational transmission of attachment," which is to say, what we do matters. Big-time. But what we *do* is not just a list of behaviors. It's a way of being. And *being* is anything but simple.

As one scholar writes:

> It should be noted that although extensive studies have been conducted to determine the epigenetic influences on maternal behavior, there have been inconsistent results, and thus this research area has remained complex. Furthermore, it is difficult to ascertain the extent to which parenting behavior is influenced by epigenetics alone and to analyze this separately from the influence of environmental factors. Therefore, it is challenging to integrate the genetic and environmental principles and identify all factors that influence the processes of attachment and maternal behavior. Understanding how these factors influence each other and eventually maternal behavior would help in developing a holistic therapeutic approach. Furthermore, given the plasticity of the

maternal brain and that epigenetic modifications can be changed or reversed through experiences, interventional programs can be developed for mothers who had experienced poor parenting once biomarkers have been established.

Raising a child and growing up as ourselves—neither is a matter of checking boxes or getting it "right." Each of us is a deep and subtle creature whose very being is the result of an infinite stream of mysterious (*I didn't ask to be born!*) and at the same time lawful causes and conditions. While the amount and type of care we receive as children is deeply impactful, what matters the most is how our caregivers feel about us, which grows out of how they feel about themselves. It is, as Mary called it, "this internal something" we call attachment that will be felt and transmitted in everything they do. And thus we will become what they feel. Which we pass on to our children. And so on.

This thing we pass on is also called sensitivity. It seems so simple, so obvious, but Mary's concept of caregiving sensitivity, which she developed after carefully watching attachments form in mothers and babies in their first year of life in Uganda and then in Baltimore, then testing it in the Strange Situation, is what brought Bowlby's idea of social releasers to life. Being an effective parent does not arise out of some special personality traits or privilege or something we learn to do, like riding a bike, but a relational suppleness, attentional flexibility, the miraculous capacity to see ourselves in another and another in ourselves. And to be honest about our capacity and willingness to do this is a task that is not for the faint of heart.

In fact, as I've said elsewhere, I'm not sure that if Mary had been a parent herself, feeling the weight and difficulty of her own mind in relation to her baby, she would have had the nerve or resolve to look so closely at this delicate operation.

LET'S FACE IT: MARY AINSWORTH'S SENSITIVITY SCALES

The Maternal Caregiving and Interaction Scales is a twenty-five-page tool Mary used when coding a mother's behavior—including both what she could see and her interpretations of what she could see—in the Baltimore Study. By plumbing the depths of embedded, entrenched, meticulous observations of mothers and babies, Mary was able to capture the heights of parental sensitivity as well as the darkest, most selfish aspects of a parent's mind in cool, explicit detail. The general construct consists of four specific evaluative scales: (1) sensitivity vs. insensitivity to the baby's signals; (2) cooperation vs. interference with baby's ongoing behavior; (3) physical and psychological availability vs. ignoring and neglecting; and (4) acceptance vs. rejection of the baby's needs. No stone is left unturned. And these scales are not just about mothers and their children, but can be applied to every single relationship we have. If we dare.

These scales, in and of themselves, form a complex and powerful document—an essay, really, revised and "mimeographed" by Mary in 1969 and published for the first time as an appendix to the 2015 edition of *Patterns of Attachment: A Psychological Study of the Strange Situation,* the report of Mary's Baltimore Study. More than anything else, these scales, in my opinion, reveal Mary's incredible (magical, mystical) powers of attention as she describes the ways we live with each other in brutally honest detail—all the spectacular ways we tune in, and all the less desirable, but utterly human ways we tune out.

Each of the four scales was broken down into nine points, and each mother in the Baltimore Study was evaluated and fell somewhere within those nine points on each scale. For instance, in the first scale, sensitivity vs. insensitivity, "the mother's ability to interpret accurately her baby's communications has three main components: (a) her awareness, as previously discussed, (b) her freedom from distortion, and (c) her empathy." The scales go from 1, for the insensitive parent who "seems geared almost exclusively to her own wishes, moods, and activity," up to 9, for "exquisite" attunement.

In the second scale, cooperation vs. interference, a "conspicuously cooperative" parent "views her infant as a separate, active, autonomous person, whose wishes and activity have validity of their own." While a "highly interfering" parent "seems to assume that the infant is hers and that she has a perfect right to do with him what she wishes."

In the third, availability vs. ignoring, the "highly accessible" parent "is very alert to his [B's] whereabouts . . . Even when he is napping in his room she has a selective filter tuned in to any sounds he might make. She is capable of distributing her attention," whereas the "highly inaccessible, ignoring or neglecting" parent is "so preoccupied with her own thoughts and activities for most of the time that she simply does not notice B."

And finally, in the fourth scale, acceptance vs. rejection, the "highly accepting" parent "values the fact that infant has a will of his own, even when it opposes hers . . . at the same time she accepts the responsibility for caring for him." And the "highly rejecting" parent may say "she is sorry that she ever had him."

On the surface, these scales appear harsh. When I first encountered them, I was haunted by my own history with Azalea—my selfishness, my tempestuous outbursts, my longing to be left alone—but I also could see that I was pretty attentive. In the *accessibility vs. ignoring and neglecting* scale (even the names!), I was pretty sure I had aspects of being a 9 (highly accessible): "M arranges things so that she can be accessible to B and B to her."

After all, I wore Azalea in a sling, then a backpack, till she was five years old. But I was also pretty 5-ish (inconsistently accessible): "M is inconsistent in her accessibility to B. Fairly long periods of close attention alternate with periods of seeming obliviousness to B." And I feared I had a good dose of 1, too (highly inaccessible, ignoring or neglecting): "This mother only responds to B when she deliberately turns her attention to do something to or for B—making a project of it." Oh, Mary— "making a project of it"! *This very book?!* How true, how painful, how *fascinating*—if I can stomach it—to see it laid out so plainly.

It took me a lot of reading and digesting to appreciate that Mary was not, as it seemed to me at first, holding mothers to some impossible standard. Because Mary spent so much time around mothers, she knew that anger was just part of the deal. But she also knew that because as a culture we find maternal anger so unacceptable, mothers might repress or avoid these feelings and express a certain kind of warmth on the surface that isn't authentic, which isn't wrong, since of course we want to present our best self to our children. But as a researcher, Mary saw this false face as so pervasive in her Baltimore Study that she cautioned her coders against getting fooled by "pseudo-accepting" mothers who responded to their babies in a "long-suffering manner." In fact, "Ainsworth had noted that emotional warmth (which can be shown without sensitivity) did not distinguish mothers of secure-attached from those of insecure-attached infants." The first time I read this, I thought of my mother, and her "honey-this" and "sweetie-that." I felt as if her kind words contradicted her emotional distance. I have since come to hear my mom's Midwestern niceties very differently—as the chirps and calls of a loving mother whose warmth is both superficial *and* deep.

As challenging as these scales are, as I have studied them over the past many years, I have come to marvel at Mary's subtle wisdom, and to agree wholeheartedly with what she saw before her. These scales are not about mothers and babies; what Mary is describing here is nothing less than an outline of what it means to love someone—anyone—including ourselves. And it's a guide—a step-by-step walk through the human mind of identifying with the self, then with the other, then with the self, then with the other. Back and forth, back and forth.

The highly sensitive mother " 'reads' B's signals and communications skillfully, and knows what the meaning is of even his subtle, minimal and understated cues . . . When she feels that it is best not to comply with his demands—for example, when he is too excited, over-imperious, or wants something he should not have—she is tactful in acknowledging his communication and in offering an acceptable alternative."

Imagine if this were how we treated ourselves. *I see that you are craving that bag of chips, Bethany, which is totally fine, and I'll love you no matter what, but what you really want is comfort. How about we try taking CC for a walk first?*

Mary gets it. "It is assumed that the arrival of a baby [or any person!] poses a potentially ambivalent situation—and for all mothers there are positive and negative aspects . . . We are concerned with how the mother [or any caregiver], given her present life situation, has been able to balance them."

How *do* we balance our positive and negative feelings as people and mothers, especially when, as Mary writes, "the social norm is that mothers love their babies and do not reject them." Being sensitive, being in the moment, being an excellent informant requires that we see ourselves clearly. Mary talks about the mothers who deny their feelings of anger, or "comply masochistically," as having "little to do with the baby except as his behavior may serve to activate this repressed aggression." Ouch. Trying to mask our rage won't do. We have to see it, acknowledge it, and accept ourselves for who we are. Like the instructions in zazen when (not *if*, but *when*) thoughts arise: *See the thought, acknowledge it, and gently let it go.* And, as in zazen, when we're truly intimate with ourselves, there's nowhere to hide. And the good news is that, "momentary outbursts of anger or irritation must not be given undue weight if they are embedded in a clearly positive, warm, loving relationship."

But, Mary, how can we know if we have a "clearly positive, warm, loving relationship"?

Even after all my asking and testing and wondering and rejoicing, there's still a quiet part of me that worries that Azalea will in fact turn out just like me—a quasi-delinquent, a wreck, an adolescent risk-taker, an insecure (maybe not technically but still!) mess—even though our relationship *appears* reasonably secure. For now. I worry about what will happen when she reads this book and has to tolerate seeing her own life and that of her mother in such stark detail. I keep telling the same old story—that I'm somehow inherently flawed—even after all these years and all this unearthing, even though I know better. I don't beat myself up like I used to—and knowing that, in a Bowlbian, one-thing, social-releasing sense, my agitation *is* Azalea's agitation really helps. I love her so much I want to protect her.

Or maybe it's me I want to protect.

Maybe like the "highly interfering mother," "the infant continues to be a narcissistic extension of herself; such a woman tends to treat him as her possession, her creature, hers."

But I don't think so, not really.

Maybe it's a little bit of both.

Maybe it's not one side or the other.

Maybe I just keep on keeping on, moving toward what I trust is good for everyone involved and certainly won't hurt. *Be sensitive, soften, soften, take it all in. Relax. I'm just a human being.* I remind myself that, like Mary said, as a species, we've got this. Even though we may not always know exactly what "this" is.

Finally, as Mary writes in the closing of *Infancy in Uganda,* "It is difficult to hold an open mind over an extended period of time—and yet, that is what's required of the scientist." This open mind—it's the heart of the matter. And it's not just for researchers. It's for mothers, fathers, children, lovers, friends, strangers. Not knowing, not clinging to what we think or what we know—as we hear in Zen all the time—is most intimate. Only when we let go of our expectations can we allow ourselves to actually be with the moment, which includes the people we see before us and who we see in the mirror.

In other words, holding our mind open is incredibly difficult. But we can do it. In a long and loving letter Mary sent to Sylvia Bell in 1968, she offers comfort and confidence to her brilliant student who was insecure about her thesis, and the general direction of her research. Mary begins, "It seems to me that you would be well-advised to reduce the pressure you have applied to yourself." Good advice for all of us.

She continues by sharing a personal story:

At some point in my analysis, my analyst, while still expressing much interest in my research, did manage to convey to me that I was attempting to plumb the most difficult of all areas of research. He did not say that I was plunging in where angels fear to tread—but I think he felt I was. Let's face it, we are in a very complex, subtle and difficult area. Conditions that, on the surface, seem negligible in their import, may be significant in their influence.

After continuing on about her own research and how "each researcher has to rise up in dignity and defend the validity of her own findings," she simply says—and it touches me so to read it again, imagining her speaking directly to me, here, at the end of this journey—"So—keep an open mind. I am very certain that your project is a significant one and that there will be discoveries of great worth."

I certainly hope so.

And then, as Mary's final reminder: "But the discoveries may not be exactly what either you or I might have expected. Discoveries do tend to be surprising at first!"

Don't they ever?

acknowledgments

This book has been over a decade in the making (if you don't count my entire life), so the list is long of people who have made it possible for me to devote myself to such a deeply personal, time-consuming, and challenging project.

The lifelong friendships I made at Zen Mountain Monastery have carried me from my tear-soaked early days in the zendo through early motherhood and toward this journey into attachment and book birthing. We've shared deep silence, excessive raucousness, young adulthood, marriage, rupture, repair, sickness, old age, death, birth, a million meals, an ocean of drinks, karaoke—the whole catastrophe. This beloved adult attachment village includes Lisa and Adam; Kirsten and Chris; Shoan and Gokan; Jodie and Andrea. And their beautiful children (*"Omwana mulungi nnyo nnyo!"*), aged three to twenty-six— Elliot, Chloe, Oona, Thea, Ella—who have helped raise me.

Thank you to Yukon for Sunday night dinners, Hojin for magic, Zuiko and Onjin for watching Strange Situations with me on the big screen.

To Daido Roshi, who convinced me to take a chance on myself. And to Shugen Roshi, who keeps every door open, including doors I didn't know existed. And to the Zen Mountain Monastery sangha for keeping the lights on.

To my incredibly smart and loving friends who have never once *appeared* tired of me or my obsession or the ups and downs of this epic process. They've listened, asked, fed, traveled far and wide, hosted more than their share of playdates, sleepovers, pickups at the bridge, drop-offs at the four corners, loved us all, and read drafts and offered feedback. Thank you to Anastasia, Holly, Dorothy and Scott, Grace and JD, Jessie and Steve, Elizabethanne (and Jakson! Che! Cosimo!), Aimee, Maya, Dawn and Andy, Adrienne, Hayley and Marlan. And Azalea's sweet young friends who supported her in their ever-evolving ways—Nadou, Iris, Sofia.

To Erica Keswin for offering me her home, her patience, her sense of humor, her wonderfully human friendship.

To Crystal for being like family.

To Katya Friedman-Bush and Laura Merando for being so sensitively attuned to Azalea while I worked.

To Thayer's family—Jean, David, Nelson, Ravinka, and Oliver Case—for welcoming me into their life and taking such good care of us all (especially Azalea) and for always asking how they can do more to help. *As if!* David and Jean specialize in going above and beyond, and this book is a testament to their generosity.

To my visionary goddess agent, Meg Thompson, for seeing something in this story and for being such a regal midwife. To my wise editor at Random House, Pamela Cannon, for choosing this book and for guiding it into being. To Nan Satter for painstakingly caring, editing, and tracking every single teeny, tiny change. To Lexi Batsides at Random House for taking care of business so graciously, and to Will Palmer, whose copyediting was over-the-top kind, careful, and correct. In a word—*intimate.*

To my hero Wednesday Martin for the title and the nerve. To my mentor Andrew Solomon for teaching me how to be searching on the page and for the encouragement (and for the tip that I could write my acknowledgments like holiday cards). To Lauren Kern, former executive editor of *New York* magazine, for teaching me how to craft my story and for showing me—by example—how to be a consummate professional.

To Sil Reynolds for putting me together (even though I'm not broken).

To Gina Essex for her special powers.

While many scholars whom I now consider friends have read versions and drafts and sections of this book, all errors, omissions, and misunderstandings belong solely to me.

With that said . . .

To Alan Sroufe for believing in Mary and Missy and me. And for reading so many versions of this book, and for the phone calls, and for always being kind, and for answering my hundreds of questions with so much heart and precision.

To Howard Steele for taking me at my word, asking profound questions, sending studies and answering *endless* "just one more thing," emails. For being there with me as I waded through studies and statistics. And for Miriam Steele for being so beautifully devoted to mothers and their babies and the work of adult attachment and for getting it when certain transcripts blew my mind.

To Bob and Cherri Marvin for welcoming me into their home, wining and dining me, and sharing their love of Mary with me, as well as boxes and boxes of notes. And to Bob for talking to me for hours, swearing he didn't remember but then telling me story after story about his beloved Mary and the history of the Strange Situation.

To the many attachment scholars who fielded my questions, sent me their studies, challenged and encouraged me. A special thank-you to Marinus van IJzendoorn, intimidating meta-analyst extraordinaire, who helped me at the last minute.

To Daniel Siegel for an early phone call about this book and earned security.

To the staff at the Cummings Center for the History of Psychology, at the University of Akron, and the Radcliffe Institute for Advanced Study, at Harvard University, for their careful assistance.

To Gracie Smith and Nina Olivetti and for early and excellent research support.

To Rachel Martin for her impeccable attentional flexibility, research, fact-checking, and bibliography building.

To Joanna Parson for her impressively attuned transcriptions of interviews.

To Tom from the Phoenicia Belle, who let me stay there for some wintry months while I wrote and for letting me burn incense in my room.

To Uncle Mike for reading on my dad's behalf and for the phone call.

For Kathy for reading on my dad's behalf and for letting me say what's true for me and for honoring our attachment, especially elbow-deep in stuffing.

To Sam and Matt for having their own stories and for being willing to tell me some of them.

To the Symon cousins and aunts and uncles who are so fun and always welcoming and so unflinching. Stacy especially, for reading. And Brent and Karen for visiting.

To Gretel Ehrlich for writing the book *This Cold Heaven: Seven Seasons in Greenland,* which imprinted me.

To Robert Karen for his perfect book *Becoming Attached: First Relationships and How They Shape Our Capacity to Love.* He's so lucky he got to meet Mary!

To CC—yes, the poodle—for sitting with me day in, day

out, comforting, queenly, silly, and devoted. And Marilyn for being her loyal auntie and attachment figure.

To Thayer, who opened the window on love the moment I saw him in the monastery dining room. And because he's read every draft, and lived them, too—the agony and the ecstasy, the love and the longing, and, between us, every single pattern of attachment under the sun. And who invited me to attend our Super Bowl party as a guest when I was deep in writing this. Because he helped me see my own ordinary meatball hero's journey clearly, and because he's the only person in the world who really gets it (*every single word* gets it) and because he told me that Mary A. was like my Yoda. And he was right.

To Azalea, who has transformed into a tremendous—whip-smart and hilarious—teenager even amid the irony of missing out on a mom who was so often gone, locked up in her study, or off somewhere in an Airbnb or bed-and-breakfast writing a book about attachment. On her thirteenth birthday, I asked her if she wanted to read the parts of the book about her and about us and she said, "Maybe later." I thank her for being too busy to be bothered, and for being the kind of person who I believe will forgive me when she does read it—for what I got wrong about her, and for what I got right about myself.

To my truly excellent informant mother, Libby Saltman, for withstanding the discomfort of reading about herself through my evolving and critical eyes—for setting the bar on love that high. For generating generational love, even over FaceTime and text. And for not asking for progress reports or details when I know she was dying to know, and for all the speakerphone calls from my car, which I know annoy the heck out of her. But for which she always says she's grateful. And because I believe her. And she, of all people, knows what it takes to convince me.

questions for discussion

1. Having her own daughter changed the way Bethany sees her mother and their relationship. If you're a parent, how has having a child affected your relationship with your parents?

2. What was it like for you to read about Bethany's struggles as a new mother? Did you identify with her or Azalea?

3. When Bethany started writing about her mother, what did you think of her? Did your opinion of her mother change? If so, what did that shift tell you about what it means to be "securely attached"?

4. In the Prologue, Bethany writes, "Anguish turns to love. Separation becomes connection. Without the pain of aloneness, I never would have discovered the depth of my relatedness." What does she mean by that? How can you relate to this experience of anguish and separation in your own life?

5. What do you think about the Strange Situation itself? Do you believe it can in fact show something so important about a relationship in just twenty minutes? Would you ever want you or your child to experience the Strange Situation in a lab?

6. Bethany experienced her childhood and teenage years as very lonely and challenging, and even describes herself as having been a delinquent. After reading the book, how do you see her childhood, especially her relationship with her mom?

7. How has reading this book changed the way you see your parents, and your children, if you have them?

8. Bethany writes, "This is the telltale heart of attachment. No matter what secure adults have been through, they are governed by a trust in the importance of love in their life. Even when it hurts." What does this mean? And how is this different for insecure/dismissing or insecure/preoccupied adults?

9. Before reading *Strange Situation,* had you heard of Dr. William Sears and his attachment parenting philosophy? How has your opinion of his books and attachment parenting changed?

10. How do you think Azalea might feel about how she is represented in the book—now, as a teenager, and as she grows up and has her own children?

11. Mary Ainsworth never got to be a mother in her own life. Near the end of the book, Bethany writes, "As sad as

I am for her, I must confess that I'm grateful, too. Had she been a mother herself, I doubt she would have had the heart to look so closely into the workings of maternal love." What do you think Bethany means by this? Do you agree with her?

12. What do you think it is about Mary Ainsworth that drew Bethany to her so passionately?

13. How does Bethany describe the relationship between attachment and Zen in the book?

14. At the end of the book, Bethany's brother Sam reflects, "Got it. So, like, the past is real, but not destiny." What did he mean by that?

endnotes

vii   **"I'm going to be interviewing"** Carol George, Nancy Kaplan, and Mary Main, *The Adult Attachment Interview* (unpublished manuscript, Stony Brook University, New York, 1985), 1, http://www.psychology.sunysb.edu /attachment/measures/content/aai_interview.pdf.

ix   **"My own peculiar addiction to science"** Mary Ainsworth to Michael Lewis, February 26, 1983.

xi   **"Things are not as they seem"** Shakyamuni Buddha, *The Lankavatara Sutra: A Mahayana Text,* translated by Daisetz Teitaro Suzuki, http://lirs.ru /do/lanka_eng/lanka-nondiacritical.htm.

Prologue

xxii   **All newborn mammals attach to their caregivers** Ruth Feldman, "The Neurobiology of Mammalian Parenting and the Biosocial Context of Human Caregiving," *Hormones and Behavior* 77 (January 2016): 3–6. I'd like to say a note here about this "caregiver." For most of the history of attachment research, the primary "caretaker" has been the mother. This is due to the reality of mothers doing the lion's share of childcare, by cultural design, if not desire. More recently, researchers have paid attention to the very important role of fathers in attachment, which I will outline in my afterword. But from the outset of this book, please know that while there are some subtle differences in the ways children appear to relate to fathers and thus their attachment patterns, there are no biological or otherwise essential differences in the way attachment functions between fathers and children, or any other primary caregiver and their charge, for that matter. Attachment is a biological function of our bodies and minds and is available to all of us. (See K. Lee Raby and Mary Dozier, "Attachment Across the Lifespan: Insights from Adoptive Families," *Current Opinion in Psychology* 25 [2019]: 81–85.) This includes fathers, adoptive parents—human beings in any and all variety of family structure one can conceive of. As will be described herein, an attachment is a relationship between two beings, and does not discriminate. With that said, the story you are about to read is mine, a woman raised in and currently living in a "traditional" family of one mother (the primary caretaker) and one father, and so that is simply the shape of my story. Please feel invited, whoever you are, to put yourself in my shoes as an attachment figure to the people you love, and who love you, and to see your own attachment figures—whoever they are—in that light. My story can and should be seen through your eyes.

xxii   **For human infants, born incapable** Jeffry A. Simpson and Jay Belsky, "Attachment Theory Within a Modern Evolutionary Framework," in *Handbook of Attachment: Theory, Research, and Clinical Applications,* eds. Jude Cassidy and Phillip R. Shaver (New York: Guilford Press, 2016), 91–111.

xxiii **inflicting upon my daughter** Attachment theory holds that babies attach to one particular person sometime within the first year. This tendency is called monotropy. The story that follows is indeed one of monotropy—beginning with my primary caregiving relationship to my daughter, but the fact that this relationship is emphasized does not imply that other relationships don't matter. John Bowlby, "The Nature of the Child's Tie to His Mother," in *Influential Papers from the 1950s* (New York: Routledge, 2018), Google Books. More on this in the afterword.

xxiii **"lady professor" named Mary Ainsworth** Bob Marvin, interview by Bethany Saltman, December 28, 2017, transcript.

xxiii **Ainsworth was born in 1913** Nick Ravo, "Mary Ainsworth, 85, Theorist on Mother-Infant Attachment," *New York Times,* April 7, 1999, https://www.nytimes.com/1999/04/07/us/mary-ainsworth-85-theorist-on-mother-infant-attachment.html.

xxiv   **Inspired both by her own questions** Mary D. Salter Ainsworth et al., *Patterns of Attachment: A Psychological Study of the Strange Situation* (New York: Psychology Press, 2015), xix.

xxiv   **Her work in Africa** Mary D. Salter Ainsworth, "A Sketch of a Career," in *Models of Achievement: Reflections of Eminent Women in Psychology,* eds. A. N. O'Connell and N. F. Russo (New York: Columbia University Press, 1983), http://www.psychology.sunysb.edu/attachment/pdf/mda_autobio.pdf.

xxv   **"it seems unlikely that"** Jude Cassidy and Phillip R. Shaver, preface to *Handbook of Attachment,* x.

xxv   **On January 2, 1968** Mary Ainsworth to Sylvia Bell, January 2, 1968. Mary D. Salter Ainsworth Papers, Cummings Center for the History of Psychology, University of Akron.

xxv   **As the boom in attachment research** See, for example: Aida Faber and Laurette Dube, "Parental Attachment Insecurity Predicts Child and Adult High-Caloric Food Consumption," *Journal of Health Psychology* 20 (May 2015): 511–24; Kara Fletcher, "Attachment, a Matter of Substance: The Potential of Attachment Theory in the Treatment of Addictions," *Clinical Social Work Journal* 43, no. 1 (March 2015): 109–17; Amy L. Gentzler et al., "College Students' Use of Electronic Communication with Parents: Links to

Loneliness, Attachment, and Relationship Quality," *Cyberpsychology, Behavior, and Social Networking* 14, no. 1–2 (February 2011), https://doi.org/10.1089/cyber.2009.0409; Pehr Granqvist, Mario Mikulincer, and Phillip R. Shaver, "Religion as Attachment: Normative Processes and Individual Differences," *Personality and Social Psychology Review* 14, no. 1 (February 2010): 49–59; Pehr Granqvist and Lee A. Kirkpatrick, "Religion, Spirituality, and Attachment," in *APA Handbook of Psychology, Religion, and Spirituality, Vol. 1: Context, Theory, and Research,* eds. K. I. Pargament, J. J. Exline, and J. W. Jones (Washington, DC: American Psychological Association, 2013), 139–55; Brittainy Kolkhorst, Ani Yazedjian, and Michelle Toews, "A Longitudinal Examination of Parental Attachment, College Adjustment, and Academic Achievement," *Journal of the First-Year Experience and Students in Transition* 22, no. 1 (January 2010): 9–25; David F. Marks, "Homeostatic Theory of Obesity," *Health Psychology Open* 2, no. 1 (June 2015), https://doi.org/10.1177/2055102915590692; Paula R. Pietromonaco and Lindsey A. Beck, "Attachment Processes in Adult Romantic Relationships," in *Interpersonal Relations*, vol. 3 of *APA Handbook of Personality and Social Psychology,* eds. Mario Mikulincer et al. (Washington, DC: American Psychological Association, 2015), 33–64; David A. Richards and Aaron C. Schat, "Attachment at (Not to) Work: Applying Attachment Theory to Explain Individual Behavior in Organizations," *Journal of Applied Psychology* 96, no. 1 (2011): 169–82; Everett Waters, Claire E. Hamilton, and Nancy S. Weinfield, "The Stability of Attachment Security from Infancy to Adolescence and Early Adulthood," *Child Development* 71, no. 3 (2000): 703–6; Nancy S. Weinfield, Gloria J. Whaley, and Byron Egeland, "Continuity, Discontinuity, and Coherence in Attachment from Infancy to Late Adolescence: Sequelae of Organization and Disorganization," *Attachment and Human Development* 6, no. 1 (2004): 73–97; Robert S. Weisskirch and Raquel Delevi, "'Sexting' and Adult Romantic Attachment," *Computers in Human Behavior* 27, no. 5 (September 2011): 1697–1701.

xxv   **And the field itself has evolved** See, for example: Peter Fonagy, *Attachment Theory and Psychoanalysis* (New York: Routledge, 2018); Peter Fonagy, Mary Target, and George Gergely, "Psychoanalytic Perspectives on Developmental Psychopathology," in *Developmental Psychopathology, Vol. One: Theory and Method,* eds. Dante Cicchetti and Donald J. Cohen (Hoboken, NJ: John Wiley and Sons, 2006), 701–49; Paula R. Pietromonaco and Sally I. Powers, "Attachment and Health-Related Physiological Stress Processes," *Current Opinion in Psychology* 1 (February 2015): 34–39; Robert Shilkret and Cynthia J. Shilkret, "Attachment Theory," in *Inside Out and Outside In: Psychodynamic Clinical Theory and Psychopathology in Contemporary Multicultural Contexts,* eds. Joan Berzoff, Laura Melano Flanagan, and Patricia Herz (Lanham, MD: Rowman and Littlefield, 2016), 196–219; Jeffry A. Simpson and W. Steven Rholes, eds., *Attachment Theory and Research: New Directions and Emerging Themes* (New York: Guilford Press, 2015); Lane Strathearn, "Exploring the Neurobiology of Attachment," in *Developmental Science and Psychoanalysis: Integration and Innovation,* eds. Linda Mayes, Peter Fonagy, and Mary Target (New York: Routledge, 2018).

xxv **While mothers were the original** See, for example: Richard P. Barth et al.,
     "Beyond Attachment Theory and Therapy: Towards Sensitive and Evidence-
     Based Interventions with Foster and Adoptive Families in Distress," *Child and
     Family Social Work* 10, no. 4 (November 2005): 257–68; Inge Bretherton, "Fa-
     thers in Attachment Theory and Research: A Review," *Early Child Develop-
     ment and Care* 180, no. 1–2 (2010): 9–23; Natasha Demidenko, Ian Manion,
     and Catherine M. Lee, "Father–Daughter Attachment and Communication
     in Depressed and Nondepressed Adolescent Girls," *Journal of Child and Family
     Studies* 24, no. 6 (June 2015): 1727–34; Wendy L. Haight, Jill Doner Kagle,
     and James E. Black, "Understanding and Supporting Parent-Child Rela-
     tionships During Foster Care Visits: Attachment Theory and Research,"
     Social Work 48, no. 2 (April 2003): 195–208; Holly Ruhl, Elaine A. Dolan,
     and Duane Buhrmester, "Adolescent Attachment Trajectories with Mothers
     and Fathers: The Importance of Parent-Child Relationship Experiences and
     Gender," *Journal of Research of Adolescence* 25, no. 3 (September 2015): 427–42;
     Miriam Steele, "The 'Added Value' of Attachment Theory and Research for
     Clinical Work in Adoption and Foster Care," in *Creating New Families: Ther-
     apeutic Approaches to Fostering, Adoption and Kinship Care,* ed. Jenny Kenrick
     (New York: Routledge, 2018); K. Chase Stovall and Mary Dozier, "Infants
     in Foster Care," *Adoption Quarterly* 2, no. 1 (1998): 55–88.

xxv **Today, researchers believe that our pattern** See, for example: R. Chris
     Fraley and Glenn I. Roisman, "Early Attachment Experiences and Roman-
     tic Functioning: Developmental Pathways, Emerging Issues, and Future Di-
     rections," in Simpson and Rholes, *Attachment Theory and Research,* 9–38;
     Ashley M. Groh et al., "Attachment and Temperament in the Early Life
     Course: A Meta-Analytic Review," *Child Development* 88, no. 3 (May/June
     2017): 770–95; Klaus E. Grossmann, Karin Grossmann, and Everett Waters,
     eds., *Attachment from Infancy to Adulthood: The Major Longitudinal Studies* (New
     York: Guilford Press, 2005); Jason D. Jones, Jude Cassidy, and Phillip R.
     Shaver, "Parents' Self-Reported Attachment Styles: A Review of Links with
     Parenting Behaviors, Emotions, and Cognitions," *Personality and Social Psychol-
     ogy Review* 19, no. 1 (2015): 44–76, https://doi.org/10.1177/1088868314541858;
     Lee A. Kirkpatrick, "God as a Substitute Attachment Figure: A Longitudi-
     nal Study of Adult Attachment Style and Religious Change in College Stu-
     dents," *Personality and Social Psychology Bulletin* 24, no. 9 (1998): 961–73,
     https://doi.org/10.1177/0146167298249004; Lee A. Kirkpatrick and Phil-
     lip R. Shaver, "Attachment Theory and Religion: Childhood Attachments,
     Religious Beliefs, and Conversion," *Journal for the Scientific Study of Reli-
     gion* 29, no. 3 (September 1990): 315–34; Jean-Pascal Lemelin, George M.
     Tarabulsy, and Marc A. Provost, "Predicting Preschool Cognitive Develop-
     ment from Infant Temperament, Maternal Sensitivity, and Psychosocial
     Risk," *Merrill-Palmer Quarterly* 52, no. 4 (October 2006): 779–806; Adriano
     Schimmenti and Antonia Bifulco, "Linking Lack of Care in Childhood to
     Anxiety Disorders in Emerging Adulthood: The Role of Attachment
     Styles," *Child and Adolescent Mental Health* 20, no. 1 (February 2015): 41–48;
     Ole Jakob Storebø, Pernille Darling Rasmussen, and Erik Simonsen, "Asso-

ciation Between Insecure Attachment and ADHD: Environmental Mediating Factors," *Journal of Attention Disorders* 20, no. 2 (2016): 187–96, https://doi.org/10.1177/1087054713501079.

xxv   **the Strange Situation has been used** Marinus van IJzendoorn, email to Bethany Saltman, February 7, 2019.

xxv   **It's simply the gold standard** Lenny van Rosmalen, Marinus van IJzendoorn, and Marian J. Bakersman-Kranenburg, "ABC+D of Attachment Theory: The Strange Situation Procedure as the Gold Standard of Attachment Assessment," in *The Routledge Handbook of Attachment: Theory,* eds. Paul Holmes and Steve Farnfield (New York: Routledge, 2014), https://doi.org/10.4324/9781315762098.

xxvi **the relationships between humans** See, for example: Marinus H. van IJzendoorn et al., "Enhancement of Attachment and Cognitive Development of Young Nursery-Reared Chimpanzees in Responsive Versus Standard Care," *Developmental Psychology* 51, no. 2 (March 2009): 173–85; Lawrence A. Kurdek, "Pet Dogs as Attachment Figures for Adult Owners," *Journal of Family Psychology* 23, no. 4 (2009): 439–46; Alice Potter and Daniel Simon Mills, "Domestic Cats (*Felis silvestris catus*) Do Not Show Signs of Secure Attachment to Their Owners," *PLoS ONE* 10, no. 9 (2015), https://journals.plos.org/plosone/article?id=10.1371/journal.pone.0135109; Iris Schöberl et al., "Social Factors Influencing Cortisol Modulation in Dogs During a Strange Situation Procedure," *Journal of Veterinary Behavior: Clinical Applications and Research* 11 (2016): 77–85; József Topál et al., "Attachment Behavior in Dogs (Canis familiaris): A New Application of Ainsworth's (1969) Strange Situation Test," *Journal of Comparative Psychology* 112, no. 3 (1998): 219–29.

xxvi **"To build a robust attachment"** Hanna Lee, Sung-Byung Yang, and Chulmo Koo, "Exploring the Effect of Airbnb Hosts' Attachment and Psychological Ownership in the Sharing Economy," *Tourism Management* 70 (February 2019): 292.

xxvi **Ainsworth was a brave intellectual** Mary Main, "Mary D. Salter Ainsworth: Tribute and Portrait," *Psychoanalytic Inquiry* 19 (1999): 685–86, 703–8.

xxviii **"It is interaction that seems"** Mary D. Salter Ainsworth, *Infancy in Uganda: Infant Care and the Growth of Love* (Baltimore: Johns Hopkins Press, 1967), 397.

xxix **Attachment is not something we *do*** Pamela C. Alexander, "Relational Trauma and Disorganized Attachment," in *Treating Complex Traumatic Stress Disorders in Children and Adolescents: Scientific Foundations and Therapeutic Models,* eds. Julian D. Ford and Christine A. Courtois (New York: Guilford Press, 2013), 40–42.

xxix **"When we understand how our mind"** Thuong Chieu, quoted in Thich Nhat Hanh, *Understanding Our Mind: 50 Verses on Buddhist Psychology* (Berkeley, CA; Parallax Press, 2002), 1.

PART I: UNTELLING

3   **"I had thought that she would"** Mary Ainsworth, "Case 18, Visit 2," July 6, 1966. Mary Ainsworth, "Baltimore Longitudinal Study of Attachment, 1963–1967," Murray Research Center, Radcliffe Institute for Advanced Study, Harvard University.

Chapter One

5   **"Seven Baby B's of Attachment Parenting"** William Sears et al., *The Baby Book: Everything You Need to Know About Your Baby from Birth to Age Two* (New York: Little, Brown, 2008), Google Books. The Seven B's are: birth bonding, breastfeeding, baby wearing, bedding close to baby, belief in the language value of your baby's cry, beware of baby trainers, and balance. Let it be known that none of these behaviors, with the exception of believing in the value of your baby's cry, has anything to do with the science of attachment.

5   **"when a hungry or an upset"** Ibid., 6, 12–13.

6   **technical term is a "set goal"** Ibid.; Jeremy Safran and Zindel V. Segal, *Interpersonal Process in Cognitive Therapy* (New York: Jason Aronson, 1996), 54–56.

6   **Caregiving, attachment, sexuality, affiliation, fear** Roger Kobak, "The Emotional Dynamics of Disruptions in Attachment Relationships: Implications for Theory, Research, and Clinical Intervention," in Cassidy and Shaver, *Handbook of Attachment,* 29–31.

7   **"felt security"** Ibid.

7   **"Studies have shown that infants"** Sears et al., *The Baby Book.*

PART II: BEAUTIFUL CHILD

23   **"In Swahili, the lingua franca"** Ainsworth, *Infancy in Uganda,* 429. "The Luganda word is *ssaffaali*" (Mary's note!).

Chapter Four

25   **One of the first phrases Mary** Ibid., 18.

25   **one of the most important studies of mothers and babies ever completed** This is my own brave assertion based on the fact that this study is what led to the Strange Situation.

25   **It was 1954** Ainsworth, "A Sketch of a Career."

25   **throughout her field notes, she manages** Ainsworth, *Infancy in Uganda,* 9–14.

26   **"not enthusiastic"** Ainsworth, "A Sketch of a Career," 8.

26   **But she had an idea** Ibid., 9.

26   **Mary had heard** Ibid., 4–5.

26   **Once she arrived** Ibid., 6.

27   **However, she soon learned** Ibid., 4–5.

27   **Her first order of business** Ibid., 8, 38–39, 42.

27   **She was led around the villages** Ibid., 20, 24, 274.

27   **Mary was riveted by the people** Ibid., 14, 234, 322.

28   **When Mary arrived in Uganda** Ainsworth, "A Sketch of a Career."

29   **She had spent the previous four years** Klaus E. Grossmann et al., introduction to the special issue "Maternal Sensitivity: Observational Studies Honoring Mary Ainsworth's 100th Year," *Attachment and Human Development* 15, no. 5–6 (2013): 443; Robert Karen, *Becoming Attached: First Relationships and How They Shape Our Capacity to Love* (New York: Oxford University Press, 1998), 40–46, 59–66; Ainsworth, "A Sketch of a Career," 9.

29   **Mary, like almost all the psychologists** Ainsworth, "A Sketch of a Career."

29   **B. F. Skinner, the behaviorist guru** Saul McLeod, "Skinner—Operant Conditioning," Simply Psychology, accessed February 20, 2019, https://www.simplypsychology.org/operant-conditioning.html.

29   **To prove his theory, he raised** B. F. Skinner, "Baby in a Box," *Ladies' Home Journal,* October 1945.

30   **the idea that children are simply** Karen, *Becoming Attached,* 7, 166.

30   **For a few very happy months** Ainsworth, *Infancy in Uganda,* 9, 32.

31   **As payment to the twenty-six families** Ibid., 22.

31   **What she learned in those hours** Ainsworth et al., *Patterns of Attachment,* xiii.

31   *Infancy in Uganda,* **the book Mary** Ainsworth, *Infancy in Uganda,* 12, 74–76, 319–27.

32   **A rather proper Canadian lady** Ibid.

32   **Some of Mary's favorite mothers** Ibid., 54, 76–87, 188.

32   **Mary was completely taken** Ibid., 13, 295.

32   **Because she was a particularly strange stranger** Ainsworth, "A Sketch of a Career"; Karen, *Becoming Attached,* 98–101.

33   **Mary also began to see** Ainsworth, *Infancy in Uganda,* 331–50.

33   **Mary began to see Bowlby's budding** Mary D. Salter Ainsworth and Robert S. Marvin, "On the Shaping of Attachment Theory and Research: An Interview with Mary D. S. Ainsworth," *Monographs on the Society for Research in Child Development* 60, no. 23 (Fall 1994): 7.

33   **"a sudden, total, and permanent change"** Ainsworth and Marvin, "On the Shaping of Attachment Theory and Research," 7.

Chapter Five

34   **When the Ainsworths left Uganda** Main, "Mary D. Salter Ainsworth," 685.

34   **Her visits in Uganda totaled hundreds** Karen, *Becoming Attached,* 143–45.

34   **She had started to sort** Ainsworth, *Infancy in Uganda,* 28.

34   ***"Juko (thirty and thirty-two weeks)"*** Ibid., 345.

35   **Around 25 percent** Ibid., 28.

35   ***"Sulaimani (forty weeks) cried immediately"*** Ibid., 349.

35   **And just a handful (five pairs)** Ibid., 28, 388.

35   **"The twins manifested very little attachment"** Ibid., 390.

35   **While we often think** Ibid., 332.

36   **attachment theory posits that children benefit** Ibid., 392.

36   **As she searched her notebooks** Ibid., 44.

36   **babies about whom she had** Ibid., 43.

36   **Some of the mothers from her study** Ibid., 44–45.

37   **"mother's excellence as informant"** Ibid., 397–400. The language Mary uses to describe the excellent informant in 1967 is a precursor to the way the secure autonomous adult's transcript will be described in the AAI twenty years later by her student Mary Main. As Main writes, "Finally, we see that the strongest correlate of the Ganda infant's security—notably, mother's excellence as an informant—anticipates the relation later found between infant strange situation response and the parent's response to the Adult Attachment Interview. Thus, excellence as an informant (regarding the infant) is described as involving sticking to the topic, volunteering information, and giving much spontaneous detail (all forms of discourse coherence as Ruth Goldwyn and I later identified them)." Main, "Mary D. Salter Ainsworth," 697–98.

38   **through these narratives, made manifest** Erik Hesse and Mary Main, "Disorganized Infant, Child, and Adult Attachment: Collapse in Behavioral and Attentional Strategies," *Journal of the American Psychoanalytic Association* 48 (2000): 1117–19.

PART III: MIRACLE

41   **"This internalized something that we call"** Ainsworth, *Infancy in Uganda,* 430.

41   **"constitute an inner program"** "Like a computer program. As many others do, I find the computer model a useful one." (Mary's note!)

Chapter Six

43   **"walk in a yellow dress"** Anne Sexton, "45 Mercy Street," in *The Complete Poems: Anne Sexton* (Boston: Mariner Books, 1999), 481.

46   **"We are rather like whirlpools"** Charlotte Joko Beck, *Nothing Special: Living Zen,* ed. Steve Smith (New York: HarperCollins, 1993), 3.

Chapter Seven

49   **The founder and abbot** Jeff Zaleski, "Straight Ahead: An Interview with John Daido Loori," *Tricycle: The Buddhist Review,* Winter 1999, https://tricycle.org/magazine/straight-ahead-interview-john-daido-loori/.

51   **at Zen Mountain Monastery, committed relationships** Andrew Hudson, "More Clouds, More Water," *Gay Buddhist Fellowship,* September 1996, 5, http://www.gaybuddhist.org/archive/1996.09%20Andrew%20Hudson%20(More%20Clouds,%20More%20Water).pdf.

Chapter Eight

57   **Turns out it is not uncommon** Kathryn Taaffe McLearn et al., "Maternal Depressive Symptoms at 2 to 4 Months Post Partum and Early Parenting Practices," *Archives of Pediatrics and Adolescent Medicine* 160, no. 3 (March 2006): 279–84.

Chapter Nine

59   **"The way baby and parents get started"** Sears et al., *The Baby Book,* 5.

60   **"there is great comfort in feeling"** Ibid., 11.

PART IV: BIRDS OF A FEATHER

65   **"The sensitive mother . . . responds socially"** Ainsworth, *Patterns of Attachment,* 359.

Chapter Ten

67   **In 1938, when John Bowlby** Karen, *Becoming Attached,* 45–46.

67   **The classic Freudian stance** Paul Mussen and Luther Distler, "Masculinity, Identification, and Father-Son Relationships," *Journal of Abnormal and Social Psychology* 59, no. 3 (1959): 350–56; W. Schindler, "The Role of the Mother in Group Psychotherapy," *International Journal of Group Psychology* 16, no. 2 (1966): 198–202.

67   **parental love was understood** Margaret Harris and George Butterworth, *Developmental Psychology: A Student's Handbook* (New York: Taylor and Francis, 2002), 132–34.

68   **"I turned out okay!" attitude** See "I got spanked and I turned out OK" thread, Gentle Discipline forum, Mothering: The Home for Inclusive Family Living, accessed February 12, 2019, www.mothering.com/forum/36-gentle-discipline/727830-i-got-spanked-i-turned-out-ok.html.

68   **"So you are leaving some room"** Peter L. Rudnytsky, *Psychoanalytic Con-*

versations: Interviews with Clinicians, Commentators, and Critics (Hillsdale, NJ: Analytic Press, 2000), 49.

69   **Regardless of what we face in adulthood** Stay tuned for a more complete treatment of this important nature/nurture question in the afterword.

69   **During the time of Bowlby's training** Karen, *Becoming Attached,* 45–53.

69   **Bowlby was an outlier** Ibid.

70   **Even when a child's home life** Ibid., 27–28.

70   **Twelve years later, in 1950** Inge Bretherton, "The Origins of Attachment Theory: John Bowlby and Mary Ainsworth," *Developmental Psychology* 28 (1992): 764.

70   **orphaned children deprived** John Bowlby, *Maternal Care and Mental Health: A Report Prepared on Behalf of the World Health Organization as a Contribution to the United Nations Programme for the Welfare of Homeless Children,* 2nd ed. (Geneva: World Health Organization, 1952), 17, https://apps.who.int /iris/handle/10665/40724.

71   **Through his research, Bowlby** John Bowlby, *Attachment* (New York: Basic Books, 2008), xxvii–xxviii.

71   **he believed that "enjoyment,"** *delight* Bretherton, "Origins of Attachment Theory," 761–62.

71   **he placed an ad** Ibid.

71   **a friend showed Mary the job** Bretherton, "Origins of Attachment Theory," 761.

71   **"What can I say?"** Ainsworth and Marvin, "On the Shaping of Attachment Theory," 4.

Chapter Eleven

72   **In the summer of 1951** Karen, *Becoming Attached,* 89–90.

72   **When the future Nobel Prize–winning scientist** Konrad Lorenz, "Biographical," Nobel Prize website, accessed February 7, 2019, https://www .nobelprize.org/prizes/medicine/1973/lorenz/biographical/; Walter Sullivan, "Konrad Lorenz, Pioneer in Study of Animal's Behavior, Dies at 85," *New York Times,* March 1, 1989, https://www.nytimes.com/1989/03/01 /obituaries/konrad-lorenz-pioneer-in-study-of-animals-behavior-dies-at-85 .html; Marga Vicedo, *The Nature and Nurture of Love: From Imprinting to Attachment in Cold War America* (Chicago: University of Chicago Press, 2013), 44–50. The brilliant work of the ethologist Konrad Lorenz figures prominently in the story of attachment. So we must know this from the outset: During World War II, Lorenz was a member of the Nazi Party and a part of the government's war efforts. He joined the party in 1938. On his membership application, he wrote that he was "always a National Socialist" and hoped his work "stands to serve National Socialist thought" (Associated Press, "Austrian University Strips Nobel Prize Winner of Honors," *Washington Post,* December 21, 2015). In 1940 and 1943, he wrote two articles using

his observations of waterfowl to support the Nazis' bans on "interbreeding." He wrote to his mentor about a duck with an "ugly Jewish nose" and speculated about when Germany would go to war with England so "that arrogant race can be taught a lesson" (Ute Deichmann, *Biologists Under Hitler* [Cambridge, MA: Harvard University Press, 1996], 261–64). When he was drafted into the Wehrmacht in 1941, he told friends that he hoped to become a motorcycle mechanic; instead he was appointed as a military psychologist in the Office of Racial Policy. He was sent to examine "German-Polish half-breeds." Anyone found unfit psychologically or physically was sent to the concentration camps. He was captured by the Russians in 1944 and was a prisoner of war until 1948. After his release, he tried to rewrite his past, insisting he had never supported the Nazis but had done only what was necessary to protect himself. He also insisted that he had been captured by the Russians in 1942, before his work in Poland (Richard W. Burkhardt and Peter Klopfer, "Konrad Lorenz and the National Socialists: On the Politics of Ethology," *International Journal of Comparative Psychology* 7 [1994]: 202–8; Boria Sax, "What Is a 'Jewish Dog'? Konrad Lorenz and the Cult of Wildness," *Society and Animals* 1 [1997]: 3–21). In the past few decades, biographers have unearthed documents contradicting his claims. In 2015, the University of Salzburg revoked his honorary doctorate after discovering his application to join the National Socialist Party (Associated Press, "Austrian University").

73   **Years later, in 1935** Cara Flanagan, *Early Socialisation: Sociability and Attachment* (New York: Routledge, 1999), 26; "Konrad Lorenz: Kindheitserinnerungen und Anfänge der Ethologie," Bernd Lötsch, Altenberg bei Wien und Grünau im Almtal, 1977, video, 19:42, https://www.youtube.com/watch?v=__Fnb3LO_-o. https://wapo.st/1U0Ihm0?tid=ss_tw&utm_term=.70e826b1caa4).

73   **When goose chicks are born** Flanagan, *Early Socialisation.* This led Bowlby and others to suggest that there was such a "sensitive period" for humans to attach, which inspired hospitals around the world to be sure babies were with their mothers after birth in order to ensure early "bonding," which is lovely, for sure, but often leads to unnecessary dread and shame for mothers who fear that they have missed the window for whatever reason. This idea has, thankfully, been thoroughly debunked. Cecilia S. Pace et al., "Adoptive Parenting and Attachment: Association of the Internal Working Models Between Adoptive Mothers and Their Late-Adopted Children During Adolescence," *Frontiers in Psychology* 6 (September 2015), https://doi.org/10.3389/fpsyg.2015.01433.

74   **For thirty years Lorenz lived** Flanagan, *Early Socialisation*; Sullivan, "Konrad Lorenz, Pioneer."

74   **In 1975, the National Geographic Society** "Konrad Lorenz: Science of Animal Behavior," National Geographic Society and Jack Kaufman Pictures, 1975, video, 13:52, https://www.clip.fail/video/IysBMqaSAC8.

75   **Imprinting changed everything for Bowlby** Bretherton, "Origins of Attachment Theory," 762–63. Please note that attachment has come a long way

in broadening and deepening this understanding of the instinctive need to attach. It is not a simple case, as Dr. Sears would have us think, of the mother sacrificing herself to the needs of her child. Attachment is, as we will see, a much more porous and flexible (and ultimately forgiving) system than what appears in these early understandings.

75   **the concept of "social releasers"** Ibid.

75   **the reaction in one body** Ibid.; Bowlby, "Nature of the Child's Tie to His Mother"; Karen, *Becoming Attached,* 6–7.

75   **A social releaser releases something** *social* Ibid.; Ainsworth et al., *Patterns of Attachment,* 356–59.

76   **Even trees relate to each other** Richard Grant, "Do Trees Talk to Each Other?" *Smithsonian,* March 2018, https://www.smithsonianmag.com /science-nature/the-whispering-trees-180968084/.

76   **she was "so brainwashed"** Ainsworth, "A Sketch of a Career," 8.

76   **When she found herself in Uganda** Ainsworth and Marvin, "On the Shaping of Attachment Theory," 7.

77   **It grabbed hold of the idea** Bowlby, "Nature of the Child's Tie to His Mother."

77   **"To this end [i.e., infant survival]"** Ibid.

77   **His colleagues were not ready** Ibid.

77   **This may not sound like much** Bretherton, "Origins of Attachment Theory," 763.

78   **"illness, hunger, pain, cold"** Ainsworth et al., *Patterns of Attachment,* 7.

78   **Bowlby describes the idea** Bowlby, "Nature of the Child's Tie to His Mother."

79   **"[A scientist] has observed"** Ibid.

Chapter Twelve

81   **"Flowers Fall: Field Notes"** Online archive at https://www.chronogram .com/hudsonvalley/ArticleArchives?author=2124779&keywords=flowers %20fall%20saltman&sortType=recent.

83   **In one, a little girl named Caroline** "Attachment Videos Library," Department of Psychology, Stony Brook University, New York, accessed February 15, 2019, http://www.psychology.sunysb.edu/attachment/video _contents/videos_index_2010_kg2_infant_script.html.

83   **"This baby appears secure"** Ibid.

83   **"Mary Ainsworth's Strange Situation"** "Mary Ainsworth's Strage [*sic*] Situation: Attachment and the Growth of Love," preview of *Mary Ainsworth: Attachment and the Growth of Love with Robert Marvin, Ph.D.* (San Luis Obispo, CA: Davidson Films, 2005), https://www.youtube.com/watch?v=SFCQLshYL6w.

84   **My favorite scenes in the video** Ibid.

85   **"at the foot of the master"** Bob Marvin, interview by Bethany Saltman, February 7, 2017, transcript.

85   **Bowlby put it this way** Bowlby, *Attachment*, 329–34.

86   **"Most people think of fear"** Hesse and Main, "Disorganized Infant, Child, and Adult Attachment," 1104.

Chapter Thirteen

87   **revealing the "internal working model"** Inge Bretherton, "Communication Patterns, Internal Working Models, and the Intergenerational Transmission of Attachment Relationships," *Infant Mental Health Journal* 11, no. 3 (Autumn 1990): 237–52.

87   **The AAI is an interview** George, Kaplan, and Main, *The Adult Attachment Interview;* Howard Steele and Miriam Steele, "Ten Clinical Uses of the Adult Attachment Interview," in *Clinical Applications of the Adult Attachment Interview,* eds. Howard Steele and Miriam Steele (New York: Guilford Press, 2008), 9–11.

88   **a massive 75 percent correlation** Peter Fonagy, Howard Steele, and Miriam Steele, "Maternal Representations of Attachment During Pregnancy Predict the Organization of Infant-Mother Attachment at One Year of Age," *Child Development* 62, no. 5 (October 1991): 891–905; Marinus van IJzendoorn, "Adult Attachment Representations, Parental Responsiveness, and Infant Attachment: A Meta-Analysis on the Predictive Validity of the Adult Attachment Interview," *Psychological Bulletin* 117, no. 3 (May 1995): 387–403. In 2016, a large-scale study was undertaken to test the previous thirty years' worth of adult attachment research and to confirm that 75 percent number that blew my mind when Azalea was a toddler asleep in her crib (Marije L. Verhage et al., "Narrowing the Transmission Gap: A Synthesis of Three Decades of Research on Intergenerational Transmission of Attachment," *Psychological Bulletin* 142, no. 4 [April 2016]: 337–66). The result of a match between maternal adult attachment representation in the AAI and infant attachment in the Strange Situation was slightly lower than previously thought—67 percent—but as Dr. Steele said in an email to me about the study, "it's still significant" (Howard Steele, email to Bethany Saltman, February 1, 2019). Because that was the number in my head during the events of this book, and because it's not far off, I will refer to 75 percent as the correlation for the remainder of the book.

88   **"mind in relation to attachment"** Arietta Slade et al., "Maternal Reflective Functioning, Attachment, and the Transmission Gap: A Preliminary Study," *Attachment and Human Development* 7, no. 3 (2005): 283–98.

88   **researchers claim to be able to track** Fonagy, Steele, and Steele, "Maternal Representations of Attachment During Pregnancy"; van IJzendoorn, "Adult Attachment Representations, Parental Responsiveness, and Infant Attachment."

89   **in the AAI, a person's story** Peter Fonagy et al., "The Relation of Attachment Status, Psychiatric Classification, and Response to Psychotherapy," *Journal of Consulting and Clinical Psychology* 64, no. 1 (1996): 22–31.

89   **One wow factor of the AAI** Ibid.; Erik Hesse, "The Adult Attachment

Interview: Protocol, Method of Analysis, and Empirical Studies," in Cassidy and Shaver, *Handbook of Attachment*, 553–97.

89   **And it's the right side** Ibid.

PART V: STRANGE SITUATION

93   **"INSTRUCTIONS TO THE MOTHER"** Ainsworth et al., "Appendix I: Instructions to the Mother," in *Patterns of Attachment*, 316.

Chapter Fourteen

95   **They even met Mary** Howard Steele, email to Bethany Saltman, March 15, 2018.

97   **65 percent of people** Virginia M. Shiller, *The Attachment Bond: Affectional Ties Across the Lifespan* (New York: Lexington Books, 2017), 27–29.

97   **securely attached kids do better** Marlene M. Moretti and Maya Peled, "Adolescent-Parent Attachment: Bonds That Support Healthy Development," *Paediatrics and Child Health* 9, no. 8 (October 2004): 551–55; Machteld Hoeve et al., "A Meta-Analysis of Attachment to Parents and Delinquency," *Journal of Abnormal Child Psychology* 40, no. 5 (July 2012): 771–85.

97   **"Attachment history itself"** L. Alan Sroufe et al., *The Development of the Person: The Minnesota Study of Risk and Adaptation from Birth to Adulthood* (New York: Guilford Press, 2005), 197; "Minnesota Longitudinal Study of Risk and Adaptation," Institute of Child Development, University of Minnesota, accessed February 13, 2019, https://innovation.umn.edu/parent-child/.

97   **Insecure attachment in adulthood** G. Camelia Adams and Lachlan McWilliams, "Relationships Between Adult Attachment Style Ratings and Sleep Disturbances in a Nationally Representative Sample," *Journal of Psychosomatic Research* 79, no. 1 (January 2015): 37–42; Yi Jinyao, "Insecure Attachment as a Predictor of Depressive and Anxious Symptomology," *Depression and Anxiety* 29, no. 9 (September 2012): 789–96; Rachel D. MacKenzie et al., "Parental Bonding and Adult Attachment Styles in Different Types of Stalker," *Journal of Forensic Sciences* 53, no. 6 (November 2008): 1443–49; Tracey T. Manning, "Leadership Across Cultures: Attachment Style Influences," *Journal of Leadership and Organizational Studies* 9, no. 3 (August 2003): 20–30; Fiona Marsa et al., "Attachment Styles and Psychological Profiles of Child Sex Offenders in Ireland," *Journal of Interpersonal Violence* 19, no. 2 (February 2004): 228–51; Ofra Mayseless and Micha Popper, "Reliance on Leaders and Social Institutions: An Attachment Perspective," *Attachment and Human Development* 9, no. 1 (2007): 73–93; Laura Palagini et al., "Adult Insecure Attachment Plays a Role in Hyperarousal and Emotion Dysregulation in Insomnia Disorder," *Psychiatry Research* 262 (April 2018): 162–67; Wendy M. Troxel et al., "Attachment Anxiety, Relationship Context, and Sleep in Women with Recurrent Major Depression," *Psychosomatic Medicine* 69, no. 7 (August 2007): 692–99.

97   **Insecure adults experience God** Victor Counted, "God as an Attachment Figure: A Case Study of the God Attachment Language and God Concepts of Anxiously Attached Christian Youths in South Africa," *Journal of Spirituality in Mental Health* 18, no. 4 (2016): 316–46; Pehr Granqvist and Jane R. Dickie, "Attachment and Spiritual Development in Childhood and Adolescence," in *The Handbook of Spiritual Development in Childhood and Adolescence,* eds. Eugene C. Roehlkepartain et al. (Thousand Oaks, CA: Sage Publications, 2006), 197–221; Pehr Granqvist, Mario Mikulincer, and Phillip R. Shaver, "Experimental Findings on God as an Attachment Figure: Normative Processes and Moderating Effects of Internal Working Models," *Journal of Personality and Social Psychology* 103, no. 5 (2012): 804–18; Jonathan T. Hart, Alicia Limke, and Phillip R. Budd, "Attachment and Faith Development," *Journal of Psychology and Theology* 38, no. 2 (June 2010): 122–28.

97   **But the biggest subfield of attachment** Judith A. Feeney and Patricia Noller, "Attachment Style as a Predictor of Adult Romantic Relationships," *Journal of Personality and Social Psychology* 58, no. 2 (1990): 281–91; R. Chris Fraley and Keith E. Davis, "Attachment Formation and Transfer in Young Adults' Close Friendships and Romantic Relationships," *Personal Relationships* 4, no. 2 (June 1997): 131–44; R. Chris Fraley, "Attachment in Adulthood: Recent Developments, Emerging Debates, and Future Directions," *Annual Review of Psychology* 70, no. 1 (January 2019): 401–22; Cindy Hazan and Phillip Shaver, "Romantic Love Conceptualized as an Attachment Process," *Journal of Personality and Social Psychology* 52, no. 3 (April 1987): 511–24; Ramona L. Paetzold, William S. Rholes, and Jamie L. Kohn, "Disorganized Attachment in Adulthood: Theory, Measurement, and Implications for Romantic Relationships," *Review of General Psychology* 19, no. 2 (June 2015): 146–56.

97   **Securely attached, autonomous adults** Marta F. Pedro, Teresa Ribeiro, and Katharine H. Shelton, "Romantic Attachment and Family Functioning: The Mediating Role of Marital Satisfaction," *Journal of Child and Family Studies* 24, no. 11 (November 2015): 3492–95; Jeffry A. Simpson, "Adult Attachment, Stress, and Romantic Relationships," *Current Opinion in Psychology* 13 (February 2017): 19–24.

98   **"Mentalization" is a Victorian term** "Peter Fonagy: What Is Mentalization?" video, 11:01, posted by Simms/Mann Institute, November 19, 2016, https://youtu.be/MJ1Y9zw-n7U.

98   **Today, researchers define mentalization** Anthony Bateman and Peter Fonagy, *Mentalization-Based Treatment for Personality Disorders: A Practical Guide* (New York: Oxford University Press, 2016), 3, 5.

98   **This ability to mentalize comes directly** Moniek A. J. Zeegers et al., "Mind Matters: A Meta-Analysis on Parental Mentalization and Sensitivity as Predictors of Infant–Parent Attachment," *Psychological Bulletin* 143, no. 12 (2017): 1245–72.

98   **At the base of all attachment behavior** John Bowlby, "The Growth of Independence in the Young Child," *Royal Society of Health Journal* 76 (1956): 588.

98   **This process begins with "co-regulation"** Phillip R. Shaver et al., "A Lifespan Perspective on Attachment and Are for Others: Empathy, Altruism, and Prosocial Behavior," in Cassidy and Shaver, *Handbook of Attachment,* 881.

98   **a solid dose of co-regulation ends** Mario Mikulincer, Phillip R. Shaver, and Dana Pereg, "Attachment Theory and Affect Regulation: The Dynamics, Development, and Cognitive Consequences of Attachment-Related Strategies," *Motivation and Emotion* 27, no. 2 (June 2003): 91–92.

99   **"Studies have shown that infants who develop"** Sears et al., *The Baby Book.*

101   **a baby should show a "differential"** Gottfried Spangler, "Emotional and Adrenocortical Responses of Infants to the Strange Situation: The Differential Function of Emotional Expression," *International Journal of Behavioral Development* 22, no. 4 (1998): 681–706.

Chapter Fifteen

105   **Mary Dinsmore Salter was born** Inge Bretherton, "Mary Ainsworth: Insightful Observer and Courageous Theoretician," in *Portraits of Pioneers in Psychology,* vol. 5, eds. Gregory A. Kimble, Michael Wertheimer, and Charlotte L. White (Hillsdale, NJ: Erlbaum, 2003), http://www.psychology.sunysb.edu/attachment/pdf/mda_inge.pdf.

105   **she described her family as "close-knit"** Ainsworth, "A Sketch of a Career," 2.

105   **Although her mother** Main, "Mary D. Salter Ainsworth," 703.

105   **One of the Salters' favorite family** Ainsworth, "A Sketch of a Career," 2.

105   **"Self-knowledge is only to be obtained"** William McDougall, *Character and Conduct of Life: Practical Psychology for Everyman,* Psychology Revivals series (New York: Routledge, 2016), Google Books.

105   **"It had not previously occurred"** Bretherton, "Mary Ainsworth: Insightful Observer."

106   **"What a vista"** Ainsworth, "A Sketch of a Career," 2.

106   **Mary's father thought** Ibid.; Bretherton, "Mary Ainsworth: Insightful Observer."

106   **Upon Blatz's suggestion** Ibid.

107   **She would eventually call her method** Inge Bretherton, "Revisiting Mary Ainsworth's Conceptualizations and Assessments of Maternal Sensitivity-Insensitivity," in *Maternal Sensitivity: Mary Ainsworth's Enduring Influence on Attachment Theory, Research and Clinical Applications,* eds. Klaus E. Grossman et al. (New York: Routledge, 2016), 21.

107   **"everyone's career plans were changed"** Ainsworth, "A Sketch of a Career," 5.

107   **In the winter of 1943–44** Ibid., 6.

107   **From 1946 to 1950, Ainsworth and Blatz** Ibid., 7.

107 **She was, by all accounts** Bob Marvin interview, February 7, 2017; Main, "Mary D. Salter Ainsworth," 698.

108 **And "with respect to sex"** Main, "Mary D. Salter Ainsworth," 707.

108 **And yet, while Mary** Ainsworth, "A Sketch of a Career," 2.

108 **Among her claims to feminist fame** Main, "Mary D. Salter Ainsworth," 689.

108 **In the 1970s, she wrote** Mary Ainsworth to John Bowlby, January 5, 1970, Mary D. Salter Ainsworth Papers, Cummings Center for the History of Psychology, University of Akron.

108 **"I am gratified that you find 'secure' "** Mary Ainsworth to John Bowlby, date unknown (not in view in the letter), Mary D. Salter Ainsworth Papers, Cummings Center for the History of Psychology, University of Akron.

109 **the one from Johns Hopkins** Ainsworth, "A Sketch of a Career"; G. Herberton Evans Jr. to Mary Ainsworth, May 15, 1961, Mary D. Salter Ainsworth Papers, Cummings Center for the History of Psychology, University of Akron.

109 **Ten years after she'd married Len** Ainsworth, "A Sketch of a Career," 10.

109 **"Briefly to bring you up to date"** Mary Ainsworth to Christopher Heinicke, November 15, 1962, Mary D. Salter Ainsworth Papers, Cummings Center for the History of Psychology, University of Akron.

110 **The stories of Len are few** Main, "Mary D. Salter Ainsworth," 700.

110 **"From the first weeks of analysis"** Ibid., 702.

110 **"With respect to infancy"** Ibid.

111 **She lived with her cat Nnyabo** Ibid., 682–83; Mary Ainsworth to Sylvia Bell, September 19, 1967, Mary D. Salter Ainsworth Papers, Cummings Center for the History of Psychology, University of Akron; Bob Marvin, interviews by Bethany Saltman, February 6–7, 2017, transcript.

111 **"She'd walk in carrying her briefcase"** Bob Marvin, interview by Bethany Saltman, December 15, 2017, transcript.

111 **"You'd sit down"** Ibid.

112 **"She was clearly refined"** Ibid.

112 **In July 1963, firmly ensconced** Mary Ainsworth to John Bowlby, July 18, 1963, Mary D. Salter Ainsworth Papers, Cummings Center for the History of Psychology, University of Akron.

112 **she simply asked local pediatricians** Bretherton, "Revisiting Mary Ainsworth's Conceptualizations and Assessments," 20; Bob Marvin interview, December 28, 2017.

113 **"You don't say no to Dr. Ainsworth"** Ibid.

Chapter Sixteen

114 **When the selected babies** Ibid.; Kristin Bernard, E. B. Meade, and Mary Dozier, "Parental Synchrony and Nurturance as Targets in an Attachment

Based Intervention: Building upon Mary Ainsworth's Insights About Mother-Infant Interaction," in *Maternal Sensitivity,* 67–68.

114   **Harry Harlow** Deborah Blum, *Love at Goon Park: Harry Harlow and the Science of Affection* (Cambridge, MA: Basic Books, 2002), 158–70; Harry F. Harlow and Stephen J. Suomi, "Nature of Love—Simplified," *American Psychologist* 25, no. 2 (1970): 161–68.

114   **"Trust yourself and your children"** Benjamin Spock and Robert Needlman, *Dr. Spock's Baby and Child Care,* 9th ed. (New York: Gallery Books, 2011), 1.

114   **Mary's team of four observers** Sylvia Bell, interview by Bethany Saltman, December 18, 2017, transcript; Bretherton, "Origins of Attachment Theory," 767; Bretherton, "Revisiting Mary Ainsworth's Conceptualizations and Assessments," 20.

115   **Observers visited the twenty-six homes** Ainsworth et al., *Patterns of Attachment,* 31, 43–45; Ainsworth, "A Sketch of a Career"; Karen, *Becoming Attached,* 145.

115   **she gave these transcribed notes** Mary Ainsworth, "Baltimore Longitudinal Study of Attachment, 1963–1967," Murray Research Center, Radcliffe Institute for Advanced Study, Harvard University.

115   **The idea of the Baltimore Study** Bob Marvin interview, December 28, 2017.

115   **"To have somebody there"** Karen, *Becoming Attached,* 145.

116   **While observers "assiduously avoided interfering"** Bretherton, "Revisiting Mary Ainsworth's Conceptualization and Assessments," 20.

116   **"cuddliness"** Karen, *Becoming Attached,* 145.

116   **As Bob Marvin described it** Bob Marvin interview, December 28, 2017.

116   **According to Sylvia** Sylvia Bell interview.

116   **But Bob remembers** Bob Marvin interview, December 28, 2017.

117   **The authors advised** Jean Kunhardt, Lisa Spiegel, and Sandra K. Bastile, *A Mother's Circle: An Intimate Dialogue on Becoming a Mother* (New York: Soho Parenting Center, 1996).

118   **"Crying is the most conspicuous"** Sylvia M. Bell and Mary D. Salter Ainsworth, "Infant Crying and Maternal Responsiveness," *Child Development* 43, no. 4 (December 1972): 1172.

118   **The authors promoting this sleep-training** Kunhardt, Spiegel, and Bastile, *A Mother's Circle.*

119   **When Mary listened to babies cry** Bell and Ainsworth, "Infant Crying and Maternal Responsiveness," 1171–90.

Chapter Seventeen

121   **"The newborn baby is not attached"** Ainsworth, *Infancy in Uganda,* 331.

122   **"on this foundation, it seems"** John Bowlby, foreword to Ainsworth, *Infancy in Uganda,* v.

122   **They were searching for a method** Sylvia Bell to Mary Ainsworth, October 2, 1967, Mary D. Salter Ainsworth Papers, Cummings Center for the History of Psychology, University of Akron.

122   **Eventually they found that more sensitive** Bell and Ainsworth, "Infant Crying and Maternal Responsiveness," 1171–90.

123   **"in general, distress behavior is incompatible"** Ainsworth et al., *Patterns of Attachment,* 84.

123   **Mary's description of a bird** Ibid., 14–15.

123   **The article that Sylvia and Mary** Bell and Ainsworth, "Infant Crying and Maternal Responsiveness," 1171–90; Kathryn M. Bigelow and Edward K. Morris, "John B. Watson's Advice on Child Rearing: Some Historical Context," *Behavioral Development Bulletin* 10, no. 1 (2001): 26–30.

123   **"it is fortunate for their survival"** Bowlby, "Nature of the Child's Tie to His Mother," 257–60.

123   **"Because it is disagreeable to adults"** Bell and Ainsworth, "Infant Crying and Maternal Responsiveness," 1172.

123   **"As a rule, crying leads"** Bowlby, *Attachment,* 347.

Chapter Eighteen

126   **"I was really very touched"** Mary D. Salter Ainsworth, "Case 18: Visit 20, June 14, 1967," Box 3, Baltimore Longitudinal Study of Attachment, 1963–1967, Murray Research Center, Radcliffe Institute for Advanced Study, Harvard University.

126   **This family was resistant** Mary Ainsworth, "Case 18: Preliminary Visit, June 6, 1966," Baltimore Longitudinal Study of Attachment.

126   **"Theresa is a real gem"** Mary Ainsworth, "Case 18, Visit 7, July 14, 1966," Baltimore Longitudinal Study of Attachment.

127   **"attachment village"** Gordon Neufeld and Gabor Maté, *Hold On to Your Kids: Why Parents Need to Matter More Than Peers* (New York: Ballantine, 2005).

127   **"B is perfectly content to be with Theresa"** "Case 18: Visit 19, May 24, 1967," Baltimore Longitudinal Study of Attachment.

127   **"I would like to consider the relation of my research"** Ainsworth, "A Sketch of a Career," 13.

128   **After much back-and-forth** Mary Ainsworth, "Case 18: Telephone Conversations, June 28, 1966," Baltimore Longitudinal Study of Attachment.

128   **In Visit 1, Dr. A** Mary Ainsworth, "Case 18, Visit 1, June 29, 1966," Baltimore Longitudinal Study of Attachment.

129   **In Visit 1, M** Ibid.

129   **"I don't believe I'm any longer"** Mary Ainsworth, "Case 18, Visit 17, April 12, 1967," Baltimore Longitudinal Study of Attachment.

129   **Starting with Visit 7** Mary Ainsworth, "Case 18, Visit 15, March 1, 1967," Baltimore Longitudinal Study of Attachment.

129   **The Baltimore Study was the first** Bob Marvin interview, December 28, 2017.

130   **"M leaves the room"** Mary Ainsworth, "Case 18, Visit 14, February 8, 1967," Baltimore Longitudinal Study of Attachment.

130   **"the Baltimore study entailed"** Ainsworth et al., *Patterns of Attachment*, xxx.

131   **While the American babies did appear** Karen, *Becoming Attached*, 147.

131   **Mary believed one reason** Ainsworth et al., *Patterns of Attachment*, 57–60.

131   **"All right," Mary said later** Karen, *Becoming Attached*, 147.

132   **"I have been focusing my thoughts"** Mary Ainsworth to John Bowlby, July 18, 1963, Mary D. Salter Ainsworth Papers, Cummings Center for the History of Psychology, University of Akron.

132   **"It is a great pity we cannot"** John Bowlby to Mary Ainsworth, July 30, 1963, Mary D. Salter Ainsworth Papers, Cummings Center for the History of Psychology, University of Akron.

132   **Others before Mary** Jean M. Arsenian, "Young Children in an Insecure Situation," *Journal of Abnormal and Social Psychology* 38, no. 2 (1943): 225–49; Harriet L. Rheingold, Jacob L. Gerwitz, and Hana Ross, "Social Conditioning of Vocalizations in the Infant," *Journal of Comparative and Physiological Psychology* 52, no. 1 (1959): 68–73.

132   **not, as Bob told me, a "de novo"** Ainsworth et al., *Patterns of Attachment*, xvii; Bob Marvin interview, February 7, 2017.

132   **"I thought, Well, let's work"** Karen, *Becoming Attached*, 147.

133   **"It was an afterthought"** Bob Marvin interview, February 7, 2017.

133   **When their mothers were nearby** Ainsworth et al., *Patterns of Attachment*, 74–80.

133   **Some babies were "lured"** Karen, *Becoming Attached*, 149.

133   **When the mother left the room** Ibid., 147–60.

133   **Mary Ainsworth's "afterthought"** Ainsworth and Marvin, "On the Shaping of Attachment Theory," 12; Margaret Talbot, "The Disconnected; Attachment Theory: The Ultimate Experiment," *New York Times Magazine*, May 24, 1988, https://nyti.ms/2v3lOhC.

Chapter Nineteen

135   **For the past forty-five years** "Minnesota Longitudinal Study of Risk and Adaptation," Institute of Child Development, University of Minnesota.

135   **Dr. Sroufe is a kind, warm** L. Alan Sroufe, email to Bethany Saltman, March 16, 2018.

136   **Because of the behavioral system** Nathan A. Fox and Judith A. Card, "Psychophysiological Measures in the Study of Attachment," in Cassidy and Shaver, *Handbook of Attachment*, 233–35.

138   **Eventually I learned how to read** L. Alan Sroufe, Brianna Coffino, and Elizabeth A. Carlson, "Conceptualizing the Role of Early Experience: Les-

sons from the Minnesota Longitudinal Study," *Developmental Review* 30, no. 1 (March 2010): 36–51.

138   **But the different ways babies responded** Bretherton, "Fathers in Attachment Theory and Research," 10.

139   **it is generally understood** Marinus H. van IJzendoorn and Pieter M. Kroonenberg, "Cross-cultural Patterns of Attachment: A Meta-Analysis of the Strange Situation," *Child Development* 59, no. 1 (1988): 147–51.

139   **"Group-B infants showed significantly"** Ainsworth et al., *Patterns of Attachment,* 125.

139   **Tens of thousands of studies** Fraley and Roisman, "Early Attachment Experiences and Romantic Functioning," 9–38; Grossmann, Grossmann, and Waters, *Attachment from Infancy to Adulthood;* Schimmenti and Bifulco, "Linking Lack of Care in Childhood to Anxiety Disorders in Emerging Adulthood," 41–48.

139   **"There seems no doubt now"** Mary Ainsworth to Michael Lewis, February 26, 1983, Mary D. Salter Ainsworth Papers, Cummings Center for the History of Psychology, University of Akron.

140   **"a robust phenomenon"** Mary Ainsworth to Michael Lewis, February 26, 1983, Mary D. Salter Ainsworth Papers, Cummings Center for the History of Psychology, University of Akron. See also: Marinus van IJzendoorn, Marian J. Bakermans-Kranenburg, and Abraham Sagi-Schwartz, "Attachment Across Diverse Sociocultural Contexts: The Limits of Universality," in *Parenting Beliefs, Behaviors, and Parent-Child Relations: A Cross-Cultural Perspective,* eds. Kenneth H. Rubin and Ock Boon Chung (New York: Psychology Press, 2006), 121.

140   **Because the B (secure) babies** Mary D. Salter Ainsworth and Sylvia M. Bell, "Attachment, Exploration, and Separation: Illustrated by the Behavior of One-Year-Olds in a Strange Situation," *Child Development* 41 (1970): 49–67.

140   **Some of these babies were completely undone** Ainsworth et al., *Patterns of Attachment,* 115–34.

141   **Another group of babies wasn't crying** Ibid., 127, 149.

141   **Contemplating this apparent contradiction** Karen, *Becoming Attached,* 154; "A Two Year Old Goes to Hospital," extract clip from *A Two-Year-Old Goes to Hospital* (Robertson Films, 1952), video, 1:34, posted by Concord Media on July 1, 2014, https://www.youtube.com/watch?v=s14Q-_Bxc_U.

141   **Mary wondered: Can one-year-olds** Mary D. Salter Ainsworth, "Infant-Mother Attachment," *American Psychologist* 34, no. 10 (October 1979): 932–33.

142   **"As for looking-away behavior"** Main, "Mary D. Salter Ainsworth," 719–20.

142   **Eventually Bowlby came around** Ibid., 721.

142   **"I expected that some children"** Karen, *Becoming Attached,* 149–54.

142   **"The thing that blew my mind"** Ibid., 150.

142   **Because we Americans tend** Yoo Rha Hong and Jae Sun Park, "Impact of Attachment, Temperament and Parenting on Human Development," *Korean Journal of Pediatrics* 55, no. 12 (December 2012): 449–54.

142   **However, by tracking the heart rate** L. Alan Sroufe and Everett Waters, "Heart Rate as a Convergent Measure in Clinical and Developmental Research," *Merrill–Palmer Quarterly* 23, no. 1 (January 1977): 3–27.

143   **"When, however, the [attachment] response"** Bowlby, "Nature of the Child's Tie to His Mother."

143   **In the end, Mary and her team** Ainsworth et al., *Patterns of Attachment,* 228–43.

143   **And, "to Ainsworth's amazement"** Karen, *Becoming Attached,* 158.

143   **In the 1980s, after hundreds** Robbie Duschinsky, "Disorganization, Fear, and Attachment: Working Towards Clarification," *Infant Mental Health Journal* 39, no. 1 (January–February 2018): 17–29; Mary Main and Hillary Morgan, "Disorganization and Disorientation in Infant Strange Situation Behavior," in *Handbook of Dissociation: Theoretical, Empirical, and Clinical Perspectives,* eds. Larry K. Michelson and William J. Ray (Boston: Springer/Verlag US, 1996), 107–38; Mary Main and Judith Solomon, "Discovery of an Insecure-Disorganized/Disoriented Attachment Pattern," in *Affective Development in Infancy,* eds. T. B. Brazelton and M. W. Yogman (Westport, CT: Ablex Publishing, 1986), 95–124.

144   **"fright without solution"** Erik Hesse and Mary Main, "Second-Generation Effects of Unresolved Trauma in Nonmaltreating Parents: Dissociated, Frightened, and Threatening Parental Behavior," *Psychoanalytic Inquiry* 19, no. 4 (1999): 481–540.

144   **Consider Mary's bird at the window** Ainsworth et al., *Patterns of Attachment,* 14–15.

144   **This "disorganization" of the attachment pattern** See, for example: Nigel P. Field, "Unresolved Grief and Continuing Bonds: An Attachment Perspective," *Death Studies* 30, no. 8 (2006): 739–56; Karlen Lyons-Ruth and Deborah Jacobvitz, "Attachment Disorganization: Unresolved Loss, Relational Violence, and Attentional Strategies," in Cassidy and Shaver, *Handbook of Attachment,* 520–54; Mary Main and Erik Hesse, "Parents' Unresolved Traumatic Experiences Are Related to Infant Disorganized Attachment Status: Is Frightened and/or Frightening Parental Behavior the Linking Mechanism?" in *Attachment in the Preschool Years: Theory, Research, and Intervention,* eds. M. T. Greenberg, D. Cicchetti, and E. M. Cummings (Chicago: University of Chicago Press, 1990), 161–82; Illene C. Noppe, "Beyond Broken Bonds and Broken Hearts: The Bonding of Theories of Attachment and Grief," *Developmental Review* 20, no. 4 (December 2000): 514–38; Paula Thomson, "Loss and Disorganization from an Attachment Perspective," *Death Studies* 34, no. 10 (2010): 893–914.

144   **Today, disorganization is usually considered** Main and Solomon, "Discovery of an Insecure-Disorganized/Disoriented Attachment Pattern," 95–124.

144   **"disorganized attachment behaviors are not"** Barry Coughlan et al., "Attachment and Autism Spectrum Conditions: Exploring Mary Main's Coding Notes," *Developmental Child Welfare* 1, no. 1 (2019): 80.

145   **I was even beginning to be able** Marinus van IJzendoorn et al., "Dependent Attachment: B-4 Children in the Strange Situation," *Psychological Reports* 57, no. 2 (October 1985): 439–51. There has been some debate in the literature about the validity of the B4 baby being considered a B at all. Because a B4 baby can so resemble a C, it is especially important to look at ecological factors, in other words, the baby in her life.

145   **the mothers who seemed best** Ainsworth et al., *Patterns of Attachment*, xx–xxi.

145   **However, some of the most efficient** Ibid., 325–40.

145   **After the first round of Strange Situations** Mary D. Salter Ainsworth, "On Security," unpublished paper, 1988, http://www.psychology.sunysb.edu/attachment/pdf/mda_security.pdf.

145   **It was in this early mirroring** Ainsworth et al., *Patterns of Attachment*, 358–60.

146   **"The term 'motherly care' is too unspecific"** Ainsworth, *Infancy in Uganda*, 397.

146   **Mary's original concept** Mary D. Salter Ainsworth, "Social Development in the First Year of Life: Maternal Influences on Infant-Mother Attachment," in *Developments in Psychiatric Research: Essays Based on the Sir Geoffrey Vickers Lectures of the Mental Health Foundation*, ed. J. M. Tanner (New York: Hodder and Stoughton, 1977), 6.

146   **Instead, "the most important aspect"** Bretherton, "Revisiting Mary Ainsworth's Conceptualization and Assessments," 21.

146   **The sensitive caregiver picks the baby up** Ainsworth et al., *Patterns of Attachment*, 359.

146   **What Mary was looking for** Bowlby, *Attachment*, 61.

146   **But as Howard and Miriam Steele** David Howe, *Attachment Across the Lifecourse: A Brief Introduction* (New York: Macmillan International, 2011), 70. Also, "coordination, regardless of infant age during the first year, is found only about 30% or less of the time in face-to-face interactions, and the transitions from coordinated to miscoordinated states and back to coordinated states occur about once every three to five seconds." Ed Tronick, *The Neurobehavioral and Social-Emotional Development of Infants and Children* (New York: W. W. Norton, 2007), 171.

147   **Instead, it was through the experience of day-in** Bretherton, "Revisiting Mary Ainsworth's Conceptualization and Assessments," 22.

147   **Within the parent-child interaction** Ibid., 21–22.

147   **For Mary, the word "delight"** Ibid., 24.

Chapter Twenty

149   **They gathered 180 children** Sroufe et al., *The Development of the Person,* 13; "Minnesota Longitudinal Study of Risk and Adaptation," Institute of Child Development, University of Minnesota. The reason for this choice as a sample is described in detail in the authors' book. In sum, this population in Minneapolis at this time had some markers for future problems such as stress, drug and alcohol addiction, and divorce, which would be important to watch unfold in light of attachment, but it was not such an "entrenched" poverty that many in the sample would not be expected to do well and break out of it.

149   **One of the most compelling findings** Jennifer Puig et al., "Predicting Adult Physical Illness from Infant Attachment: A Prospective Longitudinal Study," *Health Psychology* 32, no. 4 (2013): 409–17.

149   **From the start, these observations** Sroufe et al., *The Development of the Person,* ix, 188.

150   **A securely attached childhood led** L. Alan Sroufe and Daniel Siegel, "The Verdict Is In: The Case for Attachment Theory," *Psychotherapy Networker* 35, no. 2 (March/April 2011), https://www.drdansiegel.com/uploads /1271-the-verdict-is-in.pdf.

150   **"Nothing is more important"** Sroufe et al., *The Development of the Person,* 19.

150   **"development is not linear"** Ibid., 11.

150   **"a dream of developmental psychologists"** Ibid., ix.

151   **It opens with the sound** L. Alan Sroufe and Robert G. Cooper, *Missy: A Developmental Portrait* (Minneapolis: University of Minnesota Media Resources, 1989), DVD. I've changed the names of the children in the study, per Dr. Sroufe's request.

151   **"We're going to do this camp"** Ibid.

152   **When the interviewer asks Missy** Ibid.

152   **Missy looks pleased with herself** Ibid.

153   **"In sum, Missy had a clear sense of herself"** Ibid.

153   **Flashing to black-and-white footage** Ibid.

153   **Next we see one-year-old Missy** Ibid.

154   **During Episode 6** Ibid.

154   **The next shot is of Missy** Ibid.

154   **The next clips show Missy** Ibid.

155   **In preschool, we see Missy** Ibid.

155   **I began to wonder** In this chapter and elsewhere I focus on the connection between Azalea and myself because attachment tends to function between the child and one special other, though I am fully aware that Thayer has passed down traits to Azalea and of course plays a part in her attachment security. See the afterword for more on fathers.

156   **one of the most marked traits** Ibid.

159   **"Children with secure histories"** Nancy S. Weinfield, "The Nature of

Individual Differences in Infant-Caregiver Attachment," in Cassidy and Shaver, *Handbook of Attachment,* 77.

159 **These days we call this trait "grit"** Angela Duckworth, *Grit: The Power of Passion and Perseverance,* reprint edition (New York: Scribner, 2018).

159 **"responsible for the presence of [the] individual's long-term drive"** Jaclyn M. Levy and Howard Steele, "Attachment and Grit: Exploring Possible Contributions of Attachment Styles (from Past and Present Life) to the Adult Personality Construct of Grit," *Journal of Social & Psychological Sciences* 4, no. 2 (2011): 16–19.

160 **"She expects, if she tries"** Sroufe and Cooper, *Missy.*

Chapter Twenty-one

163 **"so I love you because"** Pablo Neruda, "Sonnet XVII," trans. Stephen Tapscott, accessed February 14, 2019, https://www.poemhunter.com/poem/xvii-i-do-not-love-you/.

PART VI: GET MOM

167 **"There is a time to nurture"** Ainsworth, *Infancy in Uganda,* 466.

Chapter Twenty-three

171 **Six years before he met Mary Ainsworth** Phyllis S. Kosminsky and John R. Jordan, *Attachment-Informed Grief Therapy: The Clinician's Guide to Foundations and Applications* (New York: Routledge, 2016), 4.

171 **"The research presented here"** John Bowlby, "Forty-Four Juvenile Thieves: Their Characters and Home-Life," *International Journal of Psychoanalysis* 25 (1944): 19–53.

171 **"There can be no doubt"** Ibid., 39; Suzan van Dijken et al., "Bowlby Before Bowlby: The Sources of an Intellectual Departure in Psychoanalysis and Psychology," *Journal of the History of the Behavioral Sciences* 34, no. 3 (Summer 1998): 247–69.

171 **"It can be concluded that"** Bowlby, "Forty-Four Juvenile Thieves."

172 **"affectionless," the "children who lack"** Ibid.

175 **And insecurely attached kids** Louise Bowers, Peter K. Smith, and Valerie Binney, "Perceived Family Relationships of Bullies, Victims and Bully/Victims in Middle Childhood," *Journal of Social and Personal Relationships* 11, no. 2 (May 1994): 216–17.

175 **"children with 'avoidant-insecure' attachment relationships"** Neville Jones and Eileen Baglin Jones, introduction to *Learning to Behave: Curriculum and Whole School Management Approaches to Discipline,* eds. Neville Jones and Eileen Baglin Jones (New York: RoutledgeFalmer, 1992), Google Books.

175 **"children who had been securely attached"** Peter K. Smith et al., "Relationships of Children Involved in Bully/Victim Problems at School," in

Making Sense of Social Development, eds. Martin Woodhead, Dorothy Faulkner, and Karen Littleton (New York: Routledge, 1999), 128.

Chapter Twenty-four

181   **In January 2018** Alex Stone, "Is Your Child Lying to You? That's Good," *New York Times,* January 6, 2018.

182   **Theory of mind is closely linked** Elizabeth Meins et al., "Maternal Mind-Mindedness and Attachment Security as Predictors of Theory of Mind Understanding," *Child Development* 73, no. 6 (November 2002): 1715–26.

182   **The reason Bowlby's early** Bowlby, "Forty-Four Juvenile Thieves."

182   **"total amount of care"** Ainsworth, "On Security."

182   **we are imprinted by our caregivers** Bowlby, "Forty-Four Juvenile Thieves."

182   **"Studies of nonclinical samples"** Moretti and Peled, "Adolescent-Parent Attachment," 551–55. A note from Alan Sroufe: "I know you use your own personal case later, but you really should acknowledge that lots of kids with secure histories get into trouble in adolescence. We don't want parents thinking that because their kid gets into drugs etc. that it means they were insecure as infants. There are 'snares,' as Moffitt calls them, that can get anyone. Secures do tend to come through it better." Alan Sroufe, email to Bethany Saltman, March 23, 2018.

182   **"In adolescence, attachment security"** Joseph P. Allen et al., "A Secure Base in Adolescence: Markers of Attachment Security in the Mother-Adolescent Relationship," *Child Development* 74, no. 1 (January–February 2003): 292–307.

183   **Alan Sroufe and his colleagues** L. Alan Sroufe, *Emotional Development: The Organization of Emotional Life in the Early Years* (New York: Cambridge University Press, 1995), 177. From another note from Alan Sroufe on "felt security": "I do think there are ways in which Bowlby's initial conceptions sold human attachment short. Humans are not geese. Our instincts are looser. A gosling sees mother move and automatically follows. With humans there is much more mediation by emotion. Mother moves, and the baby (monitoring always) looks up, perhaps with the beginnings of concern. But she smiles and nods and says it's OK and the baby relaxes and goes back to play. A major point in our 1977 paper was that it is better to think of the 'set point' for the attachment system is not physical proximity but 'felt security.' This makes the construct more developmentally robust and way less mechanical. When Azalea is off in college and gets hurt by someone she can call you; she doesn't need a literal hug (not to say that we don't sometimes). I think these changes in conceptualization are very important for clinical work. One can become secure even after one's parents are no longer alive, and a therapist can provide a secure base with no physical contact." Alan Sroufe, email to Bethany Saltman, December 7, 2017. See also L. Alan Sroufe and Everett Waters, "Attachment as an Organizational Construct," *Child Development* 48, no. 4 (December 1977): 1184–99.

183   **"felt security"** Sroufe and Waters, "Attachment as an Organizational Construct," 1184–99.

183   **"Antisocial" behavior is considered** Nathalie Fontaine et al., "Research Review: A Critical Review of Studies on the Developmental Trajectories of Antisocial Behavior in Females," *Child Psychology and Psychiatry* 50, no. 4 (2009): 363–85. Clearly there is a racial bias here, too . . . White girls like me get away with things black girls would never. Peggy McIntosh, "White Privilege: Unpacking the Invisible Knapsack," *Peace and Freedom,* July/August 1989.

184   **"the secure adolescent *tends to create"*** Allen et al., "A Secure Base in Adolescence," 292–307. Dr. Gordon Neufeld has written about the idea of "peer orientation" and how the kind of seeking I was doing is not necessarily always a good thing. When kids start orienting toward each other instead of their parents, an attachment rupture is definitely possible. I highly recommend the book *Hold On to Your Kids: Why Parents Need to Matter More Than Peers* (New York: Ballantine, 2005), by Neufeld and Gabor Maté.

185   **"Parental attunement and appropriate responsiveness"** Moretti and Peled, "Adolescent-Parent Attachment," 551–55.

185   **"In our view, the explanation"** Sroufe et al., *The Development of the Person,* 175.

185   **Was my relentless pursuit of connection** Ibid.

PART VII: A THING TO SLIP INTO

191   **"This woman won our unstinted admiration"** Ainsworth, *Infancy in Uganda,* 234.

Chapter Twenty-six

193   **an article published in 1985** Mary Main, Nancy Kaplan, and Jude Cassidy, "Security in Infancy, Childhood, and Adulthood: A Move to the Level of Representation," *Monographs of the Society for Research in Child Development* 50, no. 1/2 (1985): 66–104. On February 23, 2019, the official citation count according to Google Scholar was 6,996 times.

194   **At two years old** Mary Main, Erik Hesse, and Nancy Kaplan, "Predictability of Attachment Behavior and Representational Processes at 1, 6, and 19 Years of Age: The Berkeley Longitudinal Study," in Grossmann, Grossmann, and Waters, *Attachment from Infancy to Adulthood,* 248–49.

194   **Chomsky, born in 1928** Howard Lasnik and Terje Lohndal, "Noam Chomsky," *Oxford Research Encyclopedia of Linguistics,* August 2017, http://www.oxfordre.com/linguistics/view/10.1093/acrefore/9780199384655.001.0001/acrefore-9780199384655-e-356.

194   **Main applied to the Johns Hopkins** Main, "Mary D. Salter Ainsworth," 685.

194   **Mary Ainsworth offered Main a spot** Ibid., 682–86.

194   **Main's dissertation, completed in 1973** Main, Hesse, and Kaplan, "Predictability of Attachment Behavior," 250.

195   **a phrase Mary would throw back** Main, "Mary D. Salter Ainsworth," 13.

195   **after receiving her PhD** Main, Hesse, and Kaplan, "Predictability of Attachment Behavior," 245–95.

195   **the parents' transcripts were then classified** Ibid., 267.

196   **"one of the most robust findings"** Annie Bernier and Raphaele Milkovitch, "Intergenerational Transmission Attachment in Father-Child Dyads: The Case of Single Parenthood," *Journal of Genetic Psychology* 170, no. 1 (2009): 31–32.

196   **"the verdict is in"** Sroufe and Siegel, "The Verdict Is In."

197   **"Buddhism contains the idea"** Traleg Kyabgon Rinpoche, *Karma: What It Is, What It Isn't, Why It Matters* (Boston: Shambhala Publications, 2015), Google Books.

197   **"All that can safely be said"** Bowlby, *Attachment,* 349.

197   **"As always, adaptation is a product"** Sroufe et al., *The Development of the Person,* 150.

198   **"Karmic theory is supposed"** Traleg, *Karma.*

Chapter Twenty-seven

203   **"requir[ing] a rapid succession"** Main, Hesse, and Kaplan, "Predictability of Attachment Behavior," 291.

204   **"You mentioned that you felt"** Ibid., 265.

Chapter Twenty-eight

208   **As evidence for the adjective "loving"** Hesse, "The Adult Attachment Interview," 558–59.

209   **the way preoccupied speech incorporates** Kenneth N. Levy and Kristen M. Kelly, "Using Interviews to Assess Adult Attachment," in *Attachment Theory and Research in Clinical Work with Adults,* eds. J. H. Obegi and E. Berant (New York: Guilford Press, 2009), 121–52.

209   **whether or not a person *values*** Ibid.

210   **Securely attached adults** Ibid.

Chapter Twenty-nine

211   **"Mum was very good"** Howard and Miriam are, like Ainsworth and my mom and our good friends, Canadian, hence "Mum."

212   **an "adaptive strategy!"** Exclamation point his!

213   **a slight touch of disorganization** Remember, disorganization can appear in an otherwise secure transcript. And that's why it's so important for me to

work with—because this kind of scary behavior can also be passed down, just like security.

214   **"B4," I repeated** Marinus van IJzendoorn et al., "How B Is B4? Attachment and Security of Dutch Children in Ainsworth's Strange Situation and at Home," *Psychological Reports* 52 (1983): 683–91.

Chapter Thirty

215   **which they call "reflective functioning"** Howard Steele and Miriam Steele, "Understanding and Resolving Emotional Conflict: Findings from the London Parent-Child Project," in Grossmann, Grossmann, and Waters, *Attachment from Infancy to Adulthood: The Major Longitudinal Studies,* 157–58.

216   **one type of secure adult—the F3B** Howard Steele and Miriam Steele, "Ten Clinical Uses of the Adult Attachment Interview," 10.

216   **The problem with this "earned secure"** Glenn I. Roisman et al., "Earned-Secure Attachment Status in Retrospect and Prospect," *Child Development* 73, no. 4 (July/August 2002): 1204–19.

Chapter Thirty-one

222   **"Kabat-Zinn: The meaning of being"** Jon Kabat-Zinn, interview by Bethany Saltman, August 21, 2010, transcript.

224   **"We shall never know"** Ainsworth, *Infancy in Uganda,* 436.

224   **85 percent dark matter** Mara Johnson-Groh, "Scientists Find the 'Missing' Dark Matter from the Early Universe," *LiveScience,* January 2, 2019, https://www.livescience.com/64389-dark-matter-around-galaxies-constant.html.

225   **"All evil karma ever committed"** John Daido Loori, *Bringing the Sacred to Life: The Daily Practice of Zen Ritual* (Boston: Shambhala, 2008), 87.

225   **the relationship between "self-compassion" and "parenting"** Helena Moreira et al., "Maternal Attachment and Children's Quality of Life: The Mediating Role of Self-Compassion and Parenting Stress," *Journal of Child and Family Studies* 24, no. 8 (2015): 2332.

226   **"Parents may learn how to reduce"** Ibid., 2342.

227   **"Attachment is not a set"** Diana Divecha, "What Is a Secure Attachment? And Why Doesn't 'Attachment Parenting' Get You There?" *Developmental Science,* April 3, 2017, http://www.developmentalscience.com/blog/2017/3/31/what-is-a-secure-attachmentand-why-doesnt-attachment-parenting-get-you-there.

228   **While other video-based interventions exist** See *Promoting Positive Parenting: An Attachment-Based Intervention,* eds. Femmie Juffer, Marian J. Bakermans-Kranenburg, and Marinus H. van IJzendoorn (New York: Taylor & Francis Group/Lawrence Erlbaum Associates, 2008).

228   **theirs is unique** Howard Steele, email to Bethany Saltman, October 31, 2019.

228   **GABI (Group Attachment–Based Intervention)** Miriam Steele et al., "Looking from the Outside In: The Use of Video in Attachment-Based Interventions," *Attachment and Human Development* 16, no. 4 (2014): 412.

228   **"Randomized controlled trials have shown"** Ibid., 404.

228   **And this maternal sensitivity** Daniel J. Siegel, *The Developing Mind: How Relationships and the Brain Interact to Shape Who We Are* (New York: Guilford Press, 2012), 261.

228   **The Steeles' GABI program** Howard Steele et al., "Randomized Control Trial Report on the Effectiveness of Group Attachment-Based Intervention (GABI): Improvements in the Parent–Child Relationship Not Seen in the Control Group," *Development and Psychopathology* 31, no. 1 (2019): 3.

229   **Bob told me** Bob Marvin interview, February 7, 2017.

Chapter Thirty-two

230   **"Attachment is internal"** Ainsworth, *Infancy in Uganda,* 429–50.

231   **"Our last visit took place"** Ibid., 205.

232   **"Sister Sarah Joan: You clearly love Sacramento"** Greta Gerwig, dir., *Lady Bird* (2017; Santa Monica, CA: Lionsgate, 2018).

232   **Mary spoke of being childless** Main, "Mary D. Salter Ainsworth," 700.

233   **The babies she never had** Ainsworth, "A Sketch of a Career."

233   **"Wisdom is of the heart"** McDougall, *Character and Conduct of Life.*

PART VIII: RETELLING

237   **"After the Strange Situation we all"** Mary Ainsworth, "Case 18, Visit 20, June 14, 1967."

Chapter Thirty-three

244   **"If an evil man"** Amoghavajra, "Sutra of the Whole-Body Relic Treasure Chest Seal Dharani, the Heart Secret of All Tathagatas," in *The Teachings of the Buddha: Selected Mahyana Sutras,* trans. Rulu (Bloomington, IN: AuthorHouse, 2012), 63.

Afterword: Where Angels Fear to Tread: Attachment Today

249   **"Despite the alarming incidence of neurosis"** Ainsworth, *Infancy in Uganda,* 458.

250   **the *New York* magazine article** Bethany Saltman, "Can Attachment Theory Explain All Our Relationships?" *New York,* July 5, 2016.

250   **Maybe the 2009 article "The First"** Marian J. Bakermans-Kranenburg and Marinus H. van IJzendoorn, "The First 10,000 Attachment Interviews: Distributions of Adult Attachment Representations in Clinical and Non-Clinical Groups," *Attachment and Human Development* 11, no. 3 (2009): 223–63.

251 **"In a popular essay recently published"** Fraley, "Attachment in Adulthood," 402.

251 **"Although theories in psychology tend"** Ibid., 402–3.

252 **The article that introduced** Main, Kaplan, and Cassidy, "Security in Infancy, Childhood, and Adulthood," 66–104.

252 **"Romantic Love Conceptualized"** Hazan and Shaver, "Romantic Love Conceptualized as an Attachment Process," 511–24.

252 **the beginning of the subfield** Ibid.

253 **while babies and children rely solely** Fraley, "Attachment in Adulthood," 404.

253 **"one of the implications of these"** Ibid., 407.

253 **"early experiences should be construed"** Ibid., 407–8.

253 **nothing that "fully determines" anything** See, for example: R. Chris Fraley and Marie E. Heffernan, "Attachment and Parental Divorce: A Test of the Diffusion and Sensitive Period Hypothesis," *Personality and Social Psychology Bulletin* 39, no. 9 (September 2013): 1199–213; Hong and Park, "Impact of Attachment, Temperament, and Parenting on Human Development," 449–54; Kimberly S. Howard, "Paternal Attachment, Parenting Beliefs and Children's Attachment," *Early Child Development and Care* 180, no. 1–2 (2010): 157–71; Jason D. Jones, Jude Cassidy, and Phillip R. Shaver, "Adult Attachment Style and Parenting," in Simpson and Rholes, *Attachment Theory and Research: New Directions and Emerging Themes,* 234–60; Jason D. Jones et al., "Maternal Attachment Style and Responses to Adolescents' Negative Emotions: The Mediating Role of Maternal Emotion Regulation," *Parenting* 14, no. 3–4 (2014): 235–57.

254 **"A test of caregiver sensitivity"** Verhage et al., "Narrowing the Transmission Gap," 337.

254 **"little evidence [that] supports genetic transmission"** Ibid., 337–40.

254 **Though twin studies** Marian J. Bakermans-Kranenburg and Marinus H. van IJzendoorn, "Attachment, Parenting, and Genetics," in Cassidy and Shaver, *Handbook of Attachment,* 156.

254 **Likewise, though "everyone knows"** R. M. Pasco Fearon and Jay Belsky, "Precursors of Attachment Security," in Cassidy and Shaver, *Handbook of Attachment,* 292.

254 **One recent study found that post-adoption** Lavinia Barone, Yagmur Ozturk, and Francesca Lionetti, "The Key Role of Positive Parenting and Children's Temperament in Post-Institutionalized Children's Socio-Emotional Adjustment After Adoption Placement: A RCT Study," *Social Development* 28, no. 1 (July 27, 2018): 136–51, https://www.doi.org/10.1111/sode.12329.

255 **infants who scored low** Brian E. Vaughn and Kelly K. Bost, "Attachment and Temperament as Intersecting Developmental Products and Interacting Developmental Contexts Throughout Infancy and Childhood," in Cassidy and Shaver, *Handbook of Attachment,* 217.

255   **"Ainsworth never expressed the belief"** Fearon and Belsky, "Precursors of Attachment Security," 291.

255   **the infant comes to its attachment** Vaughn and K. Bost, "Attachment and Temperament as Intersecting Developmental," 209–12.

255   **"Indeed, adults have needs"** Howard Steele, email to Bethany Saltman, February 7, 2019.

256   **Children on the autism spectrum** Barry Coughlan et al., "Attachment and Autism Spectrum Conditions," 2, 7. Though there is some fascinating debate about how attachment and ASC are coded and might be mistaken for each other.

256   **attachment in light of environmental risk factors** Verhage et al., "Narrowing the Transmission Gap," 337–66.

257   **"change, as well as continuity"** Sroufe et al., *The Development of the Person,* 19, 36.

257   **"Future studies should focus"** Verhage et al., "Narrowing the Transmission Gap," 18.

258   **as Bowlby and Ainsworth said** Mary D. Salter Ainsworth, "Object Relations, Dependency and Attachment: A Theoretical Review of the Infant-Mother Relationship," *Child Development* 40, no. 4 (December 1969): 969–1025; John Bowlby, "Attachment and Loss: Retrospect and Prospect," *American Journal of Orthopsychiatry* 52, no. 4 (1982): 664–78; Bretherton, "Origins of Attachment Theory," 759–75; Chris G. Sibley and Nickola C. Overall, "Modeling the Hierarchical Structure of Attachment Representations: A Test of Domain Differentiation," *Personality and Individual Differences* 44, no. 1 (January 2008): 238–49.

258   **Over our lifetimes, we develop** Fraley, "Attachment in Adulthood," 408.

258   **"there should be some degree"** Ibid.

258   **"consensual non-monogamy"** Ibid., 411.

258   **I know this is something** Elisabeth A. Sheff, "Fidelity in Polyamorous Relationships: Expanding Beyond Sexual Exclusivity," *The Polyamorists Next Door* (blog), *Psychology Today,* January 29, 2019, https://www.psychologytoday.com/us/blog/the-polyamorists-next-door/201901/fidelity-in-polyamorous-relationships.

259   **CNM "appears to be common"** M. L. Haupert et al., "Prevalence of Experiences with Consensual Nonmonogamous Relationships: Findings from Two National Samples of Single Americans," *Journal of Sex and Marital Therapy* 43, no. 5 (2017): 424–40.

259   **"moreover, according to Conley et al."** Fraley, "Attachment in Adulthood," 411.

259   **CNM relationships present a real conundrum** Bowlby, "Nature of the Child's Tie to His Mother," 350–73.

259   **Monotropy is the widely accepted idea** Carollee Howes and Susan Spieker, "Attachment Relationships in the Context of Multiple Caregivers," in Cassidy and Shaver, *Handbook of Attachment,* 319.

259   **Infants and children form attachments** Susanne Bennett, "Is There a Primary Mom? Parental Perceptions of Attachment Bond Hierarchies Within Lesbian Adoptive Families," *Child and Adolescent Social Work Journal* 20, no. 3 (June 2003): 159–73; Eric Alain Feuge et al., "Adoptive Gay Fathers' Sensitivity and Child Attachment and Behavior Problems," *Attachment and Human Development* 20 (December 2018): 1–22, https://www.doi.org/10.1080/14616734.2018.1557224; Cecilia Serena Pace, Giulio Cesare Zavattini, and M. D'Alessio, "Continuity and Discontinuity of Attachment Patterns: A Short-Term Longitudinal Pilot Study Using a Sample of Late-Adopted Children and Their Adoptive Mothers," *Attachment and Human Development* 14, no. 1 (2012): 45–61; Julie Poehlmann, "An Attachment Perspective on Grandparents Raising Their Very Young Grandchildren: Implications for Intervention and Research," *Infant Mental Health Journal* 24, no. 2 (March 2003): 149–73; Lee Raby et al., "Childhood Abuse and Neglect and Insecure Attachment States of Mind in Adulthood: Prospective, Longitudinal Evidence from a High-Risk Sample," *Development and Psychopathology* 29, no. 2 (May 2017): 347–63; Christie Schoenmaker et al., "From Maternal Sensitivity in Infancy to Adult Attachment Representations: A Longitudinal Adoption Study with Secure Base Scripts," *Attachment and Human Development* 17, no. 3 (2015): 241–56; Howard Steele and Miriam Steele, "The Construct of Coherence as an Indicator of Attachment Security in Middle Childhood: The Friends and Family Interview," in *Attachment in Middle Childhood,* eds. Kathryn A. Kerns and Rhonda A. Richardson (New York: Guilford Press, 2005), 140.

259   **gay, lesbian, or trans** While there have not been any studies to date on trans parents and their children's attachment, I'm taking the liberty of extrapolating here.

259   **In a sample of 1,281 adults** Amy C. Moors et al., "Attached to Monogamy? Avoidance Predicts Willingness to Engage (But Not Actual Engagement) in Consensual Non-Monogamy," *Journal of Social and Personal Relationships* 32, no. 2 (2015): 222–40.

259   **"Given the stigma against CNM arrangements"** Fraley, "Attachment in Adulthood," 412.

260   **"when Bowlby was writing"** Ibid., 413. Of course, Sroufe and colleagues tweaked this set goal of attachment to be "felt security" instead of physical proximity. Sroufe and Waters, "Attachment as an Organizational Construct," 1184–99.

260   **I find particularly useful** Ibid., 413–14.

260   **Likewise, "Highly avoidant people"** Ibid.

261   **This wonderful twist on how** David Rock and Heidi Grant, "Why Diverse Teams Are Smarter," *Harvard Business Review,* November 4, 2016.

261   **"According to SDT, groups"** Fraley, "Attachment in Adulthood," 413–14.

261   **"thriving through relationships"** Ibid., 415.

262   **as early as Uganda, Ainsworth** Ainsworth, *Infancy in Uganda,* 352.

262   **"Bowlby assumed that the mother"** Sarah B. Hrdy, "Evolutionary Context

of Human Development: The Cooperative Breeding Model," in *Attachment and Bonding: A New Synthesis*, Dahlem Workshop Reports, eds. C. S. Carter et al. (Cambridge, MA: MIT Press, 2005), 9–10.

263   **"Although I have described these five"** Bowlby, "Nature of the Child's Tie to His Mother."

264   **since Bowlby's first formulation, recent studies** Raby and Mary Dozier, "Attachment Across the Lifespan," 81–85.

265   **The best pathway for raising** See, for example: Claire Farrow and Jackie Blisset, "Maternal Mind-Mindedness During Infancy, General Parenting Sensitivity and Observed Child Feeding Behavior: Longitudinal Study," *Attachment and Human Development* 16, no. 3 (2014): 230–41; Zhihuan Jennifer Huang et al., "Variations in the Relationship Between Maternal Depression, Maternal Sensitivity, and Child Attachment by Race/Ethnicity and Nativity: Findings from a Nationally Representative Cohort Study," *Maternal and Child Health Journal* 16, no. 1 (2012): 40–50; Jochen Kluve and Marcus Tamm, "Parental Leave Regulations, Mothers' Labor Force Attachment and Fathers' Childcare Involvement: Evidence from a Natural Experiment," *Journal of Population Economics* 26, no. 3 (July 2013): 983–1005; Allison M. Rothman and Janice M. Steil, "Adolescent Attachment and Entitlement in a World of Wealth," *Journal of Infant, Child, and Adolescent Pscyhotherapy* 11, no. 1 (2012): 53–65; Ghadir Zreik, David Oppenheim, and Abraham Sagi-Schwartz, "Infant Attachment and Maternal Sensitivity in the Arab Minority in Israel," *Child Development* 88, no. 4 (July/August 2017): 1338–49.

265   **"attentional flexibility"** Mary Main, "The Organized Categories of Infant, Child, and Adult Attachment: Flexible vs. Inflexible Attention Under Attachment-Related Stress," *Journal of the American Psychoanalytic Association* 48, no. 4 (August 2000): 1055–96.

265   **This is the term she uses** Hesse, "The Adult Attachment Interview," 558.

265   **Likewise, Main found that the adult** Ibid.

266   **Missy's ability to manage herself** Sroufe and Cooper, *Missy*.

266   **"emotional regulation"** Susanna Pallini et al., "The Relation of Attachment Security Status to Effortful Self-Regulation: A Meta-Analysis," *Psychological Bulletin* 144, no. 5 (2018): 501–31.

266   **"To the degree that we're willing"** Pema Chödrön, quoted in Mario Mikulincer and Phillip R. Shaver, *Attachment in Adulthood: Structure, Dynamics, and Change* (New York: Guilford Press, 2007), 481.

266   **many studies have found** Jon G. Caldwell and Phillip R. Shaver, "Mediators of the Link Between Adult Attachment and Mindfulness," *Interpersonal: An International Journal on Personal Relationships* 7, no. 2 (2013): 299–310, https://interpersona.psychopen.eu/article/view/133/163.

267   **Minding the Baby** To learn more, visit https://www.medicine.yale.edu/childstudy/communitypartnerships/mtb/.

267   **define RF as "the ability to imagine"** Arietta Slade et al., "Minding the Baby: Enhancing Parental Reflective Functioning and Infant Attachment in an Attachment-Based, Interdisciplinary Home Visiting Program," *Develop-*

ment and Psychopathology 14 (January 2019): 2; Lois S. Sadler et al., "Minding the Baby: Enhancing Reflectiveness to Improve Early Health and Relationship Outcomes in an Interdisciplinary Home-Visiting Program," *Infant Mental Health Journal* 34, no. 5 (2013): 391–405.

267 **As Mary put it** Ainsworth et al., *Patterns of Attachment,* 361.

267 **The nurses and social workers** Slade et al., "Minding the Baby," 2–10.

268 **an influx of relationship valuing would increase** Ibid., 1.

268 **Paul Raeburn wrote a book** Paul Raeburn, *Do Fathers Matter? What Science Is Telling Us About the Parent We've Overlooked* (New York: Scientific American, 2014). For instance, Simon Baron-Cohen, an autism expert and professor of psychopathology at the University of Cambridge (and actor Sacha Baron Cohen's cousin!), writes in an essay in *The Guardian,* "Science continues apace to unravel the functions of genes. Just last year our group published new findings of genes related to empathy—a skill that women are, on average, better at than men. Biological determinists don't dismiss the importance of culture. They simply don't deny the role of biology. It is a moderate position, recognizing the interaction of social and biological factors. Nor, in my opinion, is biological determinism necessarily sexist. It can be sexist, if it is used to claim that all women do X and all men do Y (since sex differences don't apply to all individuals of one sex) or if it is used to perpetuate social inequalities. Such sexist applications of biological determinist theories are abhorrent." Simon Baron-Cohen, "It's Not Sexist to Accept That Biology Affects Behaviour," *Guardian,* May 3, 2010.

269 **"As an aside I remark"** Main, "Mary D. Salter Ainsworth," 695.

269 **Michael Lamb, a British man** Michael E. Lamb, "Curriculum Vitae," accessed February 26, 2019, http://www.psychology.sunysb.edu/attachment /vitae/lamb_cv.pdf; Raeburn, *Do Fathers Matter?,* 81.

269 **In one epistolary exchange** The heading of Mary's letter from 1974 reads: "COMMENTS ON 'The attachment behaviors of eight-month-olds as directed toward their mothers and fathers in the home environment.'" Lamb responded quickly and in earnest. His 1976 paper "Twelve-Month-Olds and Their Parents: Interaction in a Laboratory Playroom" can be found in *Developmental Psychology* 12, no. 3 (May 1976): 237–44.

270 **"Forgive the avuncular"** Mary Ainsworth to Michael Lamb, October 27, 1974, Mary D. Salter Ainsworth Papers, Cummings Center for the History of Psychology, University of Akron.

270 **Ainsworth's beefs with Lamb's paper** Ibid.

270 **tens of thousands of studies later** With a search on Google Scholar of fathers and attachment theory, I found 37,500 hits.

270 **"The introduction rubbed me"** Mary Ainsworth to Michael Lamb, October 27, 1974, Mary D. Salter Ainsworth Papers, Cummings Center for the History of Psychology, University of Akron.

270 **"belligerent and contentious"** Lamb's original paper is not included in Mary's archive, but his response to her letter is. His tone is gracious, though not particularly detailed. He writes, "Thank you for your comments re-

ceived yesterday. I really appreciate your taking so much time, and am sure your comments will prove invaluably helpful when I come to rewrite the paper . . . Some of your criticisms will have been allayed in the second paper . . . I did not intend to imply that fathers were more important than mothers—I tried to avoid that." And then, in closing, "Again, thank you. I hope you have equally insightful comments on the other papers." Michael E. Lamb to Mary Ainsworth, November 1, 1974, Mary D. Salter Ainsworth Papers, Cummings Center for the History of Psychology, University of Akron.

271 **"If you read *Infancy*"** Ibid. Sadly, nobody ever does! This seminal book is out of print, and few of the experts I know have even read it. One of my many hopes for this book is that it might change that.

272 **"Finally, please don't think"** Ibid.

272 **"Incidentally, you skipped a step"** Ibid.

272 **"particularly boisterous, stimulating"** Michael E. Lamb, "How Do Fathers Influence Children's Development? Let Me Count the Ways," in *The Role of the Father in Child Development,* ed. Michael E. Lamb (Hoboken, NJ: John Wiley and Sons, 2010), 3.

272 **"First, fathers and mothers seem"** Ibid., 10.

273 **the link between quality of paternal care** Fearon and Belsky, "Precursors of Attachment Security," 299; Nicole Lucassen, "The Association Between Paternal Sensitivity and Infant-Father Attachment Security: A Meta-Analysis of Three Decades of Research," *Journal of Family Psychology* 25, no. 6 (December 2011): 986–92.

273 **because of the way the Strange Situation** Geoffrey L. Brown, Sarah C. Mangelsdorf, and Cynthia Neff, "Father Involvement, Paternal Sensitivity, and Father-Child Attachment Security in the First Three Years," *Journal of Family Psychology* 26, no. 3 (2012): 421–30; Michael E. Lamb, "Qualitative Aspects of Mother- and Father-Infant Attachments," *Infant Behavior and Development* 1 (1978): 264–75; Susan Spieker and Patricia McKinsey Crittenden, "Comparing Two Attachment Classification Methods Applied to Preschool Strange Situations," *Clinical Child Psychology and Psychiatry* 15, no. 1 (January 2010): 97–120.

273 **"By having the same parent–child dyads"** Daniel Paquette and Marc Bigras, "The Risky Situation: A Procedure for Assessing the Father-Child Activation Relationship," *Early Child Development and Care* 180, no. 1–2 (January 2010): 33–50.

274 **the specifics of how fathers** Geoffrey L. Brown et al., "Associations Between Father Involvement and Father-Child Attachment Security: Variations Based on Timing and Type of Involvement," *Journal of Family Psychology* 32, no. 8 (2018): 1015–24.

274 **another tracked the testosterone** Patty X. Kuo et al., "Individual Variation in Fathers' Testosterone Reactivity to Infant Distress Predicts Parenting Behaviors with Their 1-Year-Old Infants," *Developmental Psychobiology* 58, no. 3 (April 2016): 306.

274 **"fathers of daughters were more"** Ibid., 312.

274 **these children are thriving** Bennett, "Is There a Primary Mom?" 159–73; Feuge et al., "Adoptive Gay Fathers' Sensitivity and Child Attachment and Behavior Problems," 1–22; Margaret Rosario, "Implications of Childhood Experiences for the Health and Adaptation of Lesbian, Gay, and Bisexual Individuals: Sensitivity to Developmental Process in Future Research," *Psychology of Sexual Orientation and Gender Diversity* 2, no. 2 (September 2015): 214–24.

274 **While different cultures skew differently** Judi Mesman, Marinus H. van IJzendoorn, and Abraham Sagi-Schwartz, "Cross-Cultural Patterns of Attachment: Universal and Contextual Dimensions," in Cassidy and Shaver, *Handbook of Attachment,* 857, 869.

275 **attachment patterns in individuals** Anne C. Laurita, Cindy Hazan, and R. Nathan Spreng, "An Attachment Theoretical Perspective for the Neural Representation of Close Others," *Social Cognitive and Affective Neuroscience* (2019): 1–15; Elaine Scharfe and Nicole Black, "Does Love Matter to Infants' Health: Influence of Maternal Attachment Representations on Reports of Infant Health," *Journal of Relationships Research* 10 (2019): e4, https://doi.org/10.1017/jrr.2018.24; Ohad Szepsenwol and Jeffry A. Simpson, "Attachment Within Life History Theory: An Evolutionary Perspective on Individual Differences in Attachment," *Current Opinion in Psychology* 25 (February 2019): 65–70.

275 **The recent documentary** *Three Identical Strangers* Tim Wardle, dir., *Three Identical Strangers* (Universal City, CA: Universal Pictures Home Entertainment, 2018), DVD.

275 **epigenetics, the study of the role** Lawrence Harper, "Epigenetic Inheritance and the Intergenerational Transfer of Experience," *Psychological Bulletin* 131, no. 3 (2005): 340–60; Karen Jones-Mason et al., "Epigenetic Marks as the Link Between Environment and Development: Examination of the Associations Between Attachment: Socioeconomic Status, and Methylation of the SLC6A4 Gene," *Brain and Behavior* 6, no. 7 (2016): e00480, https://doi.org/10.1002/brb3.480; Maartje P. C. M. Luijk et al., "The Association Between Parenting and Attachment Security Is Moderated by a Polymorphism in the Mineralocorticoid Receptor Gene: Evidence for Differential Susceptibility," *Biological Psychology* 88, no. 1 (September 2011): 37–40; Howard Steele and Larry Siever, "An Attachment Perspective on Borderline Personality Disorder: Advances in Gene-Environment Considerations," *Current Psychiatry Reports* 12, no. 1 (February 2010): 61–67.

276 **When Dr. Nadine Burke Harris** Nadine Burke Harris, "How Childhood Trauma Affects Health Across a Lifetime," filmed September 2014, TEDMED video, 15:59, https://www.ted.com/talks/nadine_burke_harris_how_childhood_trauma_affects_health_across_a_lifetime.

276 **"something medical was happening with"** Nadine Burke Harris, *The Deepest Well: Healing the Long-Term Effects of Childhood Adversity* (Boston: Houghton Mifflin Harcourt, 2018), 5.

276 **It started with the proliferation** Ibid., 3–6.

276   **Burke Harris was struck** Ibid.

276   **Burke Harris's young patients** Ibid., 3–7.

277   **ACE is an acronym** "Got Your ACE Score?" ACES too High!, accessed February 27, 2019, https://acestoohigh.com/got-your-ace-score/.

278   **"Relationship of Childhood Abuse"** Vincent J. Felitti et al., "Relationship of Childhood Abuse and Household Dysfunction to Many of the Leading Causes of Death in Adults: The Adverse Childhood Experiences (ACE) Study," *American Journal of Preventive Medicine* 14, no. 4 (1998): 245–58.

278   **"Before he could even shut"** Burke Harris, *The Deepest Well*, 30.

279   **"If one hundred people all drink"** Ibid., 12.

279   **What the ACE study found** Ibid., 38. See also Vincent J. Felitti and Robert F. Anda, "The Relationship of Adverse Childhood Experiences to Adult Medical Disease, Psychiatric Disorders, and Sexual Behavior: Implications for Healthcare," in *The Impact of Early Life Trauma on Health and Disease: The Hidden Epidemic,* eds. Ruth A. Lanius, Eric Vermetten, and Claire Pain (Boston: Cambridge University Press, 2010), 77–87.

279   **"the more ACEs a child"** "Together We Can Build a Healthier Future for Children Exposed to Adversity," Center for Youth Wellness, accessed April 4, 2019, https://centerforyouthwellness.org.

280   **"How is it that ACEs are handed"** Burke Harris, *The Deepest Well*, 78–79.

280   **researchers noticed that rats** Dan Hurley, "Grandma's Experiences Leave a Mark on Your Genes," *Discover,* May 2013, http://www.discovermagazine.com/2013/may/13-grandmas-experiences-leave-epigenetic-mark-on-your-genes.

280   **What happened was that Dr. Meaney** Ibid.; Burke Harris, *The Deepest Well,* 81–85.

281   **Meaney and his colleague found** Burke Harris, *The Deepest Well,* 81–85. Next steps: What happened to the male pups?!

281   **the actual behavior of the parents** Ibid.

281   **a 2019 editorial** Saoud Sultan, "Healthy Parenting in the Age of the Genome: Nature or Nurture?" *Saudi Journal of Medicine and Medical Sciences* 7, no. 1 (2019): 1–2.

282   **"Studies in both animals and humans"** Ibid.

282   **"Intriguingly the results of Meany's"** Marialuigia Spinelli, "The Attachment Theory Today: From the Epigenetic Effects of Maternal Behavior to Psyco-Neuro-Endocrino-Immunology," *Journal of Clinical Epigenetics* 3, no. 43 (2017): 2.

283   **"It can be argued that this"** Ibid., 2–3.

283   **a naturally occurring "experiment of opportunity"** Brian Hopkins, "Culture, Infancy, and Education," *European Journal of Psychology of Education* 4, no. 2 (June 1989): 289–93. The Steeles have written about the importance of ACE scores, in attachment interventions, as well. "Parenting distress and ACEs were significantly higher in the low SES group; yet, even after controlling for SES, higher ACE scores added significant explained variance

in parental distress in a linear regression model. Discussion focuses on the need to administer ACE screening in prenatal and pediatric settings to identify and to offer trauma- and attachment-informed treatment, so to reduce the intergenerational transmission of risk associated with problematic parenting." Howard Steele et al., "Adverse Childhood Experiences, Poverty, and Parenting Stress," *Canadian Journal of Behavioural Science* 48, no. 1 (January 2016): 32–38.

283 **what we do matters** Mary Dozier et al., "Attachment for Infants in Foster Care: The Role of Caregiver State of Mind," in *Annual Progress in Child Psychiatry and Child Development 2002*, eds. Margaret E. Hertzig and Ellen A. Farber (New York: Routledge, 2005), 3, 15.

283 **"It should be noted that although"** Sultan, "Healthy Parenting in the Age of the Genome," 1–2.

285 **The Maternal Caregiving and Interaction Scales** Ainsworth et al., *Patterns of Attachment,* 356–79. Here is the entire scale online (a must-read!): Mary D. Salter Ainsworth, "Maternal Sensitivity Scales," accessed February 28, 2019, http://www.psychology.sunysb.edu/attachment/measures/content/ainsworth_scales.html.

285 **Each of the four scales** Ainsworth et al., *Patterns of Attachment,* 358–62.

286 **In the second scale, cooperation vs. interference** Ibid., 366–68.

286 **In the third, availability vs. ignoring** Ainsworth, "Maternal Sensitivity Scales."

286 **in the fourth scale, acceptance vs. rejection** Ibid.

286 **a 9 (highly accessible)** Ibid.

287 **Mary saw this false face** Inge Bretherton, "Revisiting Mary Ainsworth's Conceptualization and Assessments," 24.

287 **"Ainsworth had noted"** Ibid.

288 **The highly sensitive mother " 'reads' B's"** Ibid.

288 **"It is assumed that the arrival"** Ibid.

288 **How *do* we balance** Ibid.

289 **Maybe like the "highly interfering"** Ainsworth et al., *Patterns of Attachment,* 363.

290 **"It is difficult to hold"** Ainsworth, *Infancy in Uganda,* 457.

290 **She continues by sharing a personal story** Mary Ainsworth to Sylvia Bell, January 2, 1968, Mary D. Salter Ainsworth Papers, Cummings Center for the History of Psychology, University of Akron.

bibliography

FILM, VIDEO, AND ARCHIVAL SOURCES

Ainsworth, Mary D. Salter. "Baltimore Longitudinal Study of Attachment, 1963–1967." Murray Research Center, Radcliffe Institute for Advanced Study, Harvard University.

Ainsworth, Mary D. Salter. Papers, 1956–1983. Cummings Center for the History of Psychology, University of Akron.

"Attachment Videos Library." Department of Psychology, Stony Brook University, New York. Accessed February 15, 2019. http://www.psychology.sunysb.edu /attachment/video_contents/videos_index_2010_kg2_infant_script.html.

Burke Harris, Nadine. "How Childhood Trauma Affects Health Across a Lifetime." Filmed September 2014. TEDMED video, 15:59. https://www.ted.com /talks/nadine_burke_harris_how_childhood_trauma_affects_health_across_a _lifetime.

"Circle of Security." Ainsworth Attachment Clinic and the Circle of Security. Accessed February 20, 2019. http://www.theattachmentclinic.org/AboutUs /circle_of_security.html.

"Peter Fonagy: What Is Mentalization?" Video, 11:01, posted by Simms/Mann Institute on November 18, 2016. https://www.youtube.com/watch?v=MJ1Y9zw -n7U&feature=youtu.be.

Gerwig, Greta, dir. *Lady Bird*. 2017; Santa Monica, CA: Lionsgate, 2018. DVD.

"Konrad Lorenz: Kindheitserinnerungen und Anfänge der Ethologie." Altenberg bei Wien und Grünau im Almtal, 1977. Video, 19:42, posted by konrad lorenz haus altenberg on December 13, 2012. https://www.youtube.com/watch?v= __Fnb3LO_-o.

"Konrad Lorenz: Science of Animal Behavior." National Geographic Society and Jack Kaufman Pictures, 1975. Video, 13:52, posted by Biphily2. https://www .clip.fail/video/IysBMqaSAC8.

"Mary Ainsworth's Strage [*sic*] Situation: Attachment and the Growth of Love." Preview of *Mary Ainsworth: Attachment and the Growth of Love with Robert Marvin, Ph.D.,* San Luis Obispo, CA: Davidson Films, 2005. Video, 3:49, posted by Davidson Films on June 22, 2010. https://www.youtube.com/watch?v=SFCQLshYL6w.

"Minnesota Longitudinal Study of Risk and Adaptation." Institute of Child Development, University of Minnesota. Accessed February 13, 2019. https://innovation.umn.edu/parent-child/.

Sroufe, L. Alan, and Robert G. Cooper, dirs. *Missy: A Developmental Portrait.* Minneapolis: University of Minnesota Media Resources, 1989. VHS.

"A Two-Year-Old Goes to Hospital." Extract clip from *A Two-Year-Old Goes to Hospital,* Robertson Films, 1952. Video, 1:34, posted by Concord Media on July 1, 2014. https://www.youtube.com/watch?v=s14Q-_Bxc_U.

Wardle, Tim, dir. *Three Identical Strangers.* Universal City, CA: Universal Pictures Home Entertainment, 2018. DVD.

BOOKS AND PERIODICALS

ACES Too High! "Got Your ACE Score?" Accessed February 27, 2019. https://acestoohigh.com/got-your-ace-score/.

Adams, G. Camelia, and Lachlan McWilliams. "Relationships Between Adult Attachment Style Ratings and Sleep Disturbances in a Nationally Representative Sample." *Journal of Psychosomatic Research* 79, no. 1 (January 2015): 37–42.

Ainsworth, Mary D. Salter. *Infancy in Uganda: Infant Care and the Growth of Love.* Baltimore: Johns Hopkins Press, 1967.

———. "Infant-Mother Attachment." *American Psychologist* 34, no. 10 (October 1979): 932–37.

———. "Maternal Sensitivity Scales." Accessed February 28, 2019. http://www.psychology.sunysb.edu/attachment/measures/content/ainsworth_scales.html.

———. "Object Relations, Dependency, and Attachment: A Theoretical Review of the Infant-Mother Relationship." *Child Development* 40, no. 4 (December 1969): 969–1025.

———. "On Security." Unpublished paper, 1988. http://www.psychology.sunysb.edu/attachment/pdf/mda_security.pdf.

———. "A Sketch of a Career." In *Models of Achievement: Reflections of Eminent Women in Psychology,* edited by A. N. O'Connell and N. F. Russo. New York: Columbia University Press, 1983. http://www.psychology.sunysb.edu/attachment/pdf/mda_autobio.pdf.

———. "Social Development in the First Year of Life: Maternal Influences on Infant-Mother Attachment." In *Developments in Psychiatric Research: Essays Based on the Sir Geoffrey Vickers Lectures of the Mental Health Foundation,* edited by J. M. Tanner. New York: Hodder and Stoughton, 1977.

Ainsworth, Mary D. Salter, and Sylvia M. Bell. "Attachment, Exploration, and Separation: Illustrated by the Behavior of One-Year-Olds in a Strange Situation." *Child Development* 41, no. 1 (1970): 49–67.

Ainsworth, Mary D. Salter, Sylvia M. Bell, and D. J. Stayton. "Individual Differences in Strange-Situation Behavior of One-Year-Olds." In *The Origins of Human Social Relations,* edited by H. R. Schaffer. New York: Academic Press, 1971.

Ainsworth, Mary D. Salter, Mary C. Blehar, Everett Waters, and Sally N. Wall. *Patterns of Attachment: A Psychological Study of the Strange Situation*. New York: Psychology Press, 2015.

Ainsworth, Mary D. Salter, and Robert S. Marvin. "On the Shaping of Attachment Theory and Research: An Interview with Mary D. S. Ainsworth." *Monographs of the Society for Research in Child Development* 60, no. 23 (Fall 1994): 3–21.

Alexander, Pamela C. "Relational Trauma and Disorganized Attachment." In *Treating Complex Traumatic Stress Disorders in Children and Adolescents: Scientific Foundations and Therapeutic Models,* edited by Julian D. Ford and Christine A. Courtois. New York: Guilford Press, 2013.

Allen, Joseph P., Kathleen Boykin McElhaney, Deborah J. Land, Gabriel P. Kuperminc, Cynthia W. Moore, Heather O'Beirne-Kelly, and Sarah Liebman Kilmer. "A Secure Base in Adolescence: Markers of Attachment Security in the Mother-Adolescent Relationship." *Child Development* 74, no. 1 (January–February 2003): 292–307.

Amoghavajra. "Sutra of the Whole-Body Relic Treasure Chest Seal Dharani, the Heart Secret of All Tathagatas." In *The Teachings of the Buddha: Selected Mahyana Sutras,* translated by Rulu. Bloomington, IN: AuthorHouse, 2012.

Arsenian, Jean M. "Young Children in an Insecure Situation." *Journal of Abnormal and Social Psychology* 38, no. 2 (1943): 225–49.

Associated Press. "Austrian University Strips Nobel Prize Winner of Honors." *Washington Post,* December 21, 2015. https://wapo.st/1U0Ihm0?tid=ss_tw& utm_term=.70e826b1caa4.

Bakermans-Kranenburg, Marian J., and Marinus H. van IJzendoorn. "Attachment, Parenting, and Genetics." In *Handbook of Attachment: Theory, Research, and Clinical Applications,* edited by Jude Cassidy and Phillip R. Shaver. New York: Guilford Press, 2016.

———. "The First 10,000 Attachment Interviews: Distributions of Adult Attachment Representations in Clinical and Non-Clinical Groups." *Attachment and Human Development* 11, no. 3 (2009): 223–63.

Baron-Cohen, Simon. "It's Not Sexist to Accept That Biology Affects Behaviour." *Guardian,* May 3, 2010.

Barone, Lavinia, Yagmur Ozturk, and Francesca Lionetti. "The Key Role of Positive Parenting and Children's Temperament in Post-Institutionalized Children's Socio-Emotional Adjustment After Adoption Placement. A RCT Study." *Social Development* 28, no. 1 (July 27, 2018): 136–51. https://doi.org/10.1111/sode.12329.

Barth, Richard P., Thomas M. Crea, Karen John, and June Thoburn. "Beyond Attachment Theory and Therapy: Towards Sensitive and Evidence-Based Interventions with Foster and Adoptive Families in Distress." *Child and Family Social Work* 10, no. 4 (November 2005): 257–68.

Bateman, Anthony, and Peter Fonagy. *Mentalization-Based Treatment for Personality Disorders: A Practical Guide.* New York: Oxford University Press, 2016.

Beck, Charlotte Joko. *Nothing Special: Living Zen.* Edited by Steve Smith. New York: HarperCollins, 1993.

Bell, Sylvia M., and Mary D. Salter Ainsworth. "Infant Crying and Maternal Responsiveness." *Child Development* 43, no. 4 (December 1972): 1171–90.

Bennett, Susanne. "Is There a Primary Mom? Parental Perceptions of Attachment

Bond Hierarchies Within Lesbian Adoptive Families." *Child and Adolescent Social Work Journal* 20, no. 3 (June 2003): 159–73.

Bernard, Kristin, E. B. Meade, and Mary Dozier. "Parental Synchrony and Nurturance as Targets in an Attachment Based Intervention: Building upon Mary Ainsworth's Insights About Mother-Infant Interaction." In *Maternal Sensitivity: Mary Ainsworth's Enduring Influence on Attachment Theory, Research and Clinical Applications,* edited by Klaus E. Grossmann, Inge Bretherton, Everett Waters, and Karin Grossmann. New York: Routledge, 2016.

Bernier, Annie, and Raphaele Milkovitch. "Intergenerational Transmission Attachment in Father-Child Dyads: The Case of Single Parenthood." *Journal of Genetic Psychology* 170, no. 1 (2009): 31–51.

Bigelow, Kathryn M., and Edward K. Morris. "John B. Watson's Advice on Child Rearing: Some Historical Context." *Behavioral Development Bulletin* 10, no. 1 (2001): 26–30.

Blum, Deborah. *Love at Goon Park: Harry Harlow and the Science of Affection.* Cambridge, MA: Basic Books, 2002.

Bowers, Louise, Peter K. Smith, and Valerie Binney. "Perceived Family Relationships of Bullies, Victims and Bully/Victims in Middle Childhood." *Journal of Social and Personal Relationships* 11, no. 2 (May 1994): 216–17.

Bowlby, John. "Attachment and Loss: Retrospect and Prospect." *American Journal of Orthopsychiatry* 52, no. 4 (1982): 664–78.

———. *Attachment.* Vol. 1 of *Attachment and Loss.* New York: Basic Books, 2008.

———. "Forty-Four Juvenile Thieves: Their Characters and Home-Life." *International Journal of Psychoanalysis* 25 (1944): 19–53.

———. *Maternal Care and Mental Health: A Report Prepared on Behalf of the World Health Organization as a Contribution to the United Nations Programme for the Welfare of Homeless Children.* 2nd ed. Geneva: World Health Organization, 1952. https://apps.who.int/iris/handle/10665/40724.

———. "The Growth of Independence in the Young Child." *Royal Society of Health Journal* 76 (1956): 587–91.

———. "The Nature of the Child's Tie to His Mother." In *Influential Papers from the 1950s,* edited by Andrew C. Furman and Steven T. Levy. New York: Routledge, 2018. Google Books.

Bretherton, Inge. "Communication Patterns, Internal Working Models, and the Intergenerational Transmission of Attachment Relationships." *Infant Mental Health Journal* 11, no. 3 (Autumn 1990): 237–52.

———. "Fathers in Attachment Theory and Research: A Review." *Early Child Development and Care* 180, no. 1–2 (2010): 9–23.

———. "Mary Ainsworth: Insightful Observer and Courageous Theoretician." In *Portraits of Pioneers in Psychology,* edited by Gregory A. Kimble, Michael Wertheimer, and Charlotte L. White. Hillsdale, NJ: Erlbaum, 2003. http://www.psychology.sunysb.edu/attachment/pdf/mda_inge.pdf.

———. "The Origins of Attachment Theory: John Bowlby and Mary Ainsworth." *Developmental Psychology* 28 (1992): 759–75.

———. "Revisiting Mary Ainsworth's Conceptualizations and Assessments of Maternal Sensitivity-Insensitivity." *Attachment and Human Development* 15, no. 5–6: 460–84. https://doi.org/10.1080/14616734.2013.835128.

Brown, Geoffrey L., Sarah C. Mangelsdorf, and Cynthia Neff. "Father Involvement, Paternal Sensitivity, and Father-Child Attachment Security in the First Three Years." *Journal of Family Psychology* 26, no. 3 (2012): 421–30.

Brown, Geoffrey L., Sarah C. Mangelsdorf, Aya Shigeto, and Maria Wong. "Associations Between Father Involvement and Father-Child Attachment Security: Variations Based on Timing and Type of Involvement." *Journal of Family Psychology* 32, no. 8 (2018): 1015–24.

Burke Harris, Nadine. *The Deepest Well: Healing the Long-Term Effects of Childhood Adversity.* Boston: Houghton Mifflin Harcourt, 2018.

Burkhardt, Richard W., and Peter Klopfer. "Konrad Lorenz and the National Socialists: On the Politics of Ethology." *International Journal of Comparative Psychology* 7 (1994): 202–8.

Caldwell, Jon G., and Phillip R. Shaver. "Mediators of the Link Between Adult Attachment and Mindfulness." *Interpersonal: An International Journal on Personal Relationships* 7, no. 2 (2013): 299–310. https://interpersona.psychopen.eu /article/view/133/163.

Cassidy, Jude, and Phillip R. Shaver, eds. *Handbook of Attachment: Theory, Research, and Clinical Applications.* New York: Guilford Press, 2016.

Center for Youth Wellness. "Together We Can Build a Healthier Future for Children Exposed to Adversity." Accessed April 4, 2019. https://centerforyouth wellness.org.

Coughlan, Barry, Tess Marshall-Andon, Julie Anderson, Sophie Reijman, and Robbie Duschinsky. "Attachment and Autism Spectrum Conditions: Exploring Mary Main's Coding Notes." *Developmental Child Welfare* 1, no. 1 (2019): 76–93.

Counted, Victor. "God as an Attachment Figure: A Case Study of the God Attachment Language and God Concepts of Anxiously Attached Christian Youths in South Africa." *Journal of Spirituality in Mental Health* 18, no. 4 (2016): 316–46.

Dagan, Or, and Abraham Sagi-Schwartz. "Early Attachment Network with Mother and Father: An Unsettled Issue." *Child Development Perspectives* 12, no. 2 (June 2018): 115–21.

Deichmann, Ute. *Biologists Under Hitler.* Cambridge, MA: Harvard University Press, 1996.

Demidenko, Natasha, Ian Manion, and Catherine M. Lee. "Father–Daughter Attachment and Communication in Depressed and Nondepressed Adolescent Girls." *Journal of Child and Family Studies* 24, no. 6 (June 2015): 1727–34.

Dijken, Suzan van, René van der Veer, Marinus van IJzendoorn, and Hans-Jan Kuipers. "Bowlby Before Bowlby: The Sources of an Intellectual Departure in Psychoanalysis and Psychology." *Journal of the History of the Behavioral Sciences* 34, no. 3 (Summer 1998): 247–69.

Divecha, Diana. "What Is a Secure Attachment? And Why Doesn't 'Attachment Parenting' Get You There?" *Developmental Science,* April 3, 2017. https://www .developmentalscience.com/blog/2017/3/31/what-is-a-secure-attachmentand -why-doesnt-attachment-parenting-get-you-there.

Dozier, Mary, K. Chase Stovall, Kathleen E. Albus, and Brandy Bates. "Attachment for Infants in Foster Care: The Role of Caregiver State of Mind." In *Annual Progress in Child Psychiatry and Child Development 2002,* edited by Margaret E. Hertzig and Ellen A. Farber. New York: Routledge, 2005.

Duckworth, Angela. *Grit: The Power of Passion and Perseverance,* reprint edition. New York: Scribner, 2018.

Duschinsky, Robbie. "Disorganization, Fear, and Attachment: Working Towards Clarification." *Infant Mental Health Journal* 39, no. 1 (January–February 2018): 17–29.

Faber, Aida, and Laurette Dube. "Parental Attachment Insecurity Predicts Child and Adult High-Caloric Food Consumption." *Journal of Health Psychology* 20 (May 2015): 511–24.

Farrow, Claire, and Jackie Blisset. "Maternal Mind-Mindedness During Infancy, General Parenting Sensitivity and Observed Child Feeding Behavior: A Longitudinal Study." *Attachment and Human Development* 16, no. 3 (2014): 230–41.

Feeney, Judith A., and Patricia Noller. "Attachment Style as a Predictor of Adult Romantic Relationships." *Journal of Personality and Social Psychology* 58, no. 2 (1990): 281–91.

Feldman, Ruth. "The Neurobiology of Mammalian Parenting and the Biosocial Context of Human Caregiving." *Hormones and Behavior* 77 (January 2016): 3–17.

Felitti, Vincent J., and Robert F. Anda. "The Relationship of Adverse Childhood Experiences to Adult Medical Disease, Psychiatric Disorders, and Sexual Behavior: Implications for Healthcare." In *The Impact of Early Life Trauma on Health and Disease: The Hidden Epidemic,* edited by Ruth A. Lanius, Eric Vermetten, and Claire Pain. Boston: Cambridge University Press, 2010.

Felitti, Vincent J., Robert F. Anda, Dale Nordenberg, David F. Williamson, Alison M. Spitz, Valerie Edwards, Mary Koss, et al. "Relationship of Childhood Abuse and Household Dysfunction to Many of the Leading Causes of Death in Adults: The Adverse Childhood Experiences (ACE) Study." *American Journal of Preventive Medicine* 14, no. 4 (1998): 245–58.

Feuge, Eric Alain, Chantal Cyr, Louise Cossette, and Danielle Julien. "Adoptive Gay Fathers' Sensitivity and Child Attachment and Behavior Problems." *Attachment and Human Development* 20 (December 2018): 1–22. https://doi.org/10.1080/14616734.2018.1557224.

Field, Nigel P. "Unresolved Grief and Continuing Bonds: An Attachment Perspective." *Death Studies* 30, no. 8 (2006): 739–56.

Flanagan, Cara. *Early Socialisation: Sociability and Attachment.* New York: Routledge, 1999.

Fletcher, Kara. "Attachment, a Matter of Substance: The Potential of Attachment Theory in the Treatment of Addictions." *Clinical Social Work Journal* 43, no. 1 (March 2015): 109–17.

Fonagy, Peter. *Attachment Theory and Psychoanalysis.* New York: Routledge, 2018.

Fonagy, Peter, Tom Leigh, Miriam Steel, Howard Steele, Roger Kennedy, Gretta Mattoon, Mary Target, et al. "The Relation of Attachment Status, Psychiatric Classification, and Response to Psychotherapy." *Journal of Consulting and Clinical Psychology* 64, no. 1 (1996): 22–31.

Fonagy, Peter, Howard Steele, and Miriam Steele. "Maternal Representations of Attachment During Pregnancy Predict the Organization of Infant-Mother Attachment at One Year of Age." *Child Development* 62, no. 5 (October 1991): 891–905.

Fonagy, Peter, Mary Target, and George Gergely. "Psychoanalytic Perspectives on Developmental Psychopathology." In *Developmental Psychopathology, Vol. 1:*

Theory and Method, edited by Dante Cicchetti and Donald J. Cohen. Hoboken, NJ: John Wiley and Sons, 2006.

Fontaine, Nathalie M. G., Rene Carbonneau, Frank Vitaro, and Edward D. Barker. "Research Review: A Critical Review of Studies on the Developmental Trajectories of Antisocial Behavior in Females." *Child Psychology and Psychiatry* 50, no. 4 (2009): 363–85.

Fox, Nathan A., and Judith A. Card. "Psychophysiological Measures in the Study of Attachment." In *Handbook of Attachment: Theory, Research, and Clinical Applications,* edited by Jude Cassidy and Phillip R. Shaver. New York: Guilford Press, 2016.

Fraley, R. Chris. "Attachment in Adulthood: Recent Developments, Emerging Debates, and Future Directions." *Annual Review of Psychology* 70, no. 1 (January 2019): 401–22.

Fraley, R. Chris, and Keith E. Davis. "Attachment Formation and Transfer in Young Adults' Close Friendships and Romantic Relationships." *Personal Relationships* 4, no. 2 (June 1997): 131–44.

Fraley, R. Chris, and Marie E. Heffernan. "Attachment and Parental Divorce: A Test of the Diffusion and Sensitive Period Hypothesis." *Personality and Social Psychology Bulletin* 39, no. 9 (September 2013): 1199–213.

Fraley, R. Chris, and Glenn I. Roisman. "Early Attachment Experiences and Romantic Functioning: Developmental Pathways, Emerging Issues, and Future Directions." In *Attachment Theory and Research: New Directions and Emerging Themes,* edited by Jeffry A. Simpson and W. Steven Rholes. New York: Guilford Press, 2015.

Gentzler, Amy L., Ann M. Oberhauser, David Westerman, and Danielle K. Nadorff. "College Students' Use of Electronic Communication with Parents: Links to Loneliness, Attachment, and Relationship Quality." *Cyberpsychology, Behavior, and Social Networking* 14, no. 1–2 (February 2011): 71–74. https://doi.org/10.1089/cyber.2009.0409.

George, Carol, Nancy Kaplan, and Mary Main. *The Adult Attachment Interview.* Digital reproduction of unpublished manuscript. Stony Brook University, New York, 1985. Accessed February 12, 2019. http://www.psychology.sunysb.edu/attachment/measures/content/aai_interview.pdf.

Granqvist, Pehr, and Jane R. Dickie. "Attachment and Spiritual Development in Childhood and Adolescence." In *The Handbook of Spiritual Development in Childhood and Adolescence,* edited by Eugene C. Roehlkepartain, Pamela Ebstyne King, Linda Wagener, and Peter L. Benson. Thousand Oaks, CA: Sage Publications, 2006.

Granqvist, Pehr, and Lee A. Kirkpatrick. "Religion, Spirituality, and Attachment." In *APA Handbook of Psychology, Religion, and Spirituality, Vol. 1: Context, Theory, and Research,* edited by K. I. Pargament, J. J. Exline, and J. W. Jones, 139–55. Washington, DC: American Psychological Association, 2013.

Granqvist, Pehr, Mario Mikulincer, and Phillip R. Shaver. "Experimental Findings on God as an Attachment Figure: Normative Processes and Moderating Effects of Internal Working Models." *Journal of Personality and Social Psychology* 103, no. 5 (2012): 804–18.

Granqvist, Pehr, Mario Mikulincer, and Phillip R. Shaver. "Religion as Attachment: Normative Processes and Individual Differences." *Personality and Social Psychology Review* 14, no. 1 (February 2010): 49–59.

Grant, Richard. "Do Trees Talk to Each Other?" *Smithsonian,* March 2018. https://www.smithsonianmag.com/science-nature/the-whispering-trees-180968084/.

Groh, Ashley M., Angela J. Narayan, Marian Bakermans-Kranenburg, Glenn I. Roisman, Brian E. Vaughn, Richard M. Pasco Fearon, and Marinus H. van IJzendoorn. "Attachment and Temperament in the Early Life Course: A Meta-Analytic Review." *Child Development* 88, no. 3 (May/June 2017): 770–95.

Grossmann, Klaus E., Inge Bretherton, Everett Waters, and Karin Grossmann. Introduction to the special issue "Maternal Sensitivity: Observational Studies Honoring Mary Ainsworth's 100th Year." *Attachment and Human Development* 15, no. 5–6 (2013): 443–47.

Grossmann, Klaus E., Karin Grossmann, and Everett Waters, eds. *Attachment from Infancy to Adulthood: The Major Longitudinal Studies.* New York: Guilford Press, 2005.

Haight, Wendy L., Jill Doner Kagle, and James E. Black. "Understanding and Supporting Parent-Child Relationships During Foster Care Visits: Attachment Theory and Research." *Social Work* 48, no. 2 (April 2003): 195–208.

Hanh, Thich Nhat. *Understanding Our Mind: 50 Verses on Buddhist Psychology.* Berkeley, CA: Parallax Press, 2002.

Harlow, Harry F., and Stephen J. Suomi. "Nature of Love—Simplified." *American Psychologist* 25, no. 2 (1970): 161–68.

Harper, Lawrence. "Epigenetic Inheritance and the Intergenerational Transfer of Experience." *Psychological Bulletin* 131, no. 3 (2005): 340–60.

Harris, Margaret, and George Butterworth. *Developmental Psychology: A Student's Handbook.* New York: Taylor and Francis, 2002.

Hart, Jonathan T., Alicia Limke, and Phillip R. Budd. "Attachment and Faith Development." *Journal of Psychology and Theology* 38, no. 2 (June 2010): 122–28.

Haupert, M. L., Amanda N. Gesselman, Amy C. Moors, Helen E. Fisher, and Justin R. Garcia. "Prevalence of Experiences with Consensual Nonmonogamous Relationships: Findings from Two National Samples of Single Americans." *Journal of Sex and Marital Therapy* 43, no. 5 (2017): 424–40.

Hazan, Cindy, and Phillip Shaver. "Romantic Love Conceptualized as an Attachment Process." *Journal of Personality and Social Psychology* 52, no. 3 (April 1987): 511–24.

Hesse, Erik. "The Adult Attachment Interview: Protocol, Method of Analysis, and Empirical Studies." In *Handbook of Attachment: Theory, Research, and Clinical Applications,* edited by Jude Cassidy and Phillip R. Shaver. New York: Guilford Press, 2016.

Hesse, Erik, and Mary Main. "Disorganized Infant, Child, and Adult Attachment: Collapse in Behavioral and Attentional Strategies." *Journal of the American Psychoanalytic Association* 48 (2000): 1175–87.

———. "Second-Generation Effects of Unresolved Trauma in Nonmaltreating Parents: Dissociated, Frightened, and Threatening Parental Behavior." *Psychoanalytic Inquiry* 19, no. 4 (1999): 481–540.

Hoeve, Machteld, Geert Jan J. M. Stams, Claudia E. van der Put, Judith Semon Dubas, Peter H. van der Laan, and Jan R. M. Gerris. "A Meta-Analysis of Attachment to Parents and Delinquency." *Journal of Abnormal Child Psychology* 40, no. 5 (July 2012): 771–85.

Hong, Yoo Rha, and Jae Sun Park. "Impact of Attachment, Temperament and Parenting on Human Development." *Korean Journal of Pediatrics* 55, no. 12 (December 2012): 449–54.

Hopkins, Brian. "Culture, Infancy, and Education." *European Journal of Psychology of Education* 4, no. 2 (June 1989): 289–93.

Howard, Kimberly S. "Paternal Attachment, Parenting Beliefs and Children's Attachment." *Early Child Development and Care* 180, no. 1–2 (2010): 157–71.

Howe, David. *Attachment Across the Lifecourse: A Brief Introduction.* New York: Macmillan International, 2011.

Howes, Carollee, and Susan Spieker. "Attachment Relationships in the Context of Multiple Caregivers." In *Handbook of Attachment: Theory, Research, and Clinical Applications,* edited by Jude Cassidy and Phillip R. Shaver. New York: Guilford Press, 2016.

Hrdy, Sarah B. "Evolutionary Context of Human Development: The Cooperative Breeding Model." In *Attachment and Bonding: A New Synthesis,* Dahlem Workshop Reports, edited by C. S. Carter, L. Ahnert, K. E. Grossmann, S. B. Hrdy, M. E. Lamb, S. W. Porges, and N. Sachser. Cambridge, MA: MIT Press, 2005.

Huang, Zhihuan Jennifer, Amy Lewin, Stephanie J. Mitchell, and Jin Zhang. "Variations in the Relationship Between Maternal Depression, Maternal Sensitivity, and Child Attachment by Race/Ethnicity and Nativity: Findings from a Nationally Representative Cohort Study." *Maternal and Child Health Journal* 16, no. 1 (2012): 40–50.

Hudson, Andrew. "More Clouds, More Water." *Gay Buddhist Fellowship,* September 1996. http://www.gaybuddhist.org/archive/1996.09%20Andrew%20Hudson%20(More%20Clouds,%20More%20Water).pdf.

Hurley, Dan. "Grandma's Experiences Leave a Mark on Your Genes." *Discover,* May 2013. http://www.discovermagazine.com/2013/may/13-grandmas-experiences-leave-epigenetic-mark-on-your-genes.

IJzendoorn, Marinus van. "Adult Attachment Representations, Parental Responsiveness, and Infant Attachment: A Meta-Analysis on the Predictive Validity of the Adult Attachment Interview." *Psychological Bulletin* 117, no. 3 (May 1995): 387–403.

IJzendoorn, Marinus van, Marian J. Bakermans-Kranenburg, and Abraham Sagi-Schwartz. "Attachment Across Diverse Sociocultural Contexts: The Limits of Universality." In *Parenting Beliefs, Behaviors, and Parent-Child Relations: A Cross-Cultural Perspective,* edited by Kenneth H. Rubin and Ock Boon Chung. New York: Psychology Press, 2006.

IJzendoorn, Marinus H. van, Kim Bard, Marian J. Bakermans-Kranenburg, and Krisztina Ivan. "Enhancement of Attachment and Cognitive Development of Young Nursery-Reared Chimpanzees in Responsive Versus Standard Care." *Developmental Psychology* 51, no. 2 (March 2009): 173–85.

IJzendoorn, Marinus van, Frits A. Goosens, Pieter M. Kroonenberg, and Louis W. C. Tavecchio. "Dependent Attachment: B-4 Children in the Strange Situation." *Psychological Reports* 57, no. 2 (October 1985): 439–51.

IJzendoorn, Marinus H. van, and Pieter M. Kroonenberg. "Cross-cultural Patterns of Attachment: A Meta-Analysis of the Strange Situation." *Child Development* 59, no. 1 (February 1988): 147–56.

IJzendoorn, Marinus van, Louis W. C. Tavecchio, Frits Goosens, and M. M. Vergeer. "How B Is B4? Attachment and Security of Dutch Children in Ainsworth's Strange Situation and at Home." *Psychological Reports* 52 (1983): 683–91.

Jinyao, Yi. "Insecure Attachment as a Predictor of Depressive and Anxious Symptomology." *Depression and Anxiety* 29, no. 9 (September 2012): 789–96.

Johnson-Groh, Mara. "Scientists Find the 'Missing' Dark Matter from the Early Universe." *LiveScience,* January 2, 2019. https://www.livescience.com/64389 -dark-matter-around-galaxies-constant.html.

Jones, Jason D., Bonnie E. Brett, Katherine B. Ehrlich, Carl W. Lejuez, and Jude Cassidy. "Maternal Attachment Style and Responses to Adolescents' Negative Emotions: The Mediating Role of Maternal Emotion Regulation." *Parenting* 14, no. 3–4 (2014): 235–57.

Jones, Jason D., Jude Cassidy, and Phillip R. Shaver. "Adult Attachment Style and Parenting." In *Attachment Theory and Research: New Directions and Emerging Themes,* edited by Jeffry A. Simpson and W. Steven Rholes. New York: Guilford Press, 2015.

———. "Parents' Self-Reported Attachment Styles: A Review of Links with Parenting Behaviors, Emotions, and Cognitions." *Personality and Social Psychology Review* 19, no. 1 (2015): 44–76. https://doi.org/10.1177/1088868314541858.

Jones, Neville, and Eileen Baglin Jones. Introduction to *Learning to Behave: Curriculum and Whole School Management Approaches to Discipline.* Edited by Neville Jones and Eileen Baglin Jones. New York: RoutledgeFalmer, 1992. Google Books.

Jones-Mason, Karen, Isabel Elaine Allen, Nicole R. Bush, and Sharon Hamilton. "Epigenetic Marks as the Link Between Environment and Development: Examination of the Associations Between Attachment: Socioeconomic Status, and Methylation of the SLC6A4 Gene." *Brain and Behavior* 6, no. 7 (2016): e00480. https://doi.org/10.1002/brb3.480.

Juffer, Femmie, Marian J. Bakermans-Kranenburg, and Marinus H. van IJzendoorn, eds. *Promoting Positive Parenting: An Attachment-Based Intervention.* New York: Taylor & Francis Group/Lawrence Erlbaum Associates, 2008.

Karen, Robert. *Becoming Attached: First Relationships and How They Shape Our Capacity to Love.* New York: Oxford University Press, 1998.

Kirkpatrick, Lee A. "God as a Substitute Attachment Figure: A Longitudinal Study of Adult Attachment Style and Religious Change in College Students." *Personality and Social Psychology Bulletin* 24, no. 9 (1998): 961–73. https://doi.org/10 .1177/0146167298249004.

Kirkpatrick, Lee A., and Phillip R. Shaver. "Attachment Theory and Religion: Childhood Attachments, Religious Beliefs, and Conversion." *Journal for the Scientific Study of Religion* 29, no. 3 (September 1990): 315–34.

Kluve, Jochen, and Marcus Tamm. "Parental Leave Regulations, Mothers' Labor Force Attachment and Fathers' Childcare Involvement: Evidence from a Natural Experiment." *Journal of Population Economics* 26, no. 3 (July 2013): 983–1005.

Kobak, Roger. "The Emotional Dynamics of Disruptions in Attachment Relationships: Implications for Theory, Research, and Clinical Intervention." In *Handbook of Attachment: Theory, Research, and Clinical Applications,* edited by Jude Cassidy and Phillip R. Shaver. New York: Guilford Press, 2016.

Kolkhorst, Brittany, Ani Yazedjian, and Michelle Toews. "A Longitudinal Examination of Parental Attachment, College Adjustment, and Academic Achievement." *Journal of the First-Year Experience and Students in Transition* 22, no. 1 (January 2010): 9–25.

Kosminsky, Phyllis S., and John R. Jordan. *Attachment-Informed Grief Therapy: The Clinician's Guide to Foundations and Applications.* New York: Routledge, 2016.

Kunhardt, Jean, Lisa Spiegel, and Sandra K. Bastile. *A Mother's Circle: An Intimate Dialogue on Becoming a Mother.* New York: Soho Parenting Center, 1996.

Kuo, Patty X., Ekjyot K. Saini, Elizabeth Engelitsch, Oliver C. Schultheiss, Richard Gonzalez, and Brenda L. Volling. "Individual Variation in Fathers' Testosterone Reactivity to Infant Distress Predicts Parenting Behaviors with Their 1-Year-Old Infants." *Developmental Psychobiology* 58, no. 3 (April 2016): 303–14.

Kurdek, Lawrence A. "Pet Dogs as Attachment Figures for Adult Owners." *Journal of Family Psychology* 23, no. 4 (2009): 439–46.

Kyabgon, Traleg Rinpoche. *Karma: What It Is, What It Isn't, Why It Matters.* Boston: Shambhala Publications, 2015. Google Books.

Lamb, Michael E. "How Do Fathers Influence Children's Development? Let Me Count the Ways." In *The Role of the Father in Child Development,* edited by Michael E. Lamb. Hoboken, NJ: John Wiley and Sons, 2010.

Lamb, Michael E. "Qualitative Aspects of Mother- and Father-Infant Attachments." *Infant Behavior and Development* 1 (1978): 264–75.

Lasnik, Howard, and Terje Lohndal. "Noam Chomsky." *Oxford Research Encyclopedia of Linguistics,* August 2017. http://www.oxfordre.com/linguistics/view/10 .1093/acrefore/9780199384655.001.0001/acrefore-9780199384655-e-356.

Laurita, Anne C., Cindy Hazan, and R. Nathan Spreng. "An Attachment Theoretical Perspective for the Neural Representation of Close Others." *Social Cognitive and Affective Neuroscience* 14, no. 3 (March 2019): 237–51.

Lee, Hanna, Sung-Byung Yang, and Chulmo Koo. "Exploring the Effect of Airbnb Hosts' Attachment and Psychological Ownership in the Sharing Economy." *Tourism Management* 70 (February 2019): 284–94.

Lemelin, Jean-Pascal, George M. Tarabulsy, and Marc A. Provost. "Predicting Preschool Cognitive Development from Infant Temperament, Maternal Sensitivity, and Psychosocial Risk." *Merrill-Palmer Quarterly* 52, no. 4 (October 2006): 779–806.

Levy, Jaclyn M., and Howard Steele. "Attachment and Grit: Exploring Possible Contributions of Attachment Styles (from Past and Present Life) to the Adult Personality Construct of Grit. *Journal of Social & Psychological Sciences* 4, no. 2 (2011): 16–19.

Levy, Kenneth N., and Kristen M. Kelly. "Using Interviews to Assess Adult Attachment." In *Attachment Theory and Research in Clinical Work with Adults,* edited by J. H. Obegi and E. Berant. New York: Guilford Press, 2009.

Loori, John Daido. *Bringing the Sacred to Life: The Daily Practice of Zen Ritual.* Boston: Shambhala, 2008.

Lorenz, Konrad. "Biographical." Nobel Prize website. Accessed February 7, 2019. https://www.nobelprize.org/prizes/medicine/1973/lorenz/biographical/.

Lucassen, Nicole. "The Association Between Paternal Sensitivity and Infant-Father Attachment Security: A Meta-Analysis of Three Decades of Research." *Journal of Family Psychology* 25, no. 6 (December 2011): 986–92.

Luijk, Maartje P. C. M., Anne Tharner, Marian J. Bakermans-Kranenburg, Marinus H. van IJzendoorn, Vincent W. V. Jaddoe, Albert Hofman, Frank C. Verhult, et al.

"The Association Between Parenting and Attachment Security Is Moderated by a Polymorphism in the Mineralocorticoid Receptor Gene: Evidence for Differential Susceptibility." *Biological Psychology* 88, no. 1 (September 2011): 37–40.

Lyons-Ruth, Karlen, and Deborah Jacobvitz. "Attachment Disorganization: Unresolved Loss, Relational Violence, and Attentional Strategies." In *Handbook of Attachment: Theory, Research, and Clinical Applications,* edited by Jude Cassidy and Phillip R. Shaver. New York: Guilford Press, 2016.

MacKenzie, Rachel D., Paul E. Mullen, James R. P. Ogloff, Troy E. McEwan, and David V. James. "Parental Bonding and Adult Attachment Styles in Different Types of Stalker." *Journal of Forensic Sciences* 53, no. 6 (November 2008): 1443–49.

Main, Mary. "Mary D. Salter Ainsworth: Tribute and Portrait." *Psychoanalytic Inquiry* 19 (1999): 682–776.

———. "The Organized Categories of Infant, Child, and Adult Attachment: Flexible vs. Inflexible Attention Under Attachment-Related Stress." *Journal of the American Psychoanalytic Association* 48, no. 4 (August 2000): 1055–96.

Main, Mary, and Erik Hesse. "Parents' Unresolved Traumatic Experiences Are Related to Infant Disorganized Attachment Status: Is Frightened and/or Frightening Parental Behavior the Linking Mechanism?" In *Attachment in the Preschool Years: Theory, Research, and Intervention,* edited by M. T. Greenberg, D. Cicchetti, and E. M. Cummings. Chicago: University of Chicago Press, 1990.

Main, Mary, Erik Hesse, and Nancy Kaplan. "Predictability of Attachment Behavior and Representational Processes at 1, 6, and 19 Years of Age: The Berkeley Longitudinal Study." In *Attachment from Infancy to Adulthood: The Major Longitudinal Studies,* edited by Klaus E. Grossmann, Karin Grossmann, and Everett Waters. New York: Guilford Press, 2005.

Main, Mary, Nancy Kaplan, and Jude Cassidy. "Security in Infancy, Childhood, and Adulthood: A Move to the Level of Representation." *Monographs of the Society for Research in Child Development* 50, no. 1/2 (1985): 66–104.

Main, Mary, and Hillary Morgan. "Disorganization and Disorientation in Infant Strange Situation Behavior." In *Handbook of Dissociation: Theoretical, Empirical, and Clinical Perspectives,* edited by Larry K. Michelson and William J. Ray. Boston: Springer/Verlag US, 1996.

Main, Mary, and Judith Solomon. "Discovery of an Insecure-Disorganized/Disoriented Attachment Pattern." In *Affective Development in Infancy,* edited by T. B. Brazelton and M. W. Yogman. Westport, CT: Ablex Publishing, 1986.

Manning, Tracey T. "Leadership Across Cultures: Attachment Style Influences." *Journal of Leadership and Organizational Studies* 9, no. 3 (August 2003): 20–30.

Marks, David F. "Homeostatic Theory of Obesity." *Health Psychology Open* 2, no. 1 (June 2015). https://doi.org/10.1177/2055102915590692.

Marsa, Fiona, Gary O'Reilly, Alan Carr, Paul Murphy, Maura O'Sullivan, Anthony Cotter, and David Hevey. "Attachment Styles and Psychological Profiles of Child Sex Offenders in Ireland." *Journal of Interpersonal Violence* 19, no. 2 (February 2004): 228–51.

Mayseless, Ofra, and Micha Popper. "Reliance on Leaders and Social Institutions: An Attachment Perspective." *Attachment and Human Development* 9, no. 1 (2007): 73–93.

McDougall, William. *Character and Conduct of Life: Practical Psychology for Everyman.* Psychology Revivals. New York: Routledge, 2016. Google Books.

McIntosh, Peggy. "White Privilege: Unpacking the Invisible Knapsack." *Peace and Freedom,* July/August 1989.

McLearn, Kathryn Taaffe, Cynthia S. Minkovitz, Donna M. Strobino, Elisabeth Marks, and William Hou. "Maternal Depressive Symptoms at 2 to 4 Months Post Partum and Early Parenting Practices." *Archives of Pediatrics and Adolescent Medicine* 160, no. 3 (March 2006): 279–84.

McLeod, Saul. "Skinner—Operant Conditioning." Simply Psychology. Accessed February 20, 2019. https://www.simplypsychology.org/operant-conditioning .html.

Meins, Elizabeth, Charles Fernyhough, Rachel Wainwright, Mani Das Gupta, Emma Fradley, and Michelle Tuckey. "Maternal Mind-Mindedness and Attachment Security as Predictors of Theory of Mind Understanding." *Child Development* 73, no. 6 (November 2002): 1715–26.

Mesman, Judi, Marinus H. van IJzendoorn, and Abraham Sagi-Schwartz. "Cross-Cultural Patterns of Attachment: Universal and Contextual Dimensions." In *Handbook of Attachment: Theory, Research, and Clinical Applications,* edited by Jude Cassidy and Phillip R. Shaver. New York: Guilford Press, 2016.

Mikulincer, Mario, and Phillip R. Shaver. *Attachment in Adulthood: Structure, Dynamics, and Change.* New York: Guilford Press, 2007.

Mikulincer, Mario, Phillip R. Shaver, and Dana Pereg. "Attachment Theory and Affect Regulation: The Dynamics, Development, and Cognitive Consequences of Attachment-Related Strategies." *Motivation and Emotion* 27, no. 2 (June 2003): 77–102.

Moors, Amy C., Terri D. Conley, Robin S. Edelstein, and William J. Chopik. "Attached to Monogamy? Avoidance Predicts Willingness to Engage (but Not Actual Engagement) in Consensual Non-Monogamy." *Journal of Social and Personal Relationships* 32, no. 2 (2015): 222–40.

Moreira, Helena, Maria João Gouvela, Carlos Carona, Neuza Silva, and Maria Cristina Canavarro. "Maternal Attachment and Children's Quality of Life: The Mediating Role of Self-Compassion and Parenting Stress." *Journal of Child and Family Studies* 24, no. 8 (2015): 2332–44.

Moretti, Marlene M., and Maya Peled. "Adolescent-Parent Attachment: Bonds that Support Healthy Development." *Paediatrics and Child Health* 9, no. 8 (October 2004): 551–55.

Mussen, Paul, and Luther Distler. "Masculinity, Identification, and Father-Son Relationships." *Journal of Abnormal and Social Psychology* 59, no. 3 (1959): 350–56.

Neruda, Pablo. "Sonnet XVII." Translated by Stephen Tapscott. Accessed February 14, 2019. https://www.poemhunter.com/poem/xvii-i-do-not-love-you/.

Neufeld, Gordon, and Gabor Maté. *Hold On to Your Kids: Why Parents Need to Matter More Than Peers.* New York: Ballantine, 2005.

Noppe, Illene C. "Beyond Broken Bonds and Broken Hearts: The Bonding of Theories of Attachment and Grief." *Developmental Review* 20, no. 4 (December 2000): 514–38.

Pace, Cecilia Serena, Simona Di Folco, Viviana Guerriero, Santona Alessandra, and

Grazia Terrone. "Adoptive Parenting and Attachment: Association of the Internal Working Models Between Adoptive Mothers and Their Late-Adopted Children During Adolescence," *Frontiers in Psychology* 6 (September 2015). https://doi.org/10.3389/fpsyg.2015.01433.

Pace, Cecilia Serena, Giulio Cesare Zavattini, and M. D'Alessio. "Continuity and Discontinuity of Attachment Patterns: A Short-Term Longitudinal Pilot Study Using a Sample of Late-Adopted Children and Their Adoptive Mothers." *Attachment and Human Development* 14, no. 1 (2012): 45–61.

Paetzold, Ramona L., William S. Rholes, and Jamie L. Kohn. "Disorganized Attachment in Adulthood: Theory, Measurement, and Implications for Romantic Relationships." *Review of General Psychology* 19, no. 2 (June 2015): 146–56.

Palagini, Laura, Eleonora Petri, Martina Novi, Danila Caruso, Umberto Moretto, and Dieter Riemann. "Adult Insecure Attachment Plays a Role in Hyperarousal and Emotion Dysregulation in Insomnia Disorder." *Psychiatry Research* 262 (April 2018): 162–67.

Pallini, Susanna, Antonio Chirumbolo, Mara Morelli, Roberto Balocco, Florenzo Laghl, and Nancy Eisenberg. "The Relation of Attachment Security Status to Effortful Self-Regulation: A Meta-Analysis." *Psychological Bulletin* 144, no. 5 (2018): 501–31.

Paquette, Daniel, and Marc Bigras. "The Risky Situation: A Procedure for Assessing the Father-Child Activation Relationship." *Early Child Development and Care* 180, no. 1–2 (January 2010): 33–50.

Pasco Fearon, R. M., and Jay Belsky. "Precursors of Attachment Security." In *Handbook of Attachment: Theory, Research, and Clinical Applications,* edited by Jude Cassidy and Phillip R. Shaver. New York: Guilford Press, 2016.

Pedro, Marta F., Teresa Ribeiro, and Katharine H. Shelton. "Romantic Attachment and Family Functioning: The Mediating Role of Marital Satisfaction." *Journal of Child and Family Studies* 24, no. 11 (November 2015): 3492–95.

Pietromonaco, Paula R., and Lindsey A. Beck. "Attachment Processes in Adult Romantic Relationships." In *Interpersonal Relations,* vol. 3 of *APA Handbook of Personality and Social Psychology,* edited by Mario Mikulincer, Phillip R. Shaver, Jeffry A. Simpson, and John F. Dovidio. Washington, DC: American Psychological Association, 2015.

Pietromonaco, Paula R., and Sally I. Powers. "Attachment and Health-Related Physiological Stress Processes." *Current Opinion in Psychology* 1 (February 2015): 34–39.

Poehlmann, Julie. "An Attachment Perspective on Grandparents Raising Their Very Young Grandchildren: Implications for Intervention and Research." *Infant Mental Health Journal* 24, no. 2 (March 2003): 149–73.

Potter, Alice, and Daniel Simon Mills. "Domestic Cats (*Felis silvestris catus*) Do Not Show Signs of Secure Attachment to Their Owners." *PLoS ONE* 10, no. 9 (September 2015). https://journals.plos.org/plosone/article?id=10.1371/journal.pone.0135109.

Puig, Jennifer, Michelle M. Englund, Jeffry A. Simpson, and W. Andrew Collins. "Predicting Adult Physical Illness from Infant Attachment: A Prospective Longitudinal Study." *Health Psychology* 32, no. 4 (2013): 409–17.

Raby, K. Lee, Mary Dozier. "Attachment Across the Lifespan: Insights from Adoptive Families." *Current Opinion in Psychology* 25 (2019): 81–85.

Raby, K. Lee, Madelyn H. Labella, Jodi Martin, Elizabeth A. Carlson, and Glenn I. Roisman. "Childhood Abuse and Neglect and Insecure Attachment States of Mind in Adulthood: Prospective, Longitudinal Evidence from a High-Risk Sample." *Development and Psychopathology* 29, no. 2 (May 2017): 347–63.

Raeburn, Paul. *Do Fathers Matter? What Science Is Telling Us About the Parent We've Overlooked*. New York: Scientific American, 2014.

Ravo, Nick. "Mary Ainsworth, 85, Theorist on Mother-Infant Attachment." *New York Times,* April 7, 1999. https://www.nytimes.com/1999/04/07/us/mary -ainsworth-85-theorist-on-mother-infant-attachment.html.

Rheingold, Harriet L., Jacob L. Gerwitz, and Hana Ross. "Social Conditioning of Vocalizations in the Infant." *Journal of Comparative and Physiological Psychology* 52, no. 1 (1959): 68–73.

Richards, David A., and Aaron C. Schat. "Attachment at (Not to) Work: Applying Attachment Theory to Explain Individual Behavior in Organizations." *Journal of Applied Psychology* 96, no. 1 (2011): 169–82.

Rock, David, and Heidi Grant. "Why Diverse Teams Are Smarter." *Harvard Business Review,* November 4, 2016.

Roisman, Glenn I., Elena Padron, L. Alan Sroufe, and Byron Egeland. "Earned-Secure Attachment Status in Retrospect and Prospect." *Child Development* 73, no. 4 (July/August 2002): 1204–219.

Rosario, Margaret. "Implications of Childhood Experiences for the Health and Adaptation of Lesbian, Gay, and Bisexual Individuals: Sensitivity to Developmental Process in Future Research." *Psychology of Sexual Orientation and Gender Diversity* 2, no. 2 (September 2015): 214–24.

Rosmalen, Lenny van, Marinus van IJzendoorn, and Marian J. Bakersman-Kranenburg, "ABC+D of Attachment Theory: The Strange Situation Procedure as the Gold Standard of Attachment Assessment." In *The Routledge Handbook of Attachment: Theory,* edited by Paul Holmes and Steve Farnfield. New York: Routledge, 2014. https://doi.org/10.4324/9781315762098.

Rothman, Allison M., and Janice M. Steil. "Adolescent Attachment and Entitlement in a World of Wealth." *Journal of Infant, Child,* ~~……~~ *Psychol.,* 11, no. 1 (2012): 53–65.

Rudnytsky, Peter L. *Psychoanalytic Conversations: Interviews with Clinicians, Commentators, and Critics*. Hillsdale, NJ: Analytic Press, 2000.

Ruhl, Holly, Elaine A. Dolan, and Duane Buhrmester. "Adolescent Attachment Trajectories with Mothers and Fathers: The Importance of Parent-Child Relationship Experiences and Gender." *Journal of Research of Adolescence* 25, no. 3 (September 2015): 427–42.

Sadler, Lois S., Arietta Slade, Nancy Close, Denise L. Webb, Tanika Simpson, Kristopher Fennie, and Linda C. Mayes. "Minding the Baby: Enhancing Reflectiveness to Improve Early Health and Relationship Outcomes in an Interdisciplinary Home-Visiting Program." *Infant Mental Health Journal* 34, no. 5 (2013): 391–405.

Safran, Jeremy, and Zindel V. Segal. *Interpersonal Process in Cognitive Therapy*. New York: Jason Aronson, 1996.

Saltman, Bethany. "Can Attachment Theory Explain All Our Relationships?" *New York,* July 5, 2016.

Simpson, Jeffry A. "Adult Attachment, Stress, and Romantic Relationships." *Current Opinion in Psychology* 13 (February 2017): 19–24.

Simpson, Jeffry A., and Jay Belsky. "Attachment Theory Within a Modern Evolutionary Framework." In *Handbook of Attachment: Theory, Research, and Clinical Applications,* edited by Jude Cassidy and Phillip R. Shaver. New York: Guilford Press, 2016.

Simpson, Jeffry A., and W. Steven Rholes, eds. *Attachment Theory and Research: New Directions and Emerging Themes.* New York: Guilford Press, 2015.

Skinner, B. F. "Baby in a Box." *Ladies' Home Journal,* October 1945.

Slade, Arietta, John Grienenberger, Elizabeth Bernbach, Dahlia Levy, and Alison Locker. "Maternal Reflective Functioning, Attachment, and the Transmission Gap: A Preliminary Study." *Attachment and Human Development* 7, no. 3 (2005): 283–98.

Slade, Arietta, Margaret L. Holland, Monica Roosa Ordway, Elizabeth A. Carlson, Sangchoon Jeon, Nancy Close, Linda C. Mayes, et al. "Minding the Baby: Enhancing Parental Reflective Functioning and Infant Attachment in an Attachment-Based, Interdisciplinary Home Visiting Program." *Development and Psychopathology* 14 (January 2019): 1–15.

Smith, Peter K., Louise Bowers, Valerie Binney, and Helen Cowie. "Relationships of Children Involved in Bully/Victim Problems at School." In *Making Sense of Social Development,* edited by Martin Woodhead, Dorothy Faulkner, and Karen Littleton. New York: Routledge, 1999.

Spangler, Gottfried. "Emotional and Adrenocortical Responses of Infants to the Strange Situation: The Differential Function of Emotional Expression." *International Journal of Behavioral Development* 22, no. 4 (1998): 681–706.

Spieker, Susan, and Patricia McKinsey Crittenden. "Comparing Two Attachment Classification Methods Applied to Preschool Strange Situations." *Clinical Child Psychology and Psychiatry* 15, no. 1 (January 2010): 97–120.

Spinelli, Marialuigia. "The Attachment Theory Today: From the Epigenetic Effects of Maternal Behavior to Psyco-Neuro-Endocrino-Immunology," *Journal of Clinical Epigenetics* 3, no. 43 (2017): 1–3.

Spock, Benjamin, and Robert Needlman. *Dr. Spock's Baby and Child Care.* 9th ed. New York: Gallery Books, 2011.

Sroufe, L. Alan. *Emotional Development: The Organization of Emotional Life in the Early Years.* New York: Cambridge University Press, 1995.

Sroufe, L. Alan, Brianna Coffino, and Elizabeth A. Carlson. "Conceptualizing the Role of Early Experience: Lessons from the Minnesota Longitudinal Study." *Developmental Review* 30, no. 1 (March 2010): 36–51.

Sroufe, L. Alan, Byron Egeland, Elizabeth A. Carlson, and W. Andrew Collins. *The Development of the Person: The Minnesota Study of Risk and Adaptation from Birth to Adulthood.* New York: Guilford Press, 2005.

Sroufe, L. Alan, and Daniel Siegel. "The Verdict Is In: The Case for Attachment Theory." *Psychotherapy Networker* 35, no. 2 (March/April 2011). https://www.drdansiegel.com/uploads/1271-the-verdict-is-in.pdf.

Sroufe, L. Alan, and Everett Waters. "Attachment as an Organizational Construct." *Child Development* 48, no. 4 (December 1977): 1184–99.

———. "Heart Rate as a Convergent Measure in Clinical and Developmental Research." *Merrill-Palmer Quarterly* 23, no. 1 (January 1977): 3–27.

Steele, Howard, Jordan Bate, Miriam Steele, Kerri Danskin, Hannah Y. Knafo, Adella Nikitiades, Shanta Rishi Dube, et al. "Adverse Childhood Experiences, Poverty, and Parenting Stress." *Canadian Journal of Behavioural Science* 48, no. 1 (January 2016): 32–38.

Steele, Howard, Anne Murphy, Karen Bonuck, Paul Meissner, and Miriam Steele. "Randomized Control Trial Report on the Effectiveness of Group Attachment-Based Intervention (GABI): Improvements in the Parent–Child Relationship Not Seen in the Control Group." *Development and Psychopathology* 31, no. 1 (2019): 203–17.

Steele, Howard, and Larry Siever. "An Attachment Perspective on Borderline Personality Disorder: Advances in Gene-Environment Considerations." *Current Psychiatry Reports* 12, no. 1 (February 2010): 61–67.

Steele, Howard, and Miriam Steele. "The Construct of Coherence as an Indicator of Attachment Security in Middle Childhood: The Friends and Family Interview." In *Attachment in Middle Childhood,* edited by Kathryn A. Kerns and Rhonda A. Richardson. New York: Guilford Press, 2005.

———. "Ten Clinical Uses of the Adult Attachment Interview." In *Clinical Applications of the Adult Attachment Interview,* edited by Howard Steele and Miriam Steele. New York: Guilford Press, 2008.

———. "Understanding and Resolving Emotional Conflict: Findings from the London Parent-Child Project." In *Attachment from Infancy to Adulthood: The Major Longitudinal Studies,* edited by Klaus E. Grossmann, Karin Grossmann, and Everett Waters. New York: Guilford Press, 2005.

Steele, Miriam. "The 'Added Value' of Attachment Theory and Research for Clinical Work in Adoption and Foster Care." In *Creating New Families: Therapeutic Approaches to Fostering, Adoption, and Kinship Care,* edited by Jenny Kenrick. New York: Routledge, 2018.

Steele, Miriam, Howard Steele, Jordan Bate, Hannah Knafo, Michael Kinsey, Karen Bonuck, Paul Meissner, et al. "Looking from the Outside In: The Use of Video in Attachment-Based Interventions." *Attachment and Human Development* 16, no. 4 (2014): 402–15.

Stone, Alex. "Is Your Child Lying to You? That's Good." *New York Times,* January 6, 2018.

Storebø, Ole Jakob, Pernille Darling Rasmussen, and Erik Simonsen. "Association Between Insecure Attachment and ADHD: Environmental Mediating Factors." *Journal of Attention Disorders* 20, no. 2 (2016): 187–96. https://doi.org/10.1177/1087054713501079.

Stovall, K. Chase, and Mary Dozier. "Infants in Foster Care." *Adoption Quarterly* 2, no. 1 (1998): 55–88.

Strathearn, Lane. "Exploring the Neurobiology of Attachment." In *Developmental Science and Psychoanalysis: Integration and Innovation,* edited by Linda Mayes, Peter Fonagy, and Mary Target. New York: Routledge, 2018.

Sullivan, Walter. "Konrad Lorenz, Pioneer in Study of Animals' Behavior, Dies at 85." *New York Times,* March 1, 1989. http://nyti.ms/2VfLkyd.

Sultan, Saoud. "Healthy Parenting in the Age of the Genome: Nature or Nurture?" *Saudi Journal of Medicine and Medical Sciences* 7, no. 1 (2019): 1–2.

Szepsenwol, Ohad, and Jeffry A. Simpson. "Attachment Within Life History Theory: An Evolutionary Perspective on Individual Differences in Attachment." *Current Opinion in Psychology* 25 (February 2019): 65–70.

Talbot, Margaret. "The Disconnected; Attachment Theory: The Ultimate Experiment." *New York Times Magazine,* May 24, 1988. https://nyti.ms/2v3lOhC.

Thomson, Paula. "Loss and Disorganization from an Attachment Perspective." *Death Studies* 34, no. 10 (2010): 893–914.

Topál, József, Adám Miklósi, Vilmos Csányi, and Antal Dóka. "Attachment Behavior in Dogs (Canis familiaris): A New Application of Ainsworth's (1969) Strange Situation Test." *Journal of Comparative Psychology* 112, no. 3 (1998): 219–29.

Tronick, Ed. *The Neurobehavioral and Social-Emotional Development of Infants and Children.* New York: W. W. Norton, 2007.

Troxel, Wendy M., Jill M. Cyranowski, Martica Hall, Ellen Frank, and Daniel J. Buysse. "Attachment Anxiety, Relationship Context, and Sleep in Women with Recurrent Major Depression." *Psychosomatic Medicine* 69, no. 7 (August 2007): 692–99.

Vaughn, Brian E., and Kelly K. Bost. "Attachment and Temperament as Intersecting Developmental Products and Interacting Developmental Contexts Throughout Infancy and Childhood." In *Handbook of Attachment: Theory, Research, and Clinical Applications,* edited by Jude Cassidy and Phillip R. Shaver. New York: Guilford Press, 2016.

Verhage, Marije L., Carlo Scheungel, Sheri Madigan, Richard M. Pasco Fearon, Mirjam Oosterman, Cassibba Rosalinda, Marian Bakermans-Kranenburg, et al. "Narrowing the Transmission Gap: A Synthesis of Three Decades of Research on Intergenerational Transmission of Attachment." *Psychological Bulletin* 142, no. 4 (April 2016): 337–66.

Vicedo, Marga. *The Nature and Nurture of Love: From Imprinting to Attachment in Cold War America.* Chicago: University of Chicago Press, 2013.

Waters, Everett, Claire E. Hamilton, and Nancy S. Weinfield. "The Stability of Attachment Security from Infancy to Adolescence and Early Adulthood." *Child Development* 71, no. 3 (2000): 703–6.

Weinfield, Nancy S. "The Nature of Individual Differences in Infant-Caregiver Attachment." In *Handbook of Attachment: Theory, Research, and Clinical Applications,* edited by Jude Cassidy and Phillip R. Shaver. New York: Guilford Press, 2016.

Weinfield, Nancy S., Gloria J. Whaley, and Byron Egeland. "Continuity, Discontinuity, and Coherence in Attachment from Infancy to Late Adolescence: Sequelae of Organization and Disorganization." *Attachment and Human Development* 6, no. 1 (2004): 73–97.

Weisskirch, Robert S., and Raquel Delevi. " 'Sexting' and Adult Romantic Attachment." *Computers in Human Behavior* 27, no. 5 (September 2011): 1697–1701.

Zaleski, Jeff. "Straight Ahead: An Interview with John Daido Loori." *Tricycle: The Buddhist Review,* Winter 1999. https://tricycle.org/magazine/straight-ahead -interview-john-daido-loori/.

Zeegers, Moniek A. J., Christina Colonnesi, Geert-Jan J. M. Stams, and Elizabeth

Meins. "Mind Matters: A Meta-Analysis on Parental Mentalization and Sensitivity as Predictors of Infant–Parent Attachment." *Psychological Bulletin* 143, no. 12 (2017): 1245–72.

Zreik, Ghadir, David Oppenheim, and Abraham Sagi-Schwartz. "Infant Attachment and Maternal Sensitivity in the Arab Minority in Israel." *Child Development* 88, no. 4 (July/August 2017): 1338–49.

Photo: © Hillary Harvey

BETHANY SALTMAN is an author, award-winning editor, and researcher. Her work can be seen in magazines like *The New Yorker, New York, The Atlantic, Parents,* and many others. *Strange Situation* is her first book.

Bethany also works as a bestselling book coach, devoted to helping people discover, write, and share the story they can't stop telling. She works with individuals and groups on book writing, creativity, and authentic brand identity, as well as "The Secret Teachings of Mary Ainsworth," a study group open to therapists, researchers, and attachment-curious people around the world.

In 1992, Bethany graduated from Antioch College, where she was one of the architects of the nation's first affirmative consent policy. She went on to receive her MFA in poetry from Brooklyn College in 1994, where she studied with Allen Ginsberg. In 2020, Antioch awarded Bethany the Rebecca Rice Award for Achievement in Profession.

A longtime Zen student, Bethany is devoted to the fine art and game-changing effects of paying attention. She lives in a small town in the Catskills with her family.

You can learn more by visiting bethanysaltman.com.

Twitter: @BethanySaltman

Sax, Boria. "What Is a 'Jewish Dog'? Konrad Lorenz and the Cult of Wildness." *Society and Animals* 5, no. 1 (January 1997): 3–21.

Scharfe, Elaine, and Nicole Black. "Does Love Matter to Infants' Health: Influence of Maternal Attachment Representations on Reports of Infant Health." *Journal of Relationships Research* 10 (2019): e4. https://doi.org/10.1017/jrr.2018.24.

Schimmenti, Adriano, and Antonia Bifulco. "Linking Lack of Care in Childhood to Anxiety Disorders in Emerging Adulthood: The Role of Attachment Styles." *Child and Adolescent Mental Health* 20, no. 1 (February 2015): 41–48.

Schindler, W. "The Role of the Mother in Group Psychotherapy." *International Journal of Group Psychology* 16, no. 2 (1966): 198–202.

Schöberl, Iris, Andrea Beetz, Judith Solomon, Manuela Wedl, Nancy Gee, and Kurt Kotrschal. "Social Factors Influencing Cortisol Modulation in Dogs During a Strange Situation Procedure." *Journal of Veterinary Behavior: Clinical Applications and Research* 11 (2016): 77–85.

Schoenmaker, Christie, Femmie Juffer, Marinus H. van IJzendoorn, Mariëlle Linting, Anja van der Voort, and Marian J. Bakermans-Kranenburg. "From Maternal Sensitivity in Infancy to Adult Attachment Representations: A Longitudinal Adoption Study with Secure Base Scripts." *Attachment and Human Development* 17, no. 3 (2015): 241–56.

Sears, William, Martha Sears, Robert Sears, and James Sears. *The Baby Book: Everything You Need to Know About Your Baby from Birth to Age Two.* New York: Little, Brown, 2008. Google Books.

Sexton, Anne. "45 Mercy Street." In *The Complete Poems: Anne Sexton.* Boston: Mariner Books, 1999.

Shakyamuni Buddha, *The Lankavatara Sutra: A Mahayana Text,* translated by Daisetz Teitaro Suzuki. http://lirs.ru/do/lanka_eng/lanka-nondiacritical.htm.

Shaver, Phillip R., Mario Mikulincer, Jacquelyn T. Gross, Jessica A. Stern, and Jude Cassidy. "A Lifespan Perspective on Attachment and Care for Others: Empathy, Altruism, and Prosocial Behavior." In *Handbook of Attachment: Theory, Research, Applications,* edited by Jude Cassidy and Phillip R. Shaver. New York: Guilford Press, 2016.

Sheff, Elisabeth A. "Fidelity in Polyamorous Relationships: Expanding Beyond Sexual Exclusivity." *The Polyamorists Next Door* (blog), *Psychology Today,* January 29, 2019. https://www.psychologytoday.com/us/blog/the-polyamorists-next-door/201901/fidelity-in-polyamorous-relationships.

Shilkret, Robert, and Cynthia J. Shilkret. "Attachment Theory." In *Inside Out and Outside In: Psychodynamic Clinical Theory and Psychopathology in Contemporary Multicultural Contexts,* edited by Joan Berzoff, Laura Melano Flanagan, and Patricia Herz. Lanham, MD: Rowman and Littlefield, 2016.

Shiller, Virginia M. *The Attachment Bond: Affectional Ties Across the Lifespan.* New York: Lexington Books, 2017.

Sibley, Chris G,. and Nickola C. Overall. "Modeling the Hierarchical Structure of Attachment Representations: A Test of Domain Differentiation." *Personality and Individual Differences* 44, no. 1 (January 2008): 238–49.

Siegel, Daniel J. *The Developing Mind: How Relationships and the Brain Interact to Shape Who We Are.* New York: Guilford Press, 2012.